Ripley's

Believe It
or Not!®

2017

ISBN 978-1-84794-788-8
10 9 8 7 6 5 4 3 2 1

VP Intellectual Property,
Ripley Entertainment Inc.,
7576 Kingspointe Parkway, Suite 188
Orlando, Florida 32819
publishing@ripleys.com

PUBLISHER'S NOTE
While every effort has been made to verify
the accuracy of the entries in this book, the
Publishers cannot be held responsible for any
errors contained in the work. They would be
glad to receive any information from readers.

WARNING
Some of the stunts and activities in this book
are undertaken by experts and should not be
attempted by anyone without adequate training
and supervision.

Printed in China

A CIP catalogue record for this book is available
from the British Library.

Cover Artwork Sam South

Reprographics *POST LLC

Production Coordinator Amy Webb

Contributing Designers Shelley Easter, Composure Graphics

Designers Jessica Firpi, Penny Stamp, Jim Steck

Art Director Penny Stamp

Special Thanks JR Language Translation Services, Inc. and Ripley's Social Media Team

Proofreader Cynthia Roby

Indexer Johnna VanHoose Dinse

Factcheckers Alex Bazlinton, Chris Lombardi, Matthew Usher

Copy Editor Chandler Gifford

Feature Contributors Jessica Firpi, Wendy A. Reynolds, Sabrina Sieck

Text Geoff Tibballs

Researcher Sabrina Sieck

Editors Jessica Firpi, Wendy A. Reynolds, M.S.Ed.

Managing Editor Dean Miller

Director, Publishing Operations Amanda Joiner

Vice President, Exhibits and Archives Edward Meyer

Executive Vice President, Intellectual Property Norm Deska

Ripley
PUBLISHING

Ripley
PUBLISHING
a Jim Pattison Company

UNLOCK THE WEIRD!
2017

Ripley's
Believe It
or Not!®

CONTENTS

Home Delivery or Take-Out

PIZZA

REST IN

December 25, 1890 – May 27, 1949

Robert L. Ripley

ROBERT RIPLEY

Ripley entertained some of the most famous people in the world aboard the *Mon Lei*.

MON LEI

The Ultimate Voyager

Robert Ripley was as beloved as the amazing oddities featured in the Believe It or Not! cartoons he drew for newspapers around the world, and his radio and television shows. Ripley became a celebrity whose popularity rivaled even that of US presidents. When he opened his first Odditorium in 1933 in Chicago, over two million fans flocked to see the amazing human oddities and artifacts he'd collected from every corner of the planet.

Ripley found ways to discover all that was weird and wonderful in the world—including the purchase of his own Chinese junk, the *Mon Lei*. Pictured in the painting to the right (one of Ripley's few color paintings), the ship was rebuilt from an 1890s cargo junk.

Robert Ripley

Ripley's ➜ **Believe It or Not!**

www.ripleys.com/books

The Mon Lei was the pleasure craft of a Chinese warlord or merchant, and her history is shrouded in mystery. Ripley purchased the junk in 1946, and sailed her to his private island in Mamaroneck, New York. He kept the name, Mon Lei, which means "ten thousand miles" in Chinese, perhaps as a reminder of his own lifelong voyage of discovery.

This wooden model of the Mon Lei, painstakingly restored by Ripley's own Bruce Miller, was a gift to Robert Ripley in the 1940s.

Ripley decorated the Mon Lei with many of his treasures, including this intricately carved wood paneling.

Ripley's global empire today includes Odditoriums, Aquariums, Haunted Candy Factories™, Louis Tussaud's Waxworks®, Super Fun Zones, a warehouse full of artifacts, and an archive of over 25,000 photos and 100,000 cartoons—but the Mon Lei is not among them. After Ripley's death in 1949, she was purchased by Broadway impresario John Arthur, along with other items from the Ripley estate. Believe it or not, the Mon Lei—one of the most famous ships in the world, owned by one of the most famous men of the age—changed hands for the paltry sum of $5,500.

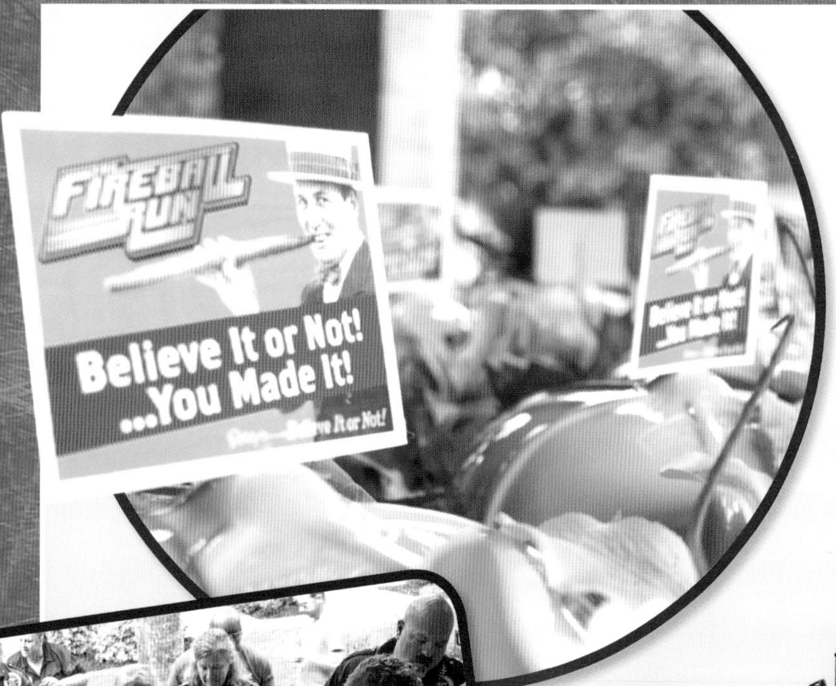
FIREBALL RUN
Believe It or Not!
...You Made It!

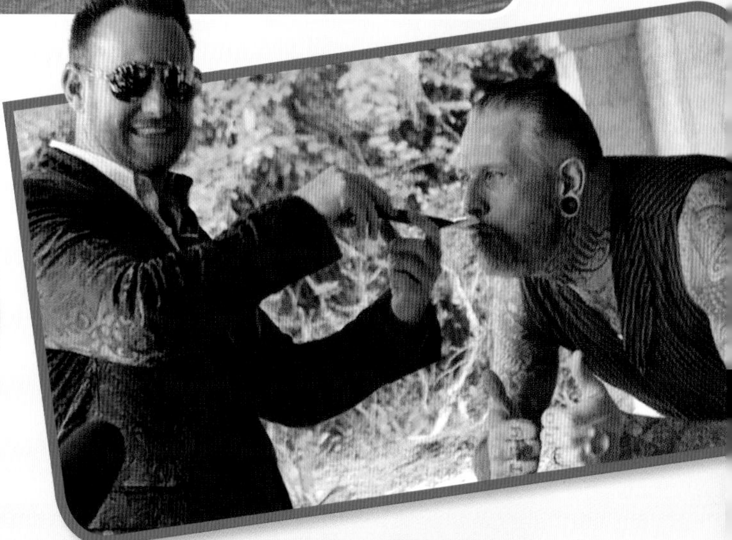

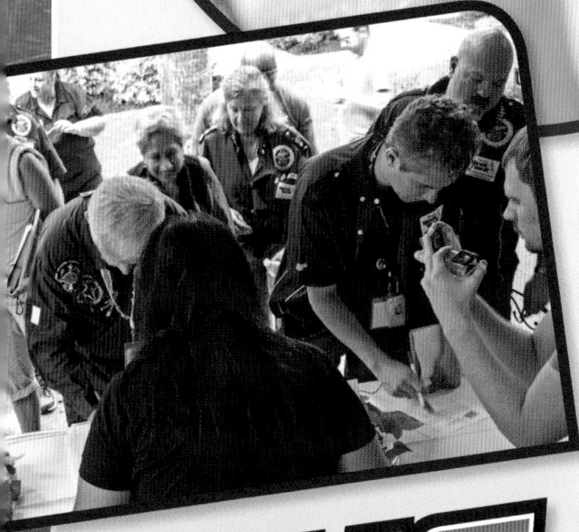

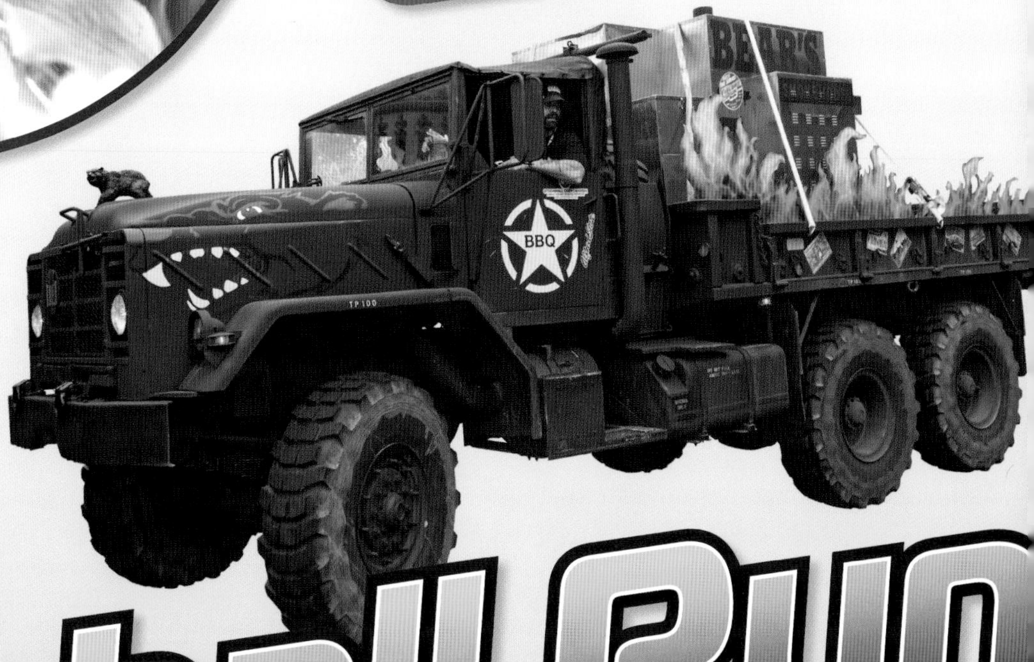
BEAR'S
BBQ

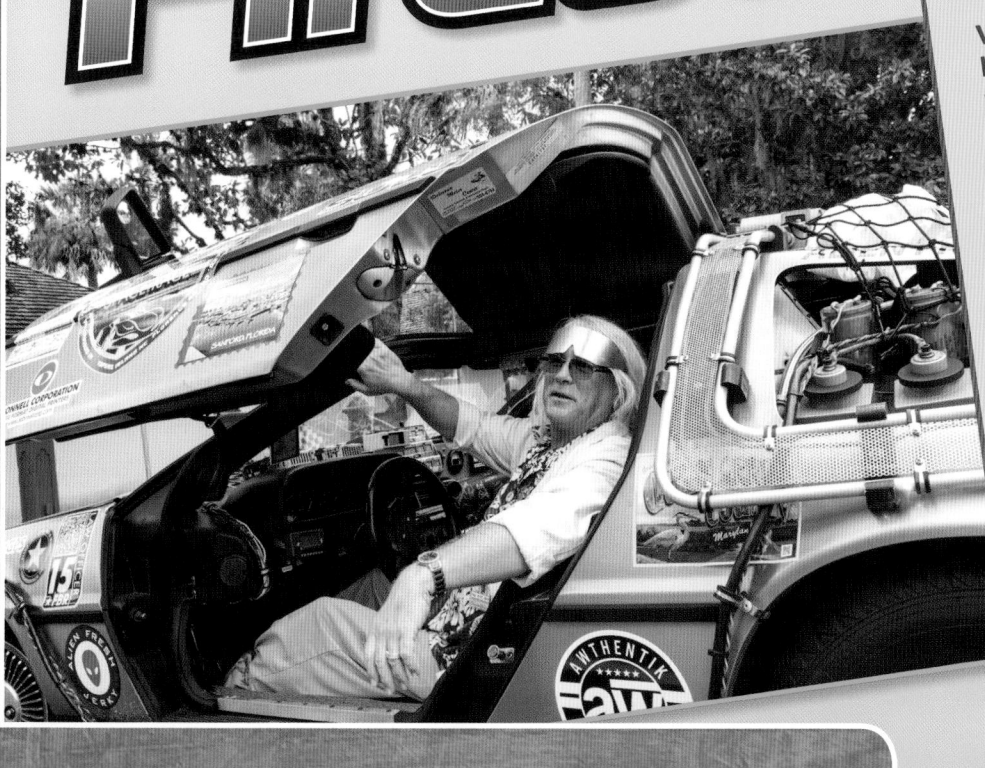

THE Fireball Run

When the Fireball Run®, one of the biggest online reality contests in the world, needed some special treasure for their 2016 hunt, the Ripley's St. Augustine Odditorium team sprang into action!

Using such special exhibits as Robert Ripley's first cartoon and a genuine shrunken head, our staff helped contestants obtain clues they needed to continue on to the next leg of the contest. After their successful Ripley's "pit stop," five-time Fireball Run participants Jim and Beth Shaver, in their 2015 Ford Mustang Convertible, went on to win the charity competition. The Fireball Run supports the Child Rescue Network in their search for missing children across the country.

AWTHENTIK

AMAZING ACQUISITIONS

With 31 Odditoriums around the world, as well as Traveling Shows to fill with the oddest items to be found, the team at Ripley's never stops looking for new and bizarre additions to expand our collection. This past year was no exception, with strange findings from all over the globe, including this Darth Vader helmet carved in the style of a ceremonial skull. This impressive piece of pop art was created by Tahe, an artist from Tahiti who likes to demonstrate how the modern world and popular culture are permanently changing indigenous culture.

RIP-ROARIN' #RIPCYCLE

When we put out the call to all our fans to send us their unbelievable upcycled creations for our 2016 Ripley's RipCycle contest, we received over 130 submissions from all over the world. Every entry stunned us with imaginative uses of bottle caps, duct tape, plastic spoons, and more. Our $2,000 (£1,400) Grand Prize Winner was this portrait of pop star Taylor Swift made from 17,625 pink, white, red, black, green, dark blue, and light blue gumballs by Andover, Maryland, artist Rob Surette!

Make sure you bookmark our website, www.ripleys.com, "like" us on Facebook, follow us on Twitter, and join us on Instagram for our next rip-roarin' contest. Maybe you'll become our next big winner!

Contest Winner!

9

PAGES 14-15

PAGE 122

PAGES 172-173

"...turn "more"

UNLOCK YOUR WEIRD!

Every year presents a new challenge here at Ripley's as we strive to uncover the bizarre, and this year was no exception. Ripley's researchers, writers, and editors spent all year collecting thousands of new stories as well as meeting some amazing people who have managed to unlock their weird!

Ripley's has a proud history of unlocking the weird! J. T. Saylors from Georgia never demonstrated his talent for contorting his face into a funny expression (aka gurning)—until he appeared at the first Ripley's Odditorium in Chicago in 1933. Robert Ripley even drew Saylors for his cartoon.

TELL US HOW YOU'VE UNLOCKED YOUR WEIRD!

If you can do something extraordinary, we'd love to know! Send us your videos or photos—we may reach out to you for an exciting opportunity.

For more information visit www.ripleys.com/unlocktheweird.

FLIGHT-SABER

PAGES 176-177

"It's important to share with other people that limitations can be pushed past, that you do have superpowers, and that they come from within you. You just need to actualize them."
—Dai Andrews

Vera Vermillion from Orlando, Florida, is a self-taught sword swallower and first learned by swallowing coat hangers!

Ripley's Believe It or Not!

On February 27, 2016, seven sword swallowers at the Ripley's Believe It or Not! Orlando, Florida, Odditorium performed a "big swallow" at exactly 2:27 pm for World Sword Swallowers Day. They swallowed a total of 17 swords!

Lady Riggy from The Schadenfreude Circus not only swallowed two swords but also walked on crushed glass at the Ripley's event!

Unlock Your Weird

www.ripleys.com/books

Ripley's — Believe It or Not!

I Believe It!

20 PENNY CIRCUS

Combining comedy, contortions, stunts, and shock tactics, Tyler Sutter and Carl Skenes—better known as 20 Penny Circus—put on quite a show! Don't be deceived by their makeup: these performers don't make balloon animals or otherwise clown around. Instead, this dark and twisted duo focus on the seedier side of magic, and aim to please "those of questionable taste!"

The pinnacle of their performance is nail gun Russian roulette, a stunt that they are now more hesitant to perform. During a 2015 show, Carl actually shot a nail through his hand! They also test the limits of the human body with such traditional stunts as sword swallowing, walking on glass, and ritualistic mutilation—all with unmistakable 20 Penny Circus flair!

20 Penny Circus performs many sideshow staples—in some cases, literally!

Onstage it is clown vs. clown—
each trying to upstage the other.
Offstage, however, Tyler and
Carl are much more friendly!

SHEEP DUNG SPITTING

Organizers had 30 pieces of sheep dung ready for the competition, thinking it would be enough, but with so many entrants, they had to recycle 18 pieces that had already been used!

In 2015, Irvinestown, Ireland's 37th Annual Lady of the Lake Festival introduced sheep dung spitting to its festivities. It is exactly what it sounds like—participants take sheep excrement into their mouths and attempt to spit it the farthest. Remarkably, 48 competitors participated, including the festival queen, the Lady of the Lake, Eimear Donnelly. After a heated tiebreaker, Mark Leonard won first place with a 29.5 ft. (9 m) spit!

Competition creator, organizer, and participant Joe Mahon was inspired by a few pints of beer and similar spitting competitions in Africa, such as Bokdrol spoeg, where participants spit kudu antelope dung. He claims that one competition entrant, Paddy McCann, spat his dung 12 ft. (4 m) with his dentures in, but when told to remove them and try again, he ended up swallowing it!

Proud of what he hopes becomes a not-so-tasty tradition, Mahon relished his role, and even sourced dung directly from the sheep!

Believe It!

Parahawking

By combining tandem paragliding and the ancient art of falconry, you get parahawking—the opportunity to soar with Egyptian vultures! Paragliders, strapped with a fanny pack full of meat, fly alongside these trained birds of prey. Passengers place small morsels of meat onto their gloved hand. When a whistle is blown, the vulture lands on the passenger's arm, quickly snatching the snack. Adam Gerber captured this action mid-flight in Pokhara, Nepal, currently the only place in the world to offer this daredevil sport.

SMALL WORLD After searching through Department of Health records to trace her birth mother who gave her up for adoption nearly 40 years ago, La-Sonya Mitchell-Clark discovered that both she and her mother worked for the same teleservices company in Youngstown, Ohio, and lived just a few minutes from each other. Not only was Mitchell-Clark reunited with her mother, Francine Simmons, but she learned that she had three sisters she knew nothing about, one of whom also worked at the same company.

GPS PROPOSAL Yasushi Takahashi spent six months trekking 4,451 miles (7,164 km) through Japan as a way of proposing to his girlfriend. Every place he visited was carefully planned so that the GPS records of his travels spelled the words "Marry Me" on a map of Japan when all the coordinates were joined together.

SWOLLEN LEGS When police officers noticed three men with unusually large legs at Mexico City's airport, a search revealed that the suspects had a total of 2.8 million pesos hidden inside their pants. The bills, worth around $190,000 (£154,000), were stuffed in socks and wrapped around their legs with elastic bandages.

OCEAN VIEW Shortly before her 101st birthday, Ruby Holt saw the ocean for the first time in her life. She had spent most of her life in rural Tennessee and could never afford to take the 400 mile (640 km) trip to the coast, but in 2014 she was taken by the Wish of a Lifetime organization from her nursing home in Columbia to the Perdido Beach Resort on the coast of the Gulf of Mexico.

WORD NAME Alexander Ek from Haninge, Sweden, has a 63-word legal name containing characters such as Iron Man, Shredder, and Yoda. He has changed his name six times before, spending over $1,000 (£641) to do so.

BAD BOUNCE A would-be thief in Drogheda, Ireland, used a brick to try and smash a car window, only to be knocked unconscious when the brick rebounded off the glass and hit him in the face. He was found lying in a pool of blood.

Ripley's Research

Soaring aircrafts and soaring birds use the same method to stay in flight. Both rely on warm pockets of rising air, called **thermals**, to achieve lift. Once a thermal is found, the pilot or bird flies within it to gain altitude before flying off to the next thermal, using them to move forward toward their destination. An incredibly energy-efficient process, thermal lift is used by many species of vultures, raptors, and storks.

DIVERTED RIVER A man in Washington State was sentenced to 30 days in jail in 2015 for trying to move a river. William Cayo Sr. used a bulldozer to fill in a section of the Tahuya River behind his Mason County home in an attempt to change its course.

100TH GRANDCHILD On April 8, 2015, Leo and Ruth Zanger of Quincy, Illinois, celebrated the birth of their 100th grandchild (53 grandchildren, 46 great-grandchildren, and one great-great-grandchild). They have been married 60 years and have 12 children, the youngest of whom, Joe, was already an uncle 10 times over when he was born.

UNIQUE NAME If parents struggling to name their baby are willing to pay $32,000 (£20,493), Erfolgswelle, a Swiss company, promises to come up with a unique baby name that will not be shared with anyone else in the whole world.

ROBBERS FOILED Two armed robbers who burst into a late-night convenience store in Berlin, Germany, fled empty-handed after the shop assistant, who was cleaning at the time, pointed the hose attachment of the vacuum cleaner she was using at them.

GRUESOME FIND The mummified body of an elderly woman was found beneath a 6 ft. (1.8 m) high mound of trash at a house in San Francisco in 2015—surrounded by black widow spiders, dog feces, rats, and 300 bottles of urine.

HEALTH TONIC While Joseph Amorese of Easton, Pennsylvania, was recovering from hernia surgery, his family sent him a get-well card with a lottery ticket inside—and when he scratched the ticket, he saw that he had won $7 million (£4,618,633).

EYE STOLEN A thief who stole a small black bag from a car parked in Boonville, New York, was probably surprised when he opened it and saw that it contained a prosthetic eye worth more than $2,000 (£1,281).

LOOM BRACELET The Hall family of Oxfordshire, England, made a loom band bracelet that measures 41,106 ft. (12,532 m) long—nearly one and a half times the height of Mt. Everest.

DOG WAR In 1925's War of the Stray Dog, Greece and Bulgaria went to war after a Greek soldier ran across the border to retrieve his dog.

For the best view in Rio De Janeiro, Brazil, climb to the top of Morro do Cantalago and don't stop there—walk a tightrope above the city! At 656 ft. (200 m) high, this rope is over five times higher in the sky than Rio's iconic Christ the Redeemer statue!

Head in the CLOUDS

Triple Vision

Identical triplets Tagiane, Rocheli, and Rafaela Bini have always shared a birthday, but now they also share another important day—their wedding day! On March 21, 2015, all three walked down the aisle of their Passo Fundo, Brazil church together. The guests as well as the grooms—Rafael, Gabriel, and Eduardo—had to pay close attention, as the sisters wore matching dresses, hairstyles, and makeup. The only difference was the color of their bouquets!

The novelty of triplet weddings dates back many years and spans many cultures, including this 1910 wedding in Burgstadt, Germany.

Singing triplets Cindy, Valerie, and Yvonne Hiles on October 18, 1975, in Folkestone, England.

SNOW SALE During the harsh 2015 US winter, enterprising Kyle Waring of Manchester-by-the-Sea, Massachusetts, shipped "historic Boston snow" to people in warmer climates at a price of $89 (£57) for 6 lb. (2.7 kg). Even if the snow had melted a little by the time it reached its destination, there was still enough left to make up to 15 snowballs.

365 PROPOSALS Dean Smith of Scottsdale, Arizona, made a video of himself secretly proposing to his girlfriend, Jennifer Kessel, every day for a year. Each day, he filmed himself holding up a whiteboard asking her to marry him, but the first she knew about it was when he played her the video on a family trip to Aruba. She said "yes."

COFFIN PICTURES Jenny Tay and Darren Cheng, who both work as undertakers in Singapore, posed for their wedding pictures inside a coffin.

CAT STATUE A supposedly worthless cat statue that Doreen Liddell had kept for years next to the fireplace of her home in Cornwall, England, turned out to be a 2,500-year-old Egyptian relic that sold at an auction in 2015 for $78,000 (£52,000).

LOST LUGGAGE In 2014, Maria Dellos of Tucson, Arizona, received a phone call from the Transportation Security Administration at Tucson International Airport to say that the luggage she had lost 20 years earlier had been found.

ESSAY CONTEST Rose and Prince Adams became the new owners of the Center Lovell Inn in Lovell, Maine, by writing a 200-word essay outlining their ambitions. The contest, which attracted thousands of entrants, was organized by previous owner Janice Sage, who herself won the inn in an essay-writing competition in 1993.

SAME NAME When William J. Danby opened an adventure book bought for him at a charity shop in Lancashire, England, he looked inside and saw that the book had previously been owned by another William J. Danby, almost a century earlier in 1919. Both boys were 13 when they were given the book, *The Young Franc-Tireurs*, by G. A. Henty.

>Extra set of fangs!

Mountain Lion Mystery

A set of teeth growing from the head of a mountain lion left experts baffled, scratching their own heads!

On December 30, 2015, an anonymous hunter began tracking the fanged feline after witnessing it attack a dog in Weston, Idaho. The dog survived the attack, but the mountain lion was not as lucky. When he captured it, the hunter was shocked by the cat's unusual deformity—fully formed teeth and white whiskers growing out of the top of its head! Experts at Idaho Fish and Game cannot definitively explain why this abnormality developed, but they believe it is either the remnants of a conjoined twin or a teratoma tumor—although both are very rare in both humans and animals.

IMPOSSIBLE ODDS Peter McCathie of Amherst Shore, Nova Scotia, Canada, won a $1 million (£641,890) lottery in 2015—years after both he and his daughter had survived separate lightning strikes. The odds against all three events happening to the same person—surviving a lightning strike, having a daughter survive a lightning strike, and winning the lottery—are 1 in 2.6 trillion!

FRUITY PROPOSAL Mr. Dong of Xi'an, China, proposed to his girlfriend in the street by creating delicate hearts and an elaborate Cupid's arrow out of her favorite fruit, lychees. Although she picked up one of the fruits and ate it, she ultimately walked off, rejecting him.

CUDDLING STORE When Samantha Hess of Portland, Oregon, opened "Cuddle Up To Me," a store charging customers $1 a minute for a therapeutic hug, she received 10,000 emails from customers in the first week, all of whom were over 18, booking hugs lasting anywhere between 15 minutes and a maximum of five hours.

PRETEND GUNFIRE After the Dutch army ran short of ammunition in 2015, its soldiers had to shout "bang, bang" during training exercises because they had no bullets.

URINE SHAMPOO Six students from the University of Reykjavik, Iceland, have created a shampoo made from cow's urine. They came up with the idea after discovering historical records detailing how women added cow's urine to their bathwater to clean their hair and make it look shiny.

"Neurons" by researcher Mehmet Berkmen and artist Maria Penil won first place. The team used yellow *Nesterenkonia*, orange *Deinococcus*, and *Sphingomonas*!

PETRI PORTRAITS

Microbes are the most diverse organisms in the world, but we usually only hear about bad ones, like bacteria. The American Society for Microbiology challenged the scientific community to help remove this stigma by turning their work into art by using microbes as paint and Petri dishes, also known as agars, as the canvas. The Agar Art competition resulted in 85 brilliant and beautiful submissions, varying from city skylines to self-portraits. Some used microbes that grew overnight, while others took weeks to come alive to create!

YANOMAMI MOM

Believe It!

avid Good comes from a broken home, but in reality, s story is much more complicated. His mother, Yarima, a member of the Yanomami tribe, living in a remote Amazonian jungle.

David's father, Kenneth, was a University of Pennsylvania anthropology student who made his first trek to the Amazon in 1975. In Venezuela, he stumbled upon Yarima's tribe. Fascinated, he returned often and became highly respected—and, years later, married Yarima from the tribe. After maintaining a long-distance relationship for several years, he brought her to Bryn Mawr, Pennsylvania, as his wife in November 1986, where David was born. Although Yarima tried to settle into American life, she longed to go home, and ultimately made the painful decision to leave David and his siblings and go back to the Yanomami.

In August 2011, David decided to find his mother. Although many years had passed, they recognized and connected with each other immediately. He now frequently visits Yarima, living like one of the tribe, dealing with the mosquitoes and parasites, and eating what they eat— monkeys, snakes, grubs, and armadillos. David has also founded The Good Project, a nonprofit organization dedicated to the education, health care, and cultural preservation of indigenous groups in South and Central America. His bond with his Yanomami heritage grows stronger with every visit.

Yarima tried to live a normal American life with her children, but the call of her native village proved too strong to overcome.

Ripley's — Asks ?

Ripley's asked David Good for more information about his reunion.

Q What was going through your mind when you were reunited with your mother?

A The moment I saw her I was immediately flooded with flashbacks and memories, briefly breaking down. But as I looked into her beautiful dark eyes, I instantly felt happy and at peace. I was finally with my mom again.

Q Did the Yanomami immediately welcome you?

A Yes, I am one of them—and my village was quick to tell me that! They also shared stories about my father and expressed their gratitude for his help. Thanks to that kinship, the Yanomami accepted me from day one, especially my brother Micashi (whom I call Ricky Martin). He has been key in teaching me the way of the Yanomami—how to hunt, how to shoot a bow and arrow, how to harvest honey, how cut down a tree, and so on.

Petrifying Well

On the banks of the river Nidd near the town of Knaresborough in North Yorkshire, England, sits a peculiar well whose water hardens any object, from teddy bears to bicycles. The lore behind the petrifying well revolves around Mother Shipton, who allegedly bewitched the well, but modern science can better explain its secret. When the well water flows over objects, its unusually high mineral content hardens them—much like the way stalactites and stalagmites form in caves. Astoundingly, objects are petrified in just three to five months!

Return to Sender

Celebrating her 90th birthday on August 24, 2015, Mary Nash Ward, affectionately called "Nashie," opened a birthday card from her best friend, Catherine Carpenter—*again*. This card, originally purchased for only a dime and posted for three cents, has been passed back and forth between them every year since 1950, when Nashie joked that Catherine could save some money by sending the card back to her for her birthday. Believe it or not, this card even survived Hurricane Katrina! It was carefully stored in a metal box with other valuables and was tossed in Nashie's trunk when she was evacuating her Long Beach, Mississippi, home.

Believe It!

BIRTHDAY MISERY Isayev Amirbek, 25, of Dushanbe, Tajikistan, was fined $600 (£389) for posting a picture on Facebook of a birthday cake in a café, thereby breaking a Tajikistani law that bans the celebration of birthdays in public. A waiter testified that no one had actually congratulated Amirbek on his birthday while he was in the café, but the judge was unmoved.

EMBARRASSING CALL A man who broke into a Laurel, Delaware, school called 911 after he became trapped in its elevator.

PRECIOUS POOP According to an Arizona State University study, gold, silver, and platinum levels are so high in human feces that a city of 1 million inhabitants flushes about $13 million (£8.7 million) worth of precious metals down toilets and sewer drains each year.

ARMLESS CARER Chen Xinyin, from Chongqing, China, cares for his 91-year-old mother even though he has no arms. He lost them in an electrical accident when he was seven years old, but has taught himself to cook, perform household chores, and raise animals on his farm using just his mouth and feet.

HIDING PLACE Upon returning to the UK after performing in France, rock band Willie and the Bandits found an illegal immigrant trying to smuggle himself into Britain by hiding in one of their guitar cases.

HORNET NESTS Terry Prouty has a collection of more than 100 giant hornet and wasp nests at his home in Tulsa, Oklahoma. He has been collecting them since 2000, buying most of them online for between $10 (£6) and $200 (£128). One of his largest is a hornet nest measuring nearly 40 inches (1 m) tall.

PAPER PRANK Professional prankster Roman Atwood vandalized the exterior of comedian and TV host Howie Mandel's California mansion with more than 4,000 rolls of toilet paper—covering it so that the building was almost completely hidden.

PRISONERS' PROTEST Eighty-six prisoners at Exeter Jail in Devon, England, signed a formal letter of complaint claiming that a Sudoku puzzle in the local newspaper—the *Exeter Express and Echo*—on May 21, 2015, was impossible to solve.

WASTED EFFORT "Tunnel Joe" Holmes spent a year and seven months tunneling out of the Maryland State Penitentiary, escaping in February 1951—but lasted only two weeks on the run before being recaptured.

GNOME INVASION In June 2015, 107 ornamental gnomes suddenly appeared in the front garden of Marcela Telehanicova's house in Devon, England. Police officers investigated, but no gnomes were reported missing in the area.

MEDIEVAL COMBAT New York City lawyer Richard Luthmann demanded the right to settle a present-day legal dispute by a medieval trial by combat, which he claimed is still legal in the United States under the Ninth Amendment. In his brief, he said he wanted to fight the duel dressed as *Game of Thrones* character Robert Baratheon and wield a war hammer.

LUCKY BREAK Tired of waiting in line at a store in Fairfield, Connecticut, Bob Sabo of Easton decided to buy two $20 (£13) lottery tickets from a vending machine instead—something he had previously never done. Since he was not wearing his glasses, he accidentally pressed the wrong button and bought a "30X Cash" ticket for $30 (£19)—but it turned out to be a $30,000 (£19,259) winner.

PENNY PROTEST In protest over a parking fine imposed by the University of North Carolina at Charlotte, student Stephen Coyle paid it in the form of 14,000 pennies (£92). It took staff 3 hours and 40 minutes to count all the coins.

FOUR CHARLOTTES In 2015, all four hair stylists working at a salon in Staffordshire, England, were named Charlotte. Manager Charlotte Roberts started the VIP Hair Salon in 2009, and has since been joined by Charlotte Thatcher, Charlotte Horrocks, and Charlotte Wagstaff.

SNOW BRIDE Minutes after getting married at a New York ski resort, Bob and Maria Reiland of Cleveland, Ohio, joined 35 of their wedding guests snowboarding on the slopes—with the bride still wearing her wedding dress.

HIGH HOPES Rossel Sabourin from Winnipeg, Manitoba, Canada, proposed to his girlfriend Shannon with a romantic dinner for two—complete with a linen tablecloth and champagne on ice—9,000 ft. (2,740 m) up a mountain in Banff National Park, Alberta. Shannon had trekked for two and a half hours to the lofty location, but had no idea what awaited her at the end of the climb. She said "yes," and the couple got married shortly afterward.

TORAJA CORPSE CLEANING RITUAL

Every August, in Toraja, South Sulawesi, Indonesia, families exhume the bodies of their dead relatives and wash, groom, and dress them in fancy new clothes in a ritual called Ma'nene, or the Ceremony of Cleaning Corpses. Damaged caskets are fixed or replaced, and the mummies are walked around their village by following a path of straight lines to honor the path of the spiritual entity Hyang.

CHANCE REUNION Two women born to the same mother in the early 1980s but adopted by different families discovered they were sisters 30 years later when both attended a Columbia University writing class in New York City. Lizzie Valverde grew up in New Jersey, while Katy Olson was raised in Florida and Iowa. Both moved to New York as adults and happened to enroll in the same course.

LOVE LETTERS Bill Bresnan of Toms River, New Jersey, has written more than 10,000 love letters to his wife Kirsten. He has penned a romantic note to her every day for almost 40 years, and most of them are filed chronologically in 25 boxes in the attic of their home.

SNEAKER SETTLEMENT Unable to pay an outstanding court fee, Jason Duval of Framingham, Massachusetts, escaped jail by offering Judge Douglas Stoddart his new pair of Nike® sneakers as bail collateral.

ADJACENT BEDS Dave O'Callaghan and Jane Hammond were born on the same day—January 26, 1955—in beds next to each other at the Mowbray Maternity Hospital in Exeter, Devon, England—but did not actually meet until they were 18. They later married and have now been together for nearly 40 years.

GOODWILL BARGAIN In 2014, Sean McEvoy of Knoxville, Tennessee, spent 58 cents on a sweater at a Goodwill store, but when he discovered that it had once been worn by Green Bay Packers coach Vince Lombardi, he was able to sell it at an auction a year later for $43,020 (£27,617).

Tibetan Sky Burial

Believe It!

Sky burials are a Vajrayana Buddhist funeral rite practiced in Tibet, Qinghai, Mongolia, and Inner Mongolia. After death, the corpse is left untouched for three days while Tibetan monks chant around it. On the fourth day, the corpse is cleaned, wrapped in white cloth, and placed in a fetal position on a pallet. Lamas, or priests, lead a funeral procession before dawn to the charnel ground, where the body is ritualistically broken into pieces and offered to the vultures who circle overhead. It is believed that the vultures are Dakinis—the Tibetan equivalent of angels—who will take the soul to heaven to be reincarnated. Tibetans are encouraged to witness this ritual so they can confront death openly and understand the impermanence of life.

GOOD DEEDS Store assistant Luke Cameron of Cheltenham, Gloucestershire, England, performed a good deed every day throughout 2014, including buying meals for strangers, helping elderly neighbors, and buying hot drinks for homeless people—and he rounded it off on New Year's Eve by handing out £365 (about $550) to 73 random people on the street, £1 for every day of the year.

AGE REWARD Moldovan businessman Dmitry Kaminskiy has offered $1 million to the first person to live to the age of 123.

DEADLY BALL Finding a large metal ball near his home in Derby, England, 10-year-old Ryan-Morgan Freeman used it to play soccer with his friends on a local basketball court. However, when Freeman's father Calvin saw the metal ball, he became suspicious of it and called the police. The ball turned out to be a 374-year-old cannonball from the English Civil War—and the bomb squad was quickly called in to blow it up.

CROSSWORD CLUES Matthew Dick of London, England, proposed marriage to his girlfriend Delyth Hughes by hiding cryptic clues in *The Times* newspaper's crossword puzzle printed June 16, 2015.

ADOPTED CHILDREN Li Li Juan, a former millionaire from Hebei Province, China, is now in debt after spending all her money adopting and raising over 75 sick and abandoned children since 1996.

MIXED MESSAGE Immediately after officiating at the marriage of Israel Silva to Ivy Koryne Smith on February 11, 2015, District Judge Steven Cranfill sentenced the groom to six to ten years in prison. Silva, who had previously been found guilty of aggravated burglary, property destruction, and driving under the influence of alcohol, wore an orange jail jumpsuit and shackles during the ceremony at a courtroom in Cody, Wyoming, and had to stay 15 ft. (4.5 m) away from his bride.

MEMENTO MORI

Art historian and self-professed "death enthusiast" Paul Koudounaris of Los Angeles, California, spent a decade visiting 250 memorial sites across 30 different countries in search of human remains concealed in historical sites, documenting how different cultures remember the dead. His book *Memento Mori* included these 19th-century remains preserved in a Capuchin monastery in Burgio, Sicily.

TWIN STRANGERS

magine how surreal it would be to meet someone that looked exactly like you. Niamh Geaney, a 26-year-old from Kerry, Ireland, set out to do just that. Using social media, she's received hundreds of submissions from around the world, and found an uncanny match in just two weeks—and she's still looking! Niamh has found two more Twin Strangers since and, through her website, is helping others find theirs.

First, Niamh found Karen, who lives just an hour away in Louth, Ireland.

Niamh's second twin stranger was Luisa from Genoa, Italy. When she met with Luisa's family and friends to get a feel for what she was like, Luisa's mother thought Niamh was her daughter from a distance.

Ripley's Asks?

Ripley's finds out more about Twin Strangers from Niamh Geaney.

Q What inspired Twin Strangers?
A The whole area of lookalikes and doppelgängers was something I always had an interest in—but it really kicked off when an Irish media company VIP approached my two friends and I to run a test on whether Twin Strangers could be found.

Q What was it like meeting your first match?
A I thought I would be fine meeting Karen until I knew I was about ten minutes away. Then I started to get ridiculously nervous, wondering how I would react to meeting someone that looks like me—I would be looking at my own face! For the entire duration of our encounter I pretty much stared at her.

Irene from Sligo, Ireland, was Niamh's third match.

Believe It!

PUZZLING JOB Every day, retired builder Michael Barry of Bath, Somerset, England, spends hours assembling jigsaw puzzles that have been donated to a charity shop to make sure that no pieces are missing. Since starting his voluntary job in 2013, he has completed more than 300 puzzles—some with up to 2,000 pieces—and rejected about half that had missing pieces.

POSTHUMOUS VICTORY Democrat Roger Freeman was reelected to the Washington State Legislature, representing the 30th District, in November 2014—even though he had died six days before Election Day.

SAUSAGE FIGHT A man named Bacon was arrested in May 2015 after a dispute over sausage. Police in Madison, New Jersey, arrested Thomas Bacon for allegedly assaulting someone for eating the last piece of sausage.

KNOTS After detailed study, Swedish mathematician Mikael Vejdemo-Johansson has concluded that there are 177,147 different ways to knot a necktie.

FLEA BOMBS In 1940 during World War II, the Imperial Japanese Army bombed the Chinese city of Ningbo with fleas carrying the bubonic plague, triggering a major outbreak that killed over 100 people.

KNIGHT SCHOOL Found wielding a 28 in. (70 cm) long samurai sword in a park in Bunbury, Western Australia, local man Guy Graham Jones told police officers that he was training to become a Jedi knight.

13 SONS In May 2015, Jay and Kateri Schwandt of Rockford, Michigan, welcomed their 13th child—and all 13 are boys.

SEEING DOUBLE When retired priest Neil Richardson moved to Raintree, Essex, England, strangers kept calling him John—and years later the reason for the confusion became apparent when he bumped into his doppelgänger neighbor, retired school principal John Jemison. Not only were the two men almost identical in appearance, they discovered that they had attended the same college and had both worked as religious education teachers.

LUCKY DAY Ken Broadwell, 75, of Dubuque, Iowa, scratched off two winning lottery tickets in one day—June 23, 2015—one winning $100,000 (£64,568), the other worth $930 (£600).

COIN TOSS Wilber Medina was elected mayor of Pillpinto, Peru, in 2014 on a coin toss after he and rival candidate Jose Cornejo had each garnered 236 votes at the ballot box.

SIGNIFICANT NUMBER The license plate of the car in which Archduke Franz Ferdinand was assassinated was AIII 118—the official end of World War I was Armistice Day, 11/11/18.

WEDDING CLIMB Dressed in their wedding clothes, climbing enthusiast Lu Chao and his fiancée, Zhang Chenyu, scaled a 100 ft. (30 m) high sheer cliff in Shaanxi Province, China, and clung to the rock face for three hours while posing for wedding pictures.

MISSING COMMA Andrea Cammelleri escaped a parking citation because an Ohio village law was missing a comma. The West Jefferson law lists several types of vehicles that cannot be parked longer than 24 hours, including a "motor vehicle camper" with the comma missing between "vehicle" and "camper." Cammelleri successfully argued that her pickup truck did not fit that definition.

SURF'S UP!

When the beach calls for "business formal" attire, Quiksilver has it covered with the True Wetsuit, a $2,500 (£1,614) wetsuit that looks like an actual suit and tie.

One of the HERD

We gave this goat man a chance to be "herd."

Q Why did you choose to assimilate with goats?

A I actually started out by trying to become an elephant, but then found that they're such emotionally complex and intelligent animals—I decided they are almost too human. So I visited a shaman, a kind of expert in human-animal relations I guess, who told me that of course I should be become a goat!

Q What was the goat farmer's initial reaction to your request?

A Well, initially he was extremely skeptical that I would be able to keep up with the goats going down the mountain, to the valley pastures, where they would spend the winter. When I was leaving, the goatherd said that he thought that the herd had accepted me!

Q What was the strangest experience during this experiment?

A There was a moment when I looked up and saw that I was in the middle of the herd—every goat had stopped chewing and was staring at me. It was like I'd committed some sort of goat faux pas, and their horns suddenly looked pretty sharp. It was scary, but then a single goat, one that seemed to have befriended me, walked right through the center of the silent, staring herd, and diffused the tension.

Q Did you still have human worries, or were you carefree?

A In the pasture, amongst the goats, I did sort of forget for a while, but when it started to rain and get cold, and my waterproof suit made with advanced technical fabrics turned out not to be so waterproof, I started shivering, and my human worries and concerns came flooding back.

Q Would you have extended the experiment if circumstances allowed?

A Yes, definitely, but my prosthetics would have had to be so good that I could truly and comfortably live my dream and gallop through the fields, enjoying just eating grass!

In September 2014, Thomas Thwaites, a designer from London, England, decided to take a break from reality and spent three days in the Swiss Alps... as a goat!

Thomas used prosthetic limbs to move on all fours to better immerse himself in the herd, and considered creating an artificial rumen (part of a goat's stomach) to eat and digest grass with actual goat gut bacteria! He's not stark-grazing mad, but studied goat behavior, locomotion, and communication to prep for the experience, and visited a behavioral psychologist and neurologist to learn how to "turn off" parts of his brain in order to think more like his four-legged friends!

2 World

IRON ILLUMINATION

At Nuanquan, China's annual Da Shuhua festival, brave blacksmiths shower themselves with molten iron that has been heated to 1,832°F (1,000°C). The tradition began over 300 years ago when local blacksmiths, unable to afford fireworks, began melting iron and throwing it at a large, cold, stone wall, producing spectacular red iron flowers that rained down on the men. For an even more colorful display, copper and aluminum are used to make green and white sparks.

TREKKIE OFFICE

Multimillionaire and *Star Trek* fan Liu Dejian spent close to $100 million (£70 million) to build an office in Fujian Province, China, designed to look like the starship *Enterprise*. His new business headquarters is the size of three soccer fields, took six years to complete, and has 30 ft. (9 m) metal slides connecting each floor, as well as automatic sliding gates between each working area. The structure is the only officially licensed *Star Trek* building in the world! Oddly enough, it even features a life-size replica of a *Tyrannosaurus rex* skeleton named Stan.

COAST TO COAST When a scale map of Alaska—at 2,364 miles (3,804 km) wide—is superimposed on a map of the 48 lower states, it actually extends from coast to coast.

FAMILY BUSINESS Founded in 718, the Hoshi Ryokan Hotel in Ishikawa Prefecture, Japan, has been run by the same family for 46 generations.

REFLECTIVE HOME Every brick on the exterior of Martin Prekop's house in Pittsburgh, Pennsylvania, is fitted with a mirror to reflect its natural surroundings. As well as attaching hundreds of mirrors to the 15-room house, he has hung brightly colored bottles and glass panels from trees on the grounds.

GATEWAY TO HELL Fumes spewing from a 3 ft. (0.9 m) wide fiery chasm that suddenly opened up on a mountainside near Urumqi, China, in 2015 have been recorded at a staggering 1,457°F (792°C)—and are so hot that tree branches burst into flames when they are held over the entrance. Locals have nicknamed the mysterious sinkhole the "Gateway to Hell."

QUICK BUILD A construction firm in Changsha, China, built an entire 57-story building in just 19 days. The Mini Sky City building, which has 800 apartments and enough office space for 4,000 people, was erected at a rate of three full stories a day.

RIVER REVIVER Because he introduced rainwater storage tanks—or *johads*—to replenish groundwater levels, and built small dams to improve the downstream flow, Rajendra Singh is credited with single-handedly reviving five rivers in Rajasthan, India, that had previously been dried up for decades. Known as the "Waterman of India," his efforts have restored water to over 1,000 villages.

BIG FREEZE When a devastating fire gutted the 124-year-old former Mulligan Elementary School in Chicago, Illinois, on November 18, 2014, fire crews doused the flames by spraying water—but as temperatures plunged, the water froze, and the exterior of the building was left covered in icicles, many several feet long.

SPLASH BACK To deter drunken revelers from urinating on street walls in Hamburg, Germany, a local community group covered the walls with hydrophobic paint that makes the urine bounce off and soak people's shoes and pants.

SUSPENDED BED Guests don't dare roll over in bed while staying at the Portaledge Hotel in Anglesey, North Wales, because the beds are small canvas platforms suspended 200 ft. (60 m) up a sheer cliff face. For $750 (£490) a night, guests rappel from the cliff top to their beds at sunset, and are then strapped into harnesses secured to the rock. Dinner is served from a cooking stove hung off the side of the ledge.

TRUCK TRANSFORMER New Zealanders Justin Hayward and Jola Siezen live in a truck that transforms into a mobile home in the shape of a fantasy castle. When everything is packed away it looks like a normal truck. Once stationary it unfolds to reveal turrets, walls, doors, and 430 sq. ft. (40 sq. m) of living space, featuring beds, a kitchen, and a rooftop bathtub.

THREE SUNS When sunlight at low altitude passes through ice crystal fragments in the Earth's atmosphere, the refracted light causes a rare optical phenomenon called a parhelion, where three suns appear in the sky at the same time, one at either side of the real sun. Known as a "sun dog" because the other two balls of light follow the sun like a dog follows its owner, it only occurs occasionally in countries such as Canada and Mongolia where daytime temperatures dip below minus 22°F (-30°C).

ARCHERY NAME There is a road in Shepshed, Leicestershire, England, called Butthole Lane—named after the targets used in archery because it was where men went to practice their archery skills in the 16th century.

WEREWOLF MUZZLE A Russian company has created a menacing muzzle that transforms placid dogs into ferocious-looking werewolves. The contraption features a snarling snout and vicious, plastic teeth, and is designed to prevent dogs and their owners from being attacked.

ANIMAL SKULLS While renovating their Auburn, Pennsylvania, home in 2015, Kajia Bretzuis and her family discovered that the walls had been insulated with dozens of dead animal carcasses wrapped in newspapers from the 1930s and 1940s.

CAT HAVEN

Just a 30-minute ferry ride off the coast of Ehime Prefecture in Japan sits a mile long (1.6 km) island swarming with 120 feral cats. The felines of Aoshima Island, known as Cat Island, were originally introduced to the ecosystem to kill mice, but after most of the 900 residents left to seek work on the mainland after World War II, the cats were left to themselves. Now outnumbering humans six to one, they rule the remote island.

DOG DETECTIVE A dog foiled a jailbreak on the Greek island of Corfu after hearing prisoners digging a tunnel. Out for a morning walk with its owner, the dog detected strange sounds coming from under the ground and refused to move. The owner eventually called the police, who discovered a tunnel already several meters long leading from Corfu prison's B wing.

ARCTIC DETOUR Among the thousands of migrants that traveled from Syria to Europe in 2015, more than 5,500 took a long detour and entered via a remote Arctic border crossing in northeastern Norway. Some arrived on bicycles because the Storskog post on the Norwegian-Russian border is not open to pedestrians.

WOLF STOLEN A 6 ft. (1.8 m) long, 100 lb. (45 kg) stuffed wolf worth $50,000 (£32,440) was stolen from the London, England, home of Charlotte Watts, granddaughter of Rolling Stones drummer Charlie Watts. The valuable taxidermy piece is an Arctic wolf, Frostbite, who died in a fight with another wolf at London Zoo during World War II.

PRIZED TOILET A chamber pot owned by Empress Elisabeth of Austria (1837–1898) sold for nearly $5,000 (£3,298) at an auction in Vienna in 2015.

SWEETHEART SMUGGLING A husband tried to smuggle his Russian wife across the border from Belarus into Poland in 2015 by squashing her tightly into his suitcase, only to learn that she was free to enter the country anyway. Suspicious Polish border guards ordered the bulky case to be opened and were shocked when the woman stepped out. However, on examining the couple's documents, they saw that the husband was French and was therefore legally entitled to bring his wife into the European Union by more comfortable and conventional means.

MOSSY BALLS Thousands of large green mossy balls suddenly washed up overnight on Dee Why Beach near Sydney, Australia, in September 2014. The rare phenomenon was caused by the movement of the ocean's waves rolling living algae into balls and depositing them ashore.

SAND HOTELS Two temporary, 26 ft. (8 m) high hotels were built out of sand in the Dutch towns of Oss and Sneek, complete with electricity, running water, glass windows, king-size beds, soft carpets, luxury bathrooms, and even Wi-Fi.

BORDER CROSSING At the Haskell Free Library and Opera House, visitors can watch a performance with one foot in Canada and the other in the United States. The building straddles the border separating Stanstead, Quebec, and Derby Line, Vermont, with the boundary marked by a thick black diagonal line across the floor. The library has a different entrance for each country, and therefore two different addresses and two different telephone area codes. Anyone exiting through the opposite door they entered from has to report to customs officers.

WOMEN ONLY Since 1990, only women have been allowed to live in the Kenyan village of Umoja—all men are banned.

CHINESE FIRE DRILL

This is not an image of a stunt show—these are Chinese students participating in a fire drill at Nanhu Vocational School near Shanghai, China. During the June 2015 mandatory event, students had to evacuate the building and run through a series of flaming poles (representing burning doorways) with napkins over their mouths to avoid smoke inhalation. Once safe from the flames, students were then expected to put out the fire. Using real fire during drills is common in Chinese schools.

FRUIT FIGHT During the Battle of Lepanto in 1571, the losing Ottoman Navy hurled oranges and lemons at Catholic soldiers when they ran out of weapons.

HALLOWEEN HORROR In 2015, the website Airbnb.com offered guests the chance to spend a spooky Halloween night in a mass grave surrounded by the bones and skulls of 200-year-old corpses in a section of the Catacombs, a vast network of burial tunnels located 66 ft. (20 m) under Paris, France. They contain the remains of more than six million people moved below ground in the late 18th century after the city's overcrowded graveyards were closed because it was thought that the decomposing bodies had caused wine and milk to go bad.

FLOATING HOME Canadian couple Wayne Adams and Catherine King have lived on a self-sustainable floating home off the coast of Tofino, British Columbia, for more than 20 years. Their house, garden, outbuildings, and greenhouses to grow food are all built on 12 floating platforms and are interconnected by wooden walkways.

EXPENSIVE WALL Part of a wall in the central business district of Melbourne, Australia, sold at auction in 2015 for over three million Australian dollars (US$2.2 million, or £1.55 million). The 1,260 sq. ft. (117 sq. m) area, which houses a digital billboard, is the side of a building overlooking the city's busiest pedestrian crossing.

ODD POLICY In 2015, to save money, police in Leicestershire, England, for three months only investigated attempted burglaries at houses with even numbers.

SPEEDING TICKET Christian Breier of Leipzig, Germany, deliberately got a speeding ticket just so that he could ask his girlfriend Anja Thomas to marry him. In Germany, the police routinely send a photograph of the driver along with the speeding notice, so he held up a banner reading "Will you marry me?" as he sped past a police camera near his home, and when the ticket duly arrived in the mail, she opened it to see a picture of him and his marriage proposal.

Ripley's —— Believe It or Not!
www.ripleys.com/books
World

Carnival of Basel

Every February, the three-day Carnival of Basel (or Fasnacht) sees 15,000 to 20,000 masked individuals take part in the largest, most popular festival in Switzerland. Fasnacht begins each day at four in the morning, when groups of musicians in costumes and masks start playing in the streets. With the entire festival meticulously organized, only members of recognized carnival groups are allowed to participate. Each of the outrageous, intricate costumes require up to 12 hours of work and often cost more than $500 (£350) to create. During the street parades and late nights of revelry, people are not allowed to unmask themselves.

STUDENT PRINCESS Princess Mako of Akishino, one of Japan's most popular royals, disguised herself as a regular student at the University of Leicester, England, for a year. She lives a life of luxury in Japan, but lived in ordinary student housing in the UK while completing a master's degree.

STALKER SQUIRREL Police officers in Bottrop, Germany, arrested a squirrel after a woman complained it was stalking her. She claimed the rodent had been pursuing her aggressively around the city streets.

APE MEN To scare away the hundreds of macaque monkeys that plague its parliament buildings in New Delhi, the Indian government hired 40 young men in ape suits. The men pose as predatory langur monkeys, making loud throaty sounds and intimidating gestures to frighten the smaller macaques that have been attacking staff for food and chewing through Internet cables.

DELAYED MESSAGE A century-old message in a bottle was found in 2015, having taken 108 years to sail 275 miles (443 km) across the North Sea from the UK to Germany. It was part of a batch of bottles launched by the Marine Biological Association to study sea currents, and, in accordance with the original promise, the woman who found it was rewarded with one old shilling (12 British pence), which had been bought on eBay.

PET TREAT A man booked the entire five-star Ocean Spring Hotel in Qingdao City, China, for two nights as a birthday treat for his pet sea lion. The animal even had its own personal chef.

BRIDGE BLAST Using vast quantities of explosives, a 3.4 mile (5.5 km) long bridge in China's Fujian Province was demolished in just four seconds in 2015.

>It's Alive!

Fascinating Fox

For the past 40 years, one of the top attractions at Pakistan's Karachi Zoo hasn't been an actual animal, but a mythical creature named "Mumtaz Begum Africa Wali."

With the body of a fox and the head of a woman, Mumtaz Begum entertains visitors for up to 12 hours a day with witty conversation and fortune telling. In reality, the performance is an optical illusion—a man inserts his head through a wooden table next to the body of a stuffed fox. The zoo has found that men are better able to respond to harassment and negative comments, so a male actor who is able to speak several local languages is always chosen to play the creature. Murad Ali, 33, currently plays Mumtaz Begum—he inherited the role from his father 16 years ago.

SLOW MOVER From the time Pluto was officially discovered in 1930 to the time its status as a planet was rescinded in 2006, it had not completed a full revolution. Pluto takes 248 years to orbit the Sun.

SMALL-TIME CRIMINALS The jailhouse in Rodney, Ontario, Canada, has only two tiny cells and covers an area of just 258 sq. ft. (24 sq. m). Originally built in 1890, it reopened as a visitor information center in 1995 after being closed for over 50 years.

OFFICIAL COMPLAINER Evansburg, Alberta, Canada, elects an official "Town Grouch" who is licensed to pester, grumble, complain, and criticize without fear of reprisal for a whole year.

UPSIDE-DOWN WATERFALL Newly discovered underwater hydrothermal vents, lying more than 12,500 ft. (3,810 m) deep in the Pescadero Basin on the Pacific seabed at the southern end of the Gulf of California, feature 35 ft. (10.6 m) high plumes of smoke and upside-down waterfalls.

THUNDER CLOUD Flying from Massachusetts to North Carolina in 1959, Lt. Colonel William Rankin, an experienced and veteran pilot of both World War II and Korea, ejected from his plane directly into a violent thunder cloud. The storm winds kept him aloft for 40 minutes, pelting him with hailstones and so much rain that he had to hold his breath at times to keep from drowning in midair.

CURIOUS COLLECTION Exhibits at the Viktor Wynd Museum of Curiosities in London, England, include a tray of 77 bat skulls, a mummified cat, a two-headed lamb, a shrunken human head, Napoleon Bonaparte's death mask, and a hairball from a cow's stomach.

ABANDONED VILLAGE Between 1985 and 2010, the entire village of Summerlands, a development of 183 homes and 774 lots on Phillip Island, Australia, was demolished and abandoned by the Victoria state government to protect a colony of little penguins.

DOLL ISLAND A small island, La Isla De Las Muñecas, in Xochimilco, Mexico, is decorated with hundred of terrifying dolls—with severed limbs, decapitated heads, and blank eyes. Legend states that after a young girl died in one of the canals that surround the island, dolls regularly began to wash ashore. The island's sole inhabitant, Don Julian Santana Barrera, then started to hang dolls from trees in memory of the girl, and although he died in 2001, visitors continue to bring dolls.

HIGH DIVE At Lake Licancabur, Chile, scuba divers can dive at an altitude of 19,409 ft. (5,916 m) above sea level. The lake is located in a crater in the Licancabur volcano and is 330 ft. (100 m) long, 230 ft. (70 m) wide with a maximum depth of 26 ft. (8 m).

SUITCASE RUN People welcome the New Year in Ecuador by taking an empty suitcase for a run around the block—a tradition that is supposed to bring the opportunity for travel in the coming 12 months.

▶▶ A PORTABLE TOILET AT THE NEWLYN FISH FESTIVAL IN CORNWALL, ENGLAND, WAS TRANSPORTED ACROSS THE HARBOR BY A FORKLIFT TRUCK—WITH A WOMAN STILL INSIDE IT.

SMALL WORLD One in every five Canadians is related to someone who emigrated to the country through Pier 21 at Halifax, Nova Scotia, which could be considered the "Ellis Island" of Canada.

FOOT CARE January 23 each year is World Measure Your Feet Day. The idea is that people should measure their feet regularly to ensure that they are not squashed inside wrong-sized shoes.

POSSUM DROP In Brasstown, North Carolina, which claims to be the "possum capital of the world," an opossum in a transparent box is carefully lowered over a crowd at midnight to mark the New Year. The drop—organized by convenience store proprietor Clay Logan—until recently used a live animal, but following complaints, a dead opossum was put in the box to herald the start of 2015.

FLOATING TREE A tree has been floating vertically in Crater Lake, Oregon, for over 100 years. The "Old Man of the Lake" is a 30 ft. (9 m) tall stump that shows about 4 ft. (1.2 m) above the surface of the 1,943 ft. (592 m) deep lake, which is the deepest lake in the United States. Bleached white by the sun, the stump moves around a lot, and during a three-month period in 1938 it traveled over 60 miles (96 km). It can drift 4 miles (6.4 km) in a single day. The stump has probably been preserved by the lake's clean, cold water in the remains of the collapsed volcano, Mount Mazama.

WEDDING PLANNERS For a fee of $153,000 (£100,000), luxury rental company Oliver's Travels will guarantee fine weather for a couple's wedding day by using the scientific technique of cloud seeding. Up to one week before the wedding, the company hires an airplane to sprinkle clouds with silver iodide crystals, thereby inducing rain and causing the clouds to disperse.

RADIATION ZONE Fifty-five-year-old rice farmer Naoto Matsumara looks after abandoned animals in Tomioka, Japan, even though radiation levels there are 17 times higher than normal. When the nearby Fukushima Daiichi nuclear plant went into meltdown following the 2011 tsunami, 57,000 residents fled, leaving their pets and livestock behind, and only Matsumara, a former construction worker, returned.

Fading Glory

Once a brilliant shade of blue, Morning Glory Pool, a hot spring in Wyoming's Yellowstone National Park, is now yellow, orange, and green. Often referred to as "Fading Glory," it has fallen victim to vandalism, as visitors over the years have thrown coins, trash, rocks, and other debris into the pool. This debris has affected water circulation and thermal energy, causing orange-colored bacteria to migrate toward the center and alter the pool's appearance.

Villagers in Kuban, Bali, uphold an ancient tradition where the dead are not buried or cremated—they are simply left to rot. When a village member dies, his or her body, except the head, is wrapped in white cloth and placed in one of 11 triangle-shaped bamboo cages in Trunyan Cemetery. After a body is completely decomposed and only bones remain, the skull is added to the stone wall shelf beneath a large banyan or "nice smell" tree, which neutralizes the stench with a pleasant, incense-like fragrance.

STACKED SKULLS

Angkor Temples

Cambodia's Angkor Wat, which means "temple city," is spread throughout 500 acres (200 hectares), making it one of the largest religious monuments ever constructed. Each structure was built using Khmer bricks that were bonded together almost invisibly with a vegetable compound instead of mortar. Angkor Wat was built between 1113 and 1150 AD as a Hindu temple site dedicated to the god Vishnu, and was later converted into a Buddhist temple site in the 14th century. Over 200 hidden paintings have been discovered in the 213 ft. (65 m) tall central tower using technology NASA developed for use on the Mars rovers, which revealed centuries-old murals of elephants, deities, boats, orchestral ensembles, and people riding horses—all invisible to the naked eye!

TWISTER HAVOC A July 2015 tornado sucked around 3,000 imperial gallons (3,600 US gallons) of water out of a garden pond in Dorset, England, and up into the sky. The twister left Celia Marker's koi carp and goldfish struggling to breathe in the shallow puddles left behind.

LOCAL DIALECTS There is no official written or spoken Norwegian language. There are so many local dialects that people can buy Norwegian-to-Norwegian dictionaries!

MERMAID CONVENTION At the annual Merfest Convention in Cary, North Carolina, as many as 300 enthusiasts dress up as mermaids and mermen in custom-made tails that cost up to $4,000 (£2,542).

SUNKEN VILLAGE The village of Curon Venosta, Italy, sits submerged underwater, but its bell tower still juts above the water's surface. The village was flooded to make way for an artificial lake shortly after World War II. During the winter, when the lake freezes over, the church tower can be reached on foot.

CRYING ROOMS The Mitsui Garden Yotsuya hotel in Shinjuku, Japan, offered special "crying rooms" in 2015 for women seeking to relieve stress. The rooms were stocked with luxury tissues and a steam eye mask to avoid the appearance of swollen eyes the following morning.

GHOST RESORT The resort city of Varosha on the coast of Cyprus is completely uninhabited, with entry forbidden to the public. It was evacuated in 1974 after Turkey invaded it, and is now a ghost city of empty high-rise hotels. Previously, Varosha had been a major tourist destination, visited by celebrities such as Elizabeth Taylor, Raquel Welch, and Brigitte Bardot.

BORDER VOLLEYBALL

Residents of both the United States and Mexico enjoyed a friendly game of volleyball at the US-Mexico border in April 2007. Made up of locals from Naco, Arizona, and Naco, Mexico, and using the border fence as the net, the match took place during the "Fiesta Bi-Nacional," a binational goodwill festival held occasionally on the border since 1979.

BIRTH BLESSING When a baby is born among the Wolof people in the North African country of Mauritania, women bless it by spitting on its face, men spit in its ear, and then they rub the saliva all over its head. The Wolof believe that human saliva has the power to retain words and feeling.

REMOTE GORGE The Yarlung Tsangpo gorge in Tibet is three times deeper than the Grand Canyon, but is so remote that it was not explored by outsiders until the 1990s.

LUCKY PANS In southern Italy, people celebrate the New Year by throwing old pots, pans, clothes, and even furniture out of their upstairs windows in order to banish past bad luck.

MINIATURE BOOKS The Baku Museum of Miniature Books in Azerbaijan contains more than 5,600 miniature books from 67 different countries. They include a 17th-century miniature copy of the Koran and a Japanese book of flowers that can only be read with a magnifying glass.

SPORTS GIANT Yankee Stadium, the Rose Bowl, Churchill Downs, the Colosseum in Rome, and Vatican City could all fit inside the 253 acre (102 hectare) space of the Indianapolis Motor Speedway oval at the same time.

ROBOT RECEPTIONIST The Mitsukoshi Nihonbashi department store in Tokyo, Japan, has a humanoid robot receptionist, Aiko Chihira, who greets customers and guides them to the building's different floors.

UNIQUE MARBLE All of the "Beulah red" marble in the world went into the Colorado State Capitol building in Denver, meaning that if the marble is damaged, it cannot be replaced at any price. It took six years, from 1894 to 1900, to cut, polish, and install the rose-colored marble.

BOTTLE HOUSE Hamidullah Ilchibaev has built a house in Chelyabinsk, Russia, from 12,000 empty champagne bottles. He collected bottles for three years to build the 1,065 sq. ft. (99 sq. m) house. He used a glass cutter to trim the bottles to size and then stacked them up like bricks to form the walls, keeping them in place with mortar.

SKY CYCLE

The Sky Cycle at Okayama Prefecture's Brazilian Washuzan Highland Park in Japan takes the thrill of roller coasters to the next level—by having you pedal a cart four stories above the ground. The bicycle cart has room for just two people, who each have a set of pedals to control the speed. Passengers need only fasten their seat belts and store their belongings in the front basket before embarking on a slow but heart-racing ride over hilly terrain toward a spectacular view of the Shimotsui-Seto Bridge on the Seto Inland Sea.

Ripley's — Believe It or Not!
www.ripleys.com/books
World

These images show the promenade steps leading down to the sandy beach before the high tide (left) and after the high tide (right), with the steps leading to a sharp drop onto rocks.

For the first time in living memory, Porthleven Beach in Cornwall, England, was stripped of all its sand overnight by a severe high tide on January 21, 2015. Equally remarkable, however, was that the sand was naturally restored back to the beach only a few hours later. A favorite vacation destination for tourists visiting Cornwall, the usually sandy location turned into a beach covered in jagged rocks and seaweed.

SHIFTING SAND

ROCKET BATTLE Every Easter on the Greek island of Chios, two rival congregations in the town of Vrontados set off tens of thousands of homemade rockets with the aim of hitting the bell tower of the opposite church. Some rocket builders have been accidentally killed while preparing for the battle.

FORTIES BAR Cahoots, a bar in London, England, is designed to resemble a World War II air raid shelter inside a 1940s London Underground station.

LUNAR RAINBOW Under a full moon on a clear night, a lunar rainbow—or moonbow— appears from the base of Cumberland Falls in Kentucky—one of only a few places in the world where the phenomenon can be seen. A moonbow occurs when light is reflected from the surface of the moon and then refracted off water droplets in the air.

OCEAN MAILBOX The Great Barrier Reef has its own mailbox. It is set on a floating platform located on the Agincourt Reef in the Coral Sea, 45 miles (72 km) off the coast of mainland Australia.

LONELY BEAT Australian Police Constable Neale McShane has spent over 10 years single-handedly patrolling the area encompassing the remote Queensland town of Birdsville—but his last arrest was in 2011. His overall jurisdiction is the size of the UK, but much of it is uninhabited desert.

WORM RAIN Thousands of live earthworms fell from the sky over a large area of southern Norway in April 2015. Scientists believe the worms could have been picked up by a storm and carried for miles.

SALAD TRAIL Police officers arrested three men on suspicion of breaking into a restaurant in Mount Morris, New York, by following a trail of macaroni salad. The burglars had stolen a large bowl of the salad and took turns eating it while making their getaway.

MODEL PRISONERS Australia's first police force, formed in Sydney in 1789, was made up of the city's 12 best-behaved convicts.

Ripley's Research

In 1876, **Sandy Island**, a tiny South Pacific island, was discovered in French territorial waters by the whaling ship *Velocity*—the ship reported "heavy breakers" and "sandy islets." However, scientists recently "undiscovered" Sandy Island after identifying a long series of inconsistencies and errors trailing back to old hard-copy charts. Although shown on maps for more than a century, Sandy Island never actually existed.

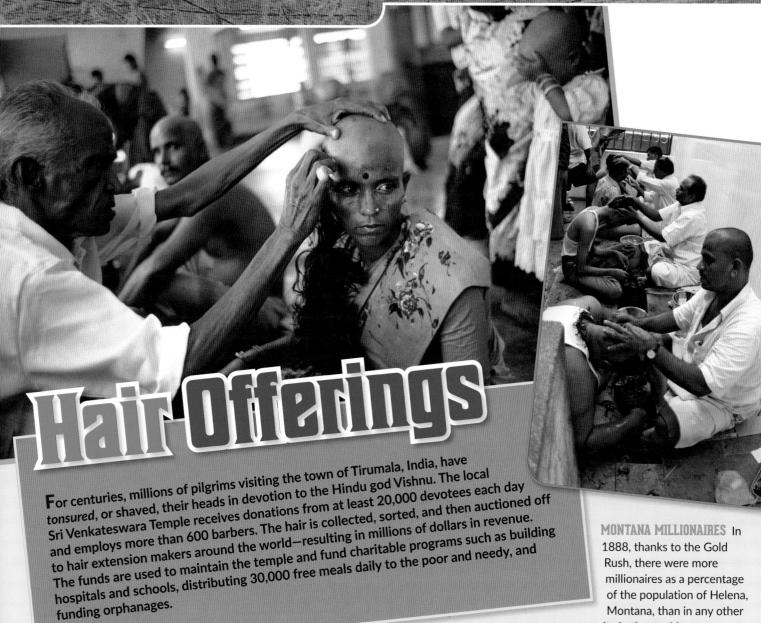

Hair Offerings

For centuries, millions of pilgrims visiting the town of Tirumala, India, have tonsured, or shaved, their heads in devotion to the Hindu god Vishnu. The local Sri Venkateswara Temple receives donations from at least 20,000 devotees each day and employs more than 600 barbers. The hair is collected, sorted, and then auctioned off to hair extension makers around the world—resulting in millions of dollars in revenue. The funds are used to maintain the temple and fund charitable programs such as building hospitals and schools, distributing 30,000 free meals daily to the poor and needy, and funding orphanages.

MONTANA MILLIONAIRES In 1888, thanks to the Gold Rush, there were more millionaires as a percentage of the population of Helena, Montana, than in any other city in the world.

POSTHUMOUS MARRIAGE In France, you can legally marry a dead person, and about 50 posthumous marriages a year now take place there. The legislation dates back to 1959 when a dam burst in southern France, killing 420 people. A pregnant woman who lost her fiancé in the disaster was so upset that President Charles de Gaulle penned a law permitting her to marry her dead lover.

DISTANT JOB For seven years, Chris Bates officially represented the British overseas territory of Tristan da Cunha, a tiny island in the South Atlantic with a population of 267—while working from his home in Birmingham, England, 6,400 miles (10,300 km) away. He arranged for items such as bus stop signs, gravestones, police badges, and dog whistles for shepherds to be delivered to the remote outpost, which can only be reached by a weeklong boat journey from Cape Town, South Africa.

BOULDER HOME Designers André Bloc and Claude Parent created a Swiss Alpine cabin that looks like a giant boulder. They sculpted and spray-painted the exterior of the cabin to resemble a rough rock, and then transported it by truck up the Swiss mountains, using a crane to lower it into position. With a concealed door and tiny window, it looks just like part of the landscape.

NEW ISLANDS In 2015, cartographers discovered that Estonia was 38.6 sq. miles (100 sq. km) larger than previously thought after 800 new islands in the Baltic Sea were officially recognized. The country now includes 2,355 islands.

HOT WATER The acidic water in the 660 ft. (200 m) wide Frying Pan Lake on New Zealand's North Island has a constant temperature of 122–140°F (50–60°C).

CURIOUS COLLECTION Canterbury Cathedral in Kent, England, houses countless curiosities collected by 17th-century traveler John Bargrave, including a chameleon pickled in brandy, the mummified finger of a Frenchman, a hippopotamus tooth, and a 12-piece anatomical model of a human eye.

THEMED MOTEL The Eden Motel in Kaohsiung City, Taiwan, has rooms themed on Batman, *The Wizard of Oz*, the horror movie *The Mummy*, and even an Alcatraz Prison room, complete with prison bars, handcuffs, and barbed wire.

NEST WRECKERS To reduce the risk of birds striking airplane engines during a large military parade in Beijing, Chinese authorities recruited a team of macaques trained to wreck nests in trees near the pilots' training areas. Five of the mischievous monkeys can dismantle 60 birds' nests in a day.

HUACACHINA OASIS

Ripley's — Believe It or Not!
www.ripleys.com/books
World

In the middle of a desert in Peru sits Huacachina, a tropical oasis home to about 100 residents and a "bucket-list" destination for tourists. Declared a national cultural heritage site, a naturally formed lake lies at the center of Huacachina, which is 2.5 miles (4 km) from the town of Ica. Visitors to the "Oasis of America" enjoy riding dune buggies and sandboards along the wind-sculpted sand dunes, as well as frequenting the rustic hotels and picturesque shops.

BODY COUNT In northeastern China in 2015, 97 human skeletons were found crammed into a 5,000-year-old house just 210 sq. ft. (19.5 sq. m) in size.

IRON RAIN Scientists in New Mexico have discovered that four billion years ago the Earth's surface was hit by showers of vaporized metal falling from the sky in the form of iron rain.

ATLANTIC CROSSING In 1973, John Soutar threw a message in a bottle into the North Sea off the east coast of Scotland—and 41 years later it was found washed up on Jones Beach, New York, 3,300 miles (5,311 km) away.

FROZEN CASKET After his wife, Yang Huiqing, died in December 2014, Jiang Maode could not bear to be without her—so for months he kept her dead body in a frozen casket at their home in Sichuan, China.

WATERFALL WALK Battling fierce winds and water spray that left them barely able to see, Austria's Reinhard Kleindl and Germany's Lukas Irmler became the first people to walk a 300 ft. (91 m) long slackline suspended 330 ft. (100 m) above Victoria Falls on the border of Zimbabwe and Zambia.

Trust Test

On May 25, 2015, hundreds of students from a vocational school's College of Nursing took part in a completely unsupervised graduation examination in an outside classroom in Baoji, Shaanxi province, China. Unsupervised exams are a growing concern in China, where the stressful, score-oriented education system has inspired the lucrative world of hired test-takers (also known as "hired guns" or "gunmen").

Battle of the ORANGES

Every year, the tiny northern city of Ivrea, Italy, celebrates the Carnevale di Ivrea by staging a re-creation of a historic fight between townsfolk and an oppressive ruler—battering each other with more than 1.1 million lbs. (500,000 kg) of fresh oranges in the Battle of the Oranges (*Battaglia delle Arance*). The battle begins the Sunday before Ash Wednesday—the "lord's henchmen" wear jester outfits and are elevated in horse-drawn carts, while the "commoners" fight at ground level in sporting uniforms. Nearly 100,000 spectators turn out to watch the competition between nine squads of almost 4,000 participants.

EXTENDED BIRTHDAY Germany's Sven Hagemeier kept his 26th birthday going for 46 hours by flying from Auckland, New Zealand, to Brisbane, Australia, and then traveling backward in time across the International Date Line to Hawaii. The actual flight time was only just over 13 hours but because he was moving between time zones, it lasted nearly two days.

SPACE CONTACT Amateur radio enthusiast Adrian Lane put out a call from his garden shed in Gloucestershire, England, and made contact with the International Space Station. He then spent 50 seconds chatting to a US astronaut as the space station flew 200 miles (320 km) overhead at a speed of 18,500 mph (30,000 km/h).

OLD NEWLYWEDS The bride and groom at a wedding in the UK had a combined age of 194. George Kirby, 103, married 91-year-old Doreen Luckie at Eastbourne, East, Sussex, England, on June 13, 2015.

OLYMPIC RINGS The 50 ton, 130 ft. (40 m) high Olympic rings that hung from Sydney Harbour Bridge during the Australia 2000 Olympics were later sold on eBay for $17,000 (£11,220).

ICE COLLECTOR At least once a week, 68-year-old Baltazar Ushca spends five hours hiking 14,700 ft. (4,482 m) up Ecuador's Mt. Chimborazo to collect ice. Continuing the family tradition, he uses a pickax to hack ice from a cave and shapes it into blocks, which sell for around $2.50 (£1.60) apiece, meaning that he rarely earns more than $25 (£16) per week. He is only 4.9 ft. (1.5 m) tall, but can carry two 66 lb. (30 kg) ice blocks on his shoulders.

WASHER RESCUE A 22-year-old man had to be rescued by firefighters in Sydney, Australia, after becoming stuck for three hours in a washing machine at his home. His entire lower body was wedged in the appliance's drum, and it took crews over an hour to extricate him.

LONG WAIT Ah Ji, a 47-year-old Taiwanese man, has been waiting for his date to show up for over 20 years. Refusing to believe that he has been rejected, he stands permanently at the Tainan train station where he had arranged to meet his girlfriend in 1995.

SHARED FOOD When Fethullah Uzumcuoglu and Esra Polat got married in Kilis, Turkey, in 2015, they shared their wedding day feast with 4,000 Syrian refugees.

TERRIFIED BURGLARS Bungling burglars who broke into a house in Derby, England, fled screaming into the night after being confronted by the owner's pet—a super-sized, 238 lb. (108 kg) Canadian pot bellied pig named Ludwig.

MUMMIFIED MONK The 200-year-old remains of a meditating monk were discovered in Mongolia in 2015—with the body still sitting in a cross-legged lotus position. The human relic had been preserved under cattle skin.

CAMEL LIFT In Chelyabinsk, Russia, in March 2015, Elbrus Nigmatullin lifted a 1,540 lb. (700 kg) adult camel that was standing atop a 440 lb. (200 kg) platform, and held the pair above his head for 44.78 seconds. Two months later in the same city, he pulled a 30 ton, two-story wooden house along a 10 ft. (3 m) track.

TRIPLET DOCTORS Born eight minutes apart on September 22, 1999, triplets Saugat, Saujan, and Sauraj Devkota from Chitwan, Nepal, all qualified to become doctors in 2015.

TOY GUILLOTINES Miniature guillotine toys that decapitated dolls were popular with children during the French Revolution.

FAMILY REUNION After having been stolen from her mother's arms as a baby, Zephany Nurse was reunited with her parents 17 years later when she ended up at the same school as her biological sister. Students at the high school in Cape Town, South Africa, noticed striking similarities between Zephany and 14-year-old Cassidy, and when Zephany was invited to meet Cassidy's parents, they immediately recognized their long-lost daughter. DNA tests confirmed her true identity.

FLUSHED PAPER The world's population flushes away 27,000 trees' worth of toilet paper every day.

THREE SINKINGS Fifteen-year-old British sailor Wenman Wykeham-Musgrave survived torpedo attacks on three different ships that were sunk in one hour off the Dutch coast on September 22, 1914, during World War I.

LIFE SAVER Retired police officer Yukio Shige patrols the Tojinbo cliffs in Japan's Fukui Prefecture—a notorious suicide spot—every day, and over the past decade he has prevented more than 500 people from jumping to their deaths.

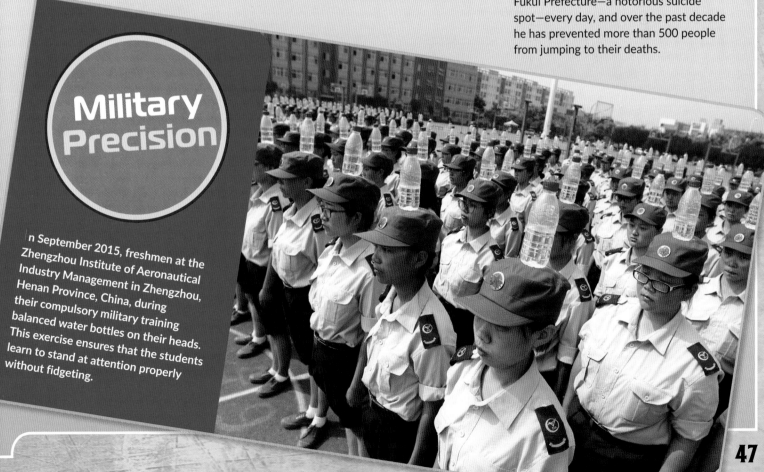

Military Precision

In September 2015, freshmen at the Zhengzhou Institute of Aeronautical Industry Management in Zhengzhou, Henan Province, China, during their compulsory military training balanced water bottles on their heads. This exercise ensures that the students learn to stand at attention properly without fidgeting.

Cliff-Hanger

Located 9,301 ft. (2,835 m) above sea level and jutting off the edge of a glacier cliff, the Bivacco Gervasutti is a solar-powered, Internet-enabled shelter for weary mountain climbers.

Opened in 2012, the tube-shaped biovac hut stands in full view of the Grandes and Petites Jorasses mountains on the Italian side of the Alps. Each segment of the 323 sq. ft. (30 sq. m), 5,512 lb. (2,500 kg) hut had to be transported by helicopter and assembled on site. Travelers must traverse steep terrain and snowfields, and then rappel down a perilous rock face to reach it.

SLOW BUILD The Duomo, the cathedral of Milan, Italy, took more than 500 years to build, and has 135 spires and over 3,000 statues.

CITY BOUNDARY Honolulu is technically the largest city in the world, spanning a distance of 1,500 miles (2,400 km)—the distance from Los Angeles, California, to Minneapolis, Minnesota. According to the Hawaii state constitution, any island not named as belonging to a county is considered part of Honolulu. Because of this, every island except Midway within the Hawaiian Archipelago is part of Honolulu, which therefore stretches all the way to the Northwestern Hawaiian Islands.

THUMBS DOWN If they walk by a graveyard or see a hearse passing, Japanese people hide their thumbs by tucking them into their pants. This is believed to protect their parents from death, because the Japanese word for "thumb" translates literally as "parent-finger."

▶▶ **TO HONOR ITS HISTORY, THE GERMAN TOWN OF BERCHTESGADEN HAS TURNED ITS OLD SALT MINE INTO A TOURIST ATTRACTION, FEATURING SLIDES, TRAINS, AND EVEN A LASER LIGHT SHOW.**

TOOTH STONE A memorial stone containing dozens of human teeth stands in Elkhart, Indiana. The Elkhart Tooth Stone was created by local dentist Dr. Joseph Stamp, who, during his 60-year practice, saved nearly every tooth he extracted and preserved them in a barrel of chemicals in his basement. When his dog, a German shepherd named Prince, died in the 1950s, Dr. Stamp created a concrete block embedded with the teeth in his memory. He enlarged the stone whenever he acquired a new batch of teeth until his own death in 1978.

RARE RAINBOW While waiting for a train at Glen Cove station on Long Island, New York, in April 2015, commuter Amanda Curtis photographed an extremely rare quadruple rainbow. Only a handful have been recorded over the past 250 years.

Figure-Eight Ferris Wheel

In 2015, the Golden Reel—the world's first figure-eight Ferris wheel—opened in China. Situated in Macau's Studio City, a $3.2 billion (£2.1 billion) casino, the wheel stands a lofty 426.5 ft. (130 m) high, making it the highest Ferris wheel in Asia. Riders enjoy spectacular views of the city and the South China Sea during their 15-minute ride in steampunk-themed cabins that rotate 23 floors above the ground.

FACE OFF Thomas Jefferson's face on Mount Rushmore was originally started on the opposite side of George Washington, but after carving for 18 months, workers realized the granite there was too weak. Consequently, Jefferson's face was blasted off with dynamite and carved on the other side.

GARDEN CHAPEL Jon Richards spent two and a half years building a miniature replica of his local parish church in the back garden of his home in Warwickshire, England, complete with stained glass windows, a bronze statue of Jesus, antique pews, prayer books, and a tapestry of *The Last Supper*. The 12 ft. x 8 ft. (3.7 m x 2.4 m) chapel can hold 12 worshippers.

FOGGY SPOT The community of Argentia in Newfoundland, Canada, experiences an average of 206 foggy days a year—caused by warm air from the Gulf Stream meeting the much colder Labrador Current. Where the two air masses collide, the water vapor that is present in the warm air suddenly cools and condenses to form fog.

HURRICANE MAGNET Nearly 40 percent of all US hurricanes hit Florida, and during the 20th century, 88 percent of major hurricanes hit either Florida or Texas.

VILLAGE VOICE In some isolated villages in New Mexico, descendants of Spanish conquistadors still speak a form of 16th-century Spanish that is spoken nowhere else in the world today.

LOTUS Building

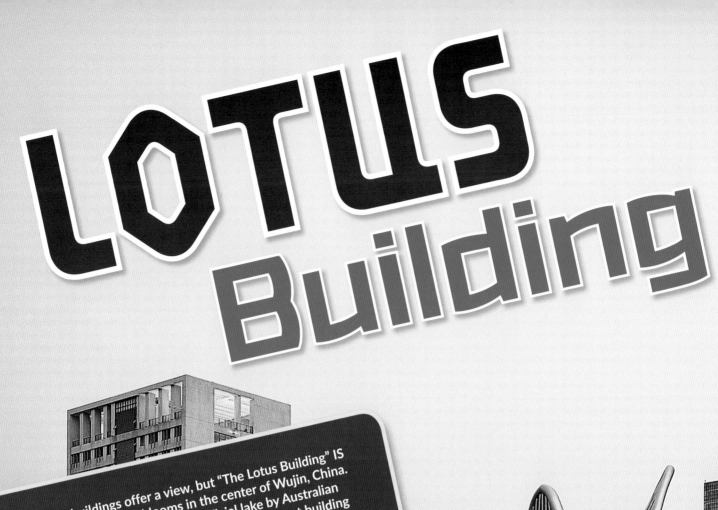

Most office buildings offer a view, but "The Lotus Building" IS the view, as it stunningly blooms in the center of Wujin, China. Designed and built in 2013 on an artificial lake by Australian architecture firm Studio 505, the unique government building takes its name and form from the lotus flower and shows the three stages of the flower's life—from a young bud to the opened bloom, which contains a seedpod. The building is designed for energy efficiency as well as beauty. The ground beneath the building pre-cools during the summer and pre-warms during the winter to facilitate the air conditioning systems.

Ripley's —— Believe It or Not!
www.ripleys.com/books
World

WRONG TIME Big Ben, the great bell inside the clock tower at the Palace of Westminster in London, England, chimed up to six seconds late for two weeks in August 2015. For over 150 years, the clock, designed to be accurate to within 1.5 seconds, has been used by people across the UK as a reliable time check, although in 1949 it slowed by four and a half minutes after a flock of starlings perched on the minute hand.

HAUNTED DOLLS Katrin Reedik, a mother of two from Glasgow, Scotland, has spent thousands of dollars on what she claims are haunted dolls. She believes that each one in her collection of 13 dolls is possessed by the spirit of a dead person, including a woman who died in a plane crash, a woman who died at age 103, and a former witch. She says the dolls once started a fire in her apartment, and she now hires a babysitter to watch them when she is out because she is afraid to leave them alone.

CHAINSAW SKATER Swedish skater Erik Sunnerheim has invented the sport of chainsaw skating. He uses the razor-sharp teeth of a chainsaw to propel him across an icy lake—but with such dexterity that he avoids slicing through the ice.

CABBIE TRICKED Two men tricked a UK taxi driver out of a $200 (£128) fare by leaving a store mannequin fully clothed and wearing a hat in his cab and pretending it was their sleeping friend. Picking up the late-night passengers in Brighton, the driver took them over 50 miles (80 km) to London, where they got out and told him that their dozing friend would pay the fare at his destination. When the cabbie reached the given address and tried to wake the friend, he discovered it was a dummy.

FLYING SNOWMOBILE Finnish daredevil Antti Pendikainen drove a snowmobile off the edge of a 5,000 ft. (1,500 m) high mountain in Sweden and paraglided to the ground. He attached a parachute to the snowmobile with duct tape for the four-minute flight.

HISTORY REWRITTEN The Greenwich Meridian Line, built in London, England, to divide the eastern and western hemispheres at zero degrees longitude, has been in the wrong place for 131 years. In 2015, researchers discovered that the steel line—a popular tourist location—should not be in the Royal Observatory, but 334 ft. (102 m) to the east inside a small café.

>It doesn't tip over

Balancing Barn

A hotel sleeping eight people, the Balancing Barn in Suffolk, England, appears to be hanging precariously over the edge of a precipice. The single-story, cantilever designed building covered in silver tiles is 100 ft. (30 m) long, but half of it hangs over a steep slope with just fresh air beneath it—like a seesaw.

THAT SUCKS! In February 2015, firefighters rescued a woman in Changwon, South Korea, after her hair was sucked up by a robotic vacuum while she was asleep.

QUICKFIRE COMIC Entertainer Clive Greenaway from Dorset, England, told 26 jokes in 60 seconds in front of a live audience, who laughed at each one. He can also perform 18 magic tricks in 60 seconds while blindfolded.

SUDDEN RECOVERY Eleven hours after a doctor had declared her dead, 91-year-old Janina Kolkiewicz from Ostrow Lubelski, Poland, awoke in a morgue complaining of feeling cold.

BURGER SCENT Burger King® in Japan launched a limited-edition cologne with the smell of grilled burgers. The "Flame Grilled" fragrance, which came with a burger, cost $40 (£26).

VAMPIRE GRAVE The grave of a suspected vampire from the 13th century was discovered in 2014 by an archaeologist in Perperikon, Bulgaria. The skeleton was found with a stake impaled in its chest—a prescribed method for killing vampires.

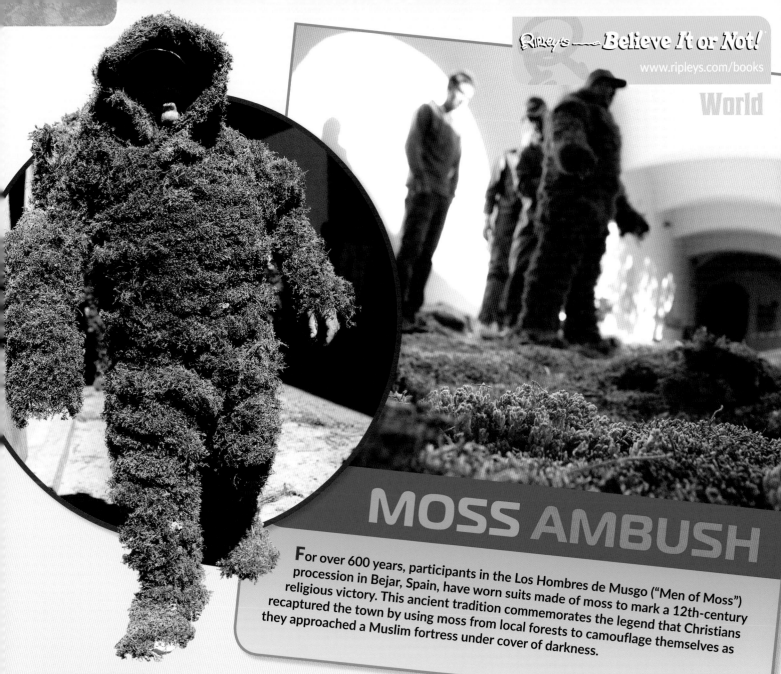

Ripley's — Believe It or Not!
www.ripleys.com/books
World

MOSS AMBUSH

For over 600 years, participants in the Los Hombres de Musgo ("Men of Moss") procession in Bejar, Spain, have worn suits made of moss to mark a 12th-century religious victory. This ancient tradition commemorates the legend that Christians recaptured the town by using moss from local forests to camouflage themselves as they approached a Muslim fortress under cover of darkness.

NAMESAKE SUBSTITUTE After buying tickets for an around-the-world tour with his girlfriend Elizabeth Gallagher, Jordan Axani of Toronto, Ontario, Canada, broke up with her, but, not wanting to waste the non-transferable ticket, he searched for another Canadian woman named Elizabeth Gallagher to take her place. His online plea attracted dozens of replies, including some from women willing to change their names, but he eventually chose Elizabeth Quinn Gallagher, a student from Cole Harbour, Nova Scotia, to accompany him on the three-week trip.

UNIQUE DOLL An extraordinarily lifelike doll of a little girl with pierced ears sold at auction in London, England, for £242,500 ($341,016) in 2014. The early 20th-century doll, made by German manufacturers Kammer & Reinhardt, is thought to be unique in its use of pierced ears and was possibly made from an experimental mold.

LATE QUADS Annegret Raunigk, a retired teacher from Berlin, Germany, gave birth to quadruplets at age 65, making her the mother of 17 children in total.

MODEL HAIR Once a month, Portuguese soccer star Cristiano Ronaldo sends his personal hairstylist to brush the hair of his wax sculpture in the Museo de Cera museum in Madrid, Spain. Ronaldo's figure at the museum has natural hair imported from India, and the player wants to ensure that it always looks perfectly groomed.

NOSE TYPIST After practicing for six hours every day for three years, Mohammed Khursheed Hussain from Hyderabad, India, is able to type a 103-character sentence with his nose in 47 seconds. He shuts one eye while doing it because it helps him locate the keys. He can also type the entire English alphabet with his fingers in under 3.5 seconds.

PLUTO CANYON Canyons on Pluto's moon Charon are up to 6 miles (9.7 km) deep—six times deeper than the Grand Canyon.

ROBOT WEDDING One hundred guests attended a wedding between two humanoid robots in Tokyo, Japan. The groom, Frois, a red and silver robot wearing a bow tie, sealed the union by extending a silver disk from his mouth in order to kiss his bride, Yukirin, who wore a long white gown with a large silk bow.

INDIAN JAILBIRD A pigeon was arrested and kept in custody by police officers in India in May 2015 on suspicion of being a Pakistani spy. The bird was spotted in the village of Manwal, near the Pakistan border, with a message written in Urdu and containing a Pakistani phone number stamped on its feathers.

GIANT ICICLE

Tree trimmer Garrick Moreland created a 45 ft. (13.7 m) tall icicle in the front yard of his mother Katherine Ragel's home near St. Elmo, Illinois, in the winter of 2014–15. As temperatures plunged, he climbed high into the tree with a hose and turned on the water. The icicle also included a mannequin of the character Elsa from the Disney® movie Frozen.

LOST LAKE Every summer, all the water from Oregon's 9 ft. (2.7 m) deep Lost Lake disappears like water in a bathtub draining through a plug hole. The natural phenomenon is caused by two hollow lava tubes at the bottom of the 85 acre (34 hectares) lake. These constantly drain the lake, but as there is less rain in summer to replenish the lost water, it eventually becomes completely dry.

TITANIC HOTEL A new hotel in Turkey is modeled after the doomed ocean liner Titanic. The Titanic Beach Lara has recreated the look of the luxury ship, which sank in 1912, allowing guests to stroll on replica decks and peer through porthole-shaped windows in their rooms. It even has its own lifeboats.

DESERT STORM A seven-day sandstorm almost the size of the United States swept across the Arabian Peninsula in April 2015, covering the region in clouds of thick yellow dust.

ROCK FACE Hundreds of visitors flocked to the San Francisco area of Putumayo, Colombia, in March 2015, after an image of what some claimed to be the face of Jesus Christ appeared in a rock formation following a landslide.

FIRST RAIN When 0.03 in. (0.7 mm) of rain fell on Phoenix, Arizona, on June 5, 2015, it was the first time that it had officially rained in the desert city on June 5 in recorded history.

SPIRAL SLIDE The RedDot Hotel in Taichung, Taiwan, has installed a 100 ft. (30 m) spiral slide to allow guests in a hurry to descend from the second to the first floor. The slide was built using 102 stainless steel sheets.

VANISHING WATER Mars has lost an entire ocean's worth of water. Although the planet's surface is now cold and dry, new maps of water in its atmosphere reveal that billions of years ago around 20 percent of Mars was covered in rivers, lakes, and seas.

SNOW MOUNTAIN After a freak storm in November 2014 buried Buffalo, New York, in up to 7 ft. (2.1 m) of snow, crews dumped 11,000 truckloads on an abandoned lot, creating a snow mountain five stories high. Eight months later, in July 2015, even though the temperature had climbed past 80°F (27°C), some of the snow still had not melted.

WARFARE MUSEUM The United States Army Chemical Corps Museum in Fort Leonard Wood, Missouri, contains over 6,000 artifacts of chemical warfare.

BALCONY PARKING Hamilton Scotts, a luxury 30-floor apartment condominium in Singapore, allows residents to park their cars on their balconies—often hundreds of feet above ground. Each apartment has an internal two-car garage, which is separated from the living room by a glass wall. Drivers park their vehicles on the ground floor inside a glass elevator shaft, which then takes the cars up to the desired levels.

GARGOYLE TRIBUTE Retired school principal Dr. Richard Shephard, who was in charge of the Minster School in York, England, for 19 years, was honored in 2015 with a stone gargoyle depicting his face on the historic Minster building. The carved figure depicts him conducting music and overlooks the school.

Ripley's —— Believe It or Not!
www.ripleys.com/books
World

Ice Hotel

First featured in the 2004 annual *Ripley's Believe It or Not!*, Quebec's luxurious Ice Hotel continues to offer visitors the coziness of an igloo. Rebuilt each year on the shores of Lake St. Joseph and only open from January to March, the hotel is constructed from 30,000 tons of snow and 500 tons of ice. Hotel guests sleep on mattresses over solid blocks of ice and keep warm with polar fleeces and deerskins. With an average temperature of around 27°F (–3°C), the hotel also features ice-carving art galleries, an ice bar, and even an ice chapel.

CAVE HOUSE Xu Wenyi, a farmer, spent six years digging his own cave house in the side of a hill in Xiangtan County, Hunan Province, China. It measures 100 ft. (30 m) deep and 13 ft. (4 m) wide and has concrete-reinforced walls, a stone kitchen, and a proper front door.

UNDERWATER TOWN Once a popular tourist resort, the town of Villa Epecuen, Argentina, was flooded in 1985 with saltwater after a nearby dam broke, and remained under as much as 33 ft. (10 m) of water for a quarter of a century. When the water slowly receded, finally exposing the ruins of the town, only one resident, Pablo Novak, returned to live there.

UMBRELLA NEEDED It rains an average of 330 days a year in Ocean Falls, British Columbia, Canada, producing more than 172 in. (4,390 mm) of rainfall.

> ▶▶ THE HOOVER DAM CONTAINS 87,750,000 CUBIC FT. (2,480,000 CUBIC M) OF CONCRETE—ENOUGH TO PAVE A TWO-LANE HIGHWAY FROM SAN FRANCISCO TO NEW YORK.

BLOOD BATTLE Every year in May as part of an ancient festival, men, women, and children of the Nahua Indian community in Guerrero, Mexico, challenge each other to brutal fistfights in the street. All the blood they spill during the fights is collected in buckets to be used to water their lands. The villagers believe that the ritual will guarantee rain and produce excellent harvests.

ICE VOLCANO Several days of subzero temperatures in February 2015 turned a geyser at Letchworth State Park, New York, into a 50 ft. (15 m) high ice volcano. The geyser froze solid to form a cone of ice several feet thick, but water still spouted out of the top.

HOUSE MOVE Wanting to move home from Wiltshire, England, to the neighboring county of Gloucestershire, Adam and Sarah Howard were unable to find a property they liked—so they had their old five-bedroom Georgian manor house carefully dismantled and rebuilt brick by brick in its new location across the county border 30 miles (48 km) away.

SHORT RIVER The Roe River in Great Falls, Montana, is only 201 ft. (60 m) long and up to 8 ft. (2.4 m) deep in places. Its entire length can be walked in one minute.

COPPER ROOF The amount of copper on the roof of Arizona's State Capitol building in Phoenix is equivalent to 4,800,000 pennies.

@ in the World

In Czech, the @ sign is called "zavinac" (pronounced ZAHV-in-ach), meaning **ROLLED PICKLED HERRING**

The French sometimes call the @ symbol "petit escargot," or **LITTLE SNAIL**

The Finnish call the @ symbol "miuku mauku" after what it looks like—**A CURLED UP, SLEEPING CAT**.

Hungarians call the @ sign "kukac" (pronounced KOO-kots), meaning **WORM OR MAGGOT**.

@ Sign Plants →

To help **PURIFY WATER QUALITY**, a local farmer in Jiaxing, China, decided to plant three kinds of water plants in the shape of an "at" sign.

The Dutch, the Germans, and the Polish refer to the @ sign as a **MONKEY OR MONKEY'S TAIL**.

In Sweden and Denmark, the most common term for the @ sign is "snabel-a," or "a with an **ELEPHANT'S TRUNK**."

In Russian, the @ symbol is usually called "sobachka"—**LITTLE DOG** or puppy.

CHEATING PARENTS

India's high-pressure 10th-grade examinations can tempt students to cheat in order to pass, but in March 2015, about two dozen parents also got in on the act, scaling the outside of the school to pass cheat sheets to their children inside. The police in Bihar, India, detained the parents and about 600 high school students were expelled for cheating. Students must pass the test in order to continue on with their high school education.

HISTORIC HOUSE The nine-bedroom Grange Farm in Warwickshire, England, was left untouched for 70 years. Farmer Jack Newton and his sister Audrey moved in during the 1940s, but they rejected nearly all modern innovations, and so when the house went up for sale in 2015 following their deaths, nothing inside had changed for seven decades. It contained such antique items as 1920s musical instruments and sheet music, old teddy bears and typewriters, and even a wartime amputation kit.

SOLE RESIDENT Elsie Eiler is the sole inhabitant of the town of Monowi, Nebraska, and serves as mayor, librarian, and bar owner. The population was 150 in the 1930s, but younger people were lured to the cities with the promise of better jobs, and since her husband Rudy died in 2004, she has been the only resident.

STAR TRIBUTE A recently discovered, 13-billion-year-old galaxy containing some of the very first stars ever formed in the universe has been named CR7 in honor of Spanish soccer club Real Madrid's own star, Portuguese forward Cristiano Ronaldo, who wears the number 7 on his uniform.

NEW NATION On April 13, 2015, Czech politician and activist Vit Jedlicka claimed a small piece of disputed land between the border of Croatia and Serbia and declared it to be a new nation, the Free Republic of Liberland. He created a Liberland flag under the motto, "To live and let live," and announced himself as the country's first ruler, even though the 2.7 sq. mile (7 sq. km) area of land is covered almost entirely in forest and has no residents.

Phone Smuggler

In March 2015, a man traveling from Hong Kong to the Chinese mainland was stopped at a Customs checkpoint after setting off a metal detector. Chan Shih, 30, was caught with 146 smuggled iPhones®—126 were strapped to his waist, while 20 more were attached to his legs. Chan Shih now holds a record in phone smuggling for a single person, as he has been caught trying to smuggle a total of 511 iPhones and 127 CPUs strapped to his body on five separate occasions. Chan Shih tried to convince the authorities that his gold bracelet had set off the metal detector, but a more thorough search revealed the contraband.

CRYING CONTEST During Japan's Nakizumo festival, two Sumo wrestlers face each other in a ring and bounce babies up and down and make faces at them to make them cry as quickly as possible. The 400-year-old crying contest takes place with the full approval of the babies' parents, as it is believed the infants' screams will reach the gods and help them to grow up strong and healthy.

BURNING LAKE Bellandur Lake in Bangalore, India, is so polluted that it sometimes catches fire. Decades of untreated chemical waste and sewage have poured into the lake, and every time it rains, the water surface is churned into a white froth as thick as shaving foam. This froth contains highly combustible methane gas, which in May 2015 caught fire and burned for hours.

MOVING MOUNTAIN The huge 7.8-magnitude earthquake that hit Nepal on April 25, 2015, caused Mt. Everest to move 1.2 in. (3 cm) to the southwest.

COKE HOME Lillian O'Donoghue has turned the kitchen of her home in County Cork, Ireland, into a shrine for Coca-Cola®. The floor, walls, and cupboards are all in the company's red and white colors, and the room is decorated with dozens of cans, advertising posters, and the brand logo. Her husband, Barry, has even made two chandeliers out of Coca-Cola bottles. Lillian has been collecting different Coke cans from around the world for 30 years, and the couple's outdoor summerhouse is also bedecked in various items of Coca-Cola memorabilia.

TOXIC ISLAND The Japanese government only allows adults over 19 to live on the island of Miyakejima, where houses are located at the foot of an active volcano, Mt. Oyama. As residents are constantly exposed to high levels of sulfur dioxide, they have to carry a gas mask at all times.

NO BARKING The Italian town of Controne has banned all dogs from barking between 2 pm and 4 pm so that residents are not disturbed while taking their regular afternoon nap in the summer.

ORANGE DESIGN If all the sails of the Sydney Opera House roof were joined together, they would form a perfect sphere. The architect, Jørn Utzon, was inspired to create the design of the Australian landmark while eating an orange.

> ►► THE LITHUANIAN VILLAGE OF RAMYGALA HOLDS AN ANNUAL BEAUTY PAGEANT FOR GOATS DRESSED IN NATIONAL COSTUME.

BURNING TOWN The town of Jharia in India's Jharkhand state has burned for 100 years because it is built above more than 70 underground coal mine fires. More than 80,000 people live there, even though the fires cause toxic fumes and dangerous sinkholes. In 1995, 250 homes were swallowed by sinkholes in just four hours.

TRANSATLANTIC NEIGHBORS Halifax, Nova Scotia, Canada, is closer to Dublin, Ireland, than it is to Victoria, British Columbia—by a distance of 187 miles (300 km).

SNAIL FOUNTAIN Heavy rain falling on a beach in Exmouth, Devon, England, in July 2015 caused a 15 ft. (4.5 m) wide and 15 ft. (4.5 m) deep sinkhole to open up and spew water and dozens of snails into the sky.

DOOMSDAY BUNKER A luxury bunker condominium extending 15 stories below ground level in Kansas is designed so that its residents can survive any disaster. It has 9 ft. (2.7 m) thick concrete walls to withstand a direct hit from a nuclear missile, can resist 500 mph (800 km/h) winds, accommodates 70 people, and has enough food and water to keep them alive for five years. Originally built in the 1960s by the US Army to house a ballistic missile, all of the condos have been sold for up to $3 million (£1.9 million) each. One executive paid $12 million (£8 million) in cash for four entire floors so that he could keep all his family and friends safe in the event of an emergency.

BULL JUMPING Among the Hamer tribe of Ethiopia, young men prove they are adults by running, jumping, and landing on the back of a bull—and then attempting to run across the backs of several bulls.

CANNIBAL MONKS Although there are very few practicing members left in the world, the feared Aghori monks of Varanasi, India, feast on human flesh, drink from human skulls, bite the heads off live animals, and sleep in cemeteries. Tribe members cut and eat the human flesh from corpses floating down the sacred Ganges River. They also eat putrefied garbage, feces, and rotten food, and drink urine. They often wear jewelry made from human bones, and some use walking sticks made from human femur bones.

TOOTH TOSS When a Greek child loses a tooth, the tooth is thrown onto the roof of his or her home to bring good luck to the family and a healthy replacement tooth for the child.

SNAP JUDGMENT In Louisiana, biting someone with your natural teeth is considered a simple assault, but biting someone with false teeth is classified as a more serious, aggravated assault.

VILLAGE HIRE The entire village of Megyer, Hungary (population 18), was made available to hire for $750 (£477) a day in 2015. The rental included legal rights to use and change the names of its four streets, as well as access to the mayor's office, the cultural center, the village's seven houses, six horses, three sheep, two cows, and a bus stop.

UNDERGROUND WATERFALL The Gaping Gill cave in Yorkshire, England, features a waterfall that is 365 ft. (111 m) tall—more than twice the height of Niagara Falls.

PLANET RINGS The planet J1407b, discovered 420 light years away, has over 30 huge rings, each tens of millions of miles wide and about 200 times larger than Saturn's rings.

SNOW TUNNEL When Ari Goldberger found his cycle route to work in Boston, Massachusetts, blocked by a 15 ft. (4.6 m) high mountain of snow, he and fellow cycling enthusiasts dug a 40 ft. (12 m) long tunnel that was high and wide enough to ride through.

Vine Bridge

Iya Kazurabashi, or Kazura Bridge, in Tokushima Prefecture, Japan, is no ordinary suspension bridge—it's made from mountain vines (Actinidia arguta) and must be rebuilt every three years! Measuring 148 ft. (45 m) long, 6.5 ft. (2 m) wide, and poised 46 ft. (14 m) above the water, the bridge was once part of a network of 13 bridges used to transport people and goods across the Iya River. The number of vine bridges has now dwindled to three, with the Kazura Bridge being the largest and most accessible.

3 Animals

Left for dead by poachers who ruthlessly cut off her keratin horn, this 12-year-old rhinoceros in the KwaZulu-Natal province of South Africa was given a second chance thanks to innovative veterinarians—and a fellow thick-skinned species. Rather than risk poachers making a second attempt on a rebuilt horn, veterinarian Dr. Johan Marais and his team debated and settled on what the best "bandage" would be—a skin graft from an elephant that died of natural causes. After an hour and a half, the first-ever operation of its kind saved the life of a member of one of the world's most endangered species.

Before surgery, the rhino's wound had to be cleared of infection and maggots, and then sterilized.

Rhino-Plasty

Cat Kimonos

Pet owners around the world show their affection in many different ways, from spoiling their loves with luxury goods to pet spa trips, but most obsessed owners love to dress their cherished animals in a great outfit! Fashionista felines in Japan know this all too well, and often rock custom-made elaborate kimonos, or traditional Japanese robes, for special occasions.

HELPFUL HOUND In Lancashire, England, Basil—a Bichon Frise-cross poodle dog owned by wheelchair-bound Deborah Cornwall—opens and empties the washing machine, fetches the mail, and even goes shopping with her, picking up items that she is unable to reach.

FERRET BAN Although legal in the rest of New York State, people in New York City have been banned from keeping ferrets as pets since 1959. California and Hawaii are the only US states where keeping a ferret is totally prohibited.

PRESERVED COAT After being buried beneath the ice for 34,000 years, the body of a baby woolly rhinoceros was discovered in Siberia in September 2014—and it was so well preserved by the frozen conditions that it still had its woolly coat.

MANY MUSCLES Many caterpillars have as many as six times more muscles in their body than humans. Some caterpillar species have 4,000 muscles, compared to 639 in humans. Some caterpillars have 248 muscles in their heads.

MANATEE RESCUE Nineteen manatees were rescued from a storm drain in Satellite Beach, Florida, in February 2015. The sea cows often leave the nearby Indian River Lagoon during cold snaps in search of warmer waters and had probably followed each other into the 150 ft. (45 m) long pipe.

HEAVY LOAD Although just 3 in. (7.5 cm) wide, the female common shore crab can carry up to 185,000 eggs when pregnant.

ELECTRIC SHOCK Liam, a 17 lb. (7.7 kg) Siamese cat owned by Jennifer and Jeff Kagay, survived after receiving an electric shock from a power pole in Grants Pass, Oregon, and crashing 25 ft. (7.6 m) to the ground.

Cannibal CROCS

Crocodiles will eat anything... even their own kind! When an unsuspecting juvenile croc accidentally swam into the jaws of its elder at the Sweni Bird Hide in South Africa's Kruger National Park, it learned this the hard way. The ravenous river monster quickly chomped down on it with its razor-sharp teeth, swallowing it whole!

An almost tragic accident led to the diving horse act! In 1881, a wooden bridge collapsed under William F. "Doc" Carver during Buffalo Bill's Wild West Show. As they fell, his trusty steed dove headfirst into the river below, which inspired Carver to perform this death-defying stunt across the United States until his death in 1927. The practice of a horse and rider leaping from a high-rise tower into a small pool continued well after Carver's death, eventually fizzling out in the 1970s. Here, Eunice Winkless and her horse thrilled a Pueblo, Colorado, audience on Independence Day 1905 as they plunged into a pool below.

High-Dive Horse

Octopus Wrestling

The odd sport of octopus wrestling captivated spectators in the 1950s and 1960s. In 1963, over 5,000 fans attended the World Octopus Wrestling Championships in Puget Sound, Washington, where 111 divers wrestled and captured over 20 Giant Pacific octopuses.

Descending as deep as 60 ft. (18 m) to find an octopus, a small team of divers would then wrestle it all the way to the surface and bring it to shore for judging. Points were awarded for the animal's weight, along with bonuses for such risks as diving without breathing equipment. Under pressure from animal rights activists, lawmakers made it a misdemeanor to "molest" or "harass" an octopus, bringing the strange sport to an end in 1976.

Jumbo the seal finished his stint at the 1949 Chicago Sportsman's Show undefeated. Racing both Olympic swim champion Ann Curtis and 1936 Olympic gold medal winner Adolph Kiefer 20 yards (18 m) twice a day was nothing for the marine mammal—who finished in half their time every round!

Winning two Olympic gold medals in 1948 as well as 34 US championships, Ann Curtis is regarded as one of the greatest female swimmers of all time, but she was no match for Jumbo!

65

LAST SUPPER

After a meal that clearly "stuck to its ribs," a 13 ft. (4 m) long African rock python died when dozens of quills from the 30 lb. (14 kg) porcupine it had just eaten apparently pierced its digestive tract from the inside. The bloated remains of the snake were found in Lake Eland Game Reserve, South Africa.

PINK DOLPHIN Angel, a rare albino bottlenose dolphin at the Taiji Whale Museum in Japan, turns pink when she is angry or sad. Her thin skin means that her blood vessels can cause a change in skin tone when she is emotional, just like in humans.

EXTRA HORN A goat in Saudi Arabia has an extra horn growing out of its back. The strange 3 in. (7.5 cm) long growth, located just to the side of the animal's spine, appears to be harmless. Animals with multiple horns are called *polycerate*.

DOUBLE TADPOLE A two-headed Near Eastern fire salamander tadpole was discovered in a laboratory at the University of Haifa, Israel. Both heads of the tadpole— called Arne and Sebastian—moved independently, but only one was able to eat.

TOUGH TEETH Although less than 0.02 in. (0.5 mm) long, the teeth of a limpet are the strongest biological material ever tested—five times stronger than spider silk and stronger than all but the toughest man-made materials. Before breaking, a limpet's teeth can withstand pressure equal to a single string of spaghetti holding up 3,000 lbs (1,361 kg).

Phantom of the Flock

FISHY STORY Sixty-two-year-old accountant Dan Carlin was injured after being pulled into the water by a hungry sea lion that jumped out of the water at a marina in San Diego, California, and grabbed a fish he was holding. Carlin, who was treated for bites, cuts, and shock, was aboard his boat posing for a picture with his biggest catch when the sea lion snatched it.

LAST LAUGH Zookeepers at Maruyama Zoo in Sapporo, Japan, abandoned their four-year attempt to mate a pair of spotted hyenas after discovering that both animals were male.

TOILET PYTHON Rampeung Onlamai from Samkok, Thailand, was bitten by a python that suddenly emerged from her toilet bowl. The huge snake sank its fangs into her and tried to drag her down the toilet, but she hit it with a broom. Her daughter eventually managed to pry the snake's head off her mother's right hand, which needed 20 stitches.

CHIMP CHAT Chimpanzees change their accents to fit in with new friends. Scientists studied two groups of chimps at Scotland's Edinburgh Zoo and found that the high-pitched calls of one group adapted to the lower-pitched calls of the second group as they got to know each other, until the sounds were identical.

Farmer Paul Phillips has a sheep with unusual markings that have earned him the name The Phantom. Bearing an uncanny resemblance to the two-toned face of the Phantom of the Opera, this sheep was born in 2015 in Kimbolton, England. The Phantom is a pedigree Texel breed, which leads Phillips to believe that his "mask" is due to a recessive trait.

KILLER SPIDER A redback spider was strong enough to trap a young venomous snake many times its size in its web, then lift it off the ground and throw it backward up into its nest, which was located on the underside of a car on Neale Postlethwaite's farm in Gooroc, Victoria, Australia. With the snake hanging in the web, the deadly spider made short work of it by delivering a venomous bite. The venom caused the snake's insides to break apart and turn to liquid, which the spider then drank.

LONG DISTANCE Giant prehistoric pterosaurs had wingspans of over 30 ft. (9 m) and may have been able to fly distances of more than 10,000 miles (16,000 km) nonstop.

INGESTED VENOM The venomous tiger keelback snake of Japan gets its venom from eating toxic toads. Pregnant snakes stock up on toads to equip their newborns with venom.

These gleaming creepy crawlies were recently discovered by wildlife photographer Jeff Cremer during a night hike through the Peruvian Amazon rainforest. Cremer enlisted three entomologists to help figure out what they were. Together, they determined that these predatory "glow worms" (a catch-all phrase for bioluminescent larvae) glow to attract their prey. They bury their bodies in dirt walls with just their heads sticking out and mandibles wide open, ready to chomp on whatever meal may come their way!

PREDATORY GLOW WORM

In September 2015, James Bristle of Lima Township, Michigan, was digging in a soybean field when he pulled up a piece of history. What he thought was an old, muddy fence post was actually a woolly mammoth rib! Bristle immediately contacted University of Michigan Museum paleontologist Dan Fisher, who led the excavation. Compared to most mammoth discoveries in the area, this is part of a whole skeleton—complete with a skull and tusks!

Mammoth Discovery

DRUNK CHIMPS Chimpanzees in Guinea, West Africa, have been getting drunk by frequently drinking the fermented sap of raffia palms that can contain up to 6.9 percent alcohol, making it stronger than most beers.

TWO-HEADED CALF A two-headed calf was born on Dwight Crews's farm in Baker County, Florida, in April 2015—a 400-million-to-one chance. The calf, named Annabel, had four eyes, two noses, two ears, and two mouths. While one mouth fed, the other mouth suckled in unison.

SNAKE HOUSE After Jeff and Jody Brooks moved into a house in Annapolis, Maryland, in December 2014, they said they found that the walls and the basement were infested with snakes. During the four months they stayed in the house, they say they discovered eight non-venomous black rat snakes, one measuring 7 ft. (2.1 m) long.

BOLD BEAR Peter Rizzuto, 77, woke from a nap on the deck of his mountain home in Snowmass, Colorado, to find a black bear nibbling at his ankle. Half asleep, he petted it, thinking it was a large dog, but then saw the bear's big claws. The animal wrapped its mouth around Rizzuto's ankle, but quickly released it without breaking the skin and wandered off.

SURROGATE MOM Edward, a seven-week-old baby sloth at London Zoo, England, was given a teddy bear as a replacement mother so that he could build up his strength. Sloths develop their muscles by clambering over their mothers but since his mom, Marilyn, had stopped producing milk, keepers bought a teddy from the zoo gift shop and fitted it with special clips so that it could be hung from a branch, enabling Edward to climb on and strengthen his limbs.

UFO TURTLE

In July 2015, scientists found the first ever biofluorescent reptile—a hawksbill sea turtle! Gliding through the water like an alien spaceship, this unique creature was spotted by marine biologist David Gruber and his team off the coast of the Solomon Islands. It reflected the blue light aimed at its shell in a variety of colors—red, green, and orange—making it different from bioluminescence, in which light is produced through a series of chemical reactions.

RIPLEY's —◯— *Believe It or Not!*
www.ripleys.com/books
Animals

Sky Hive

Over 700 man-made beehives hang 4,000 ft. (1,219 m) above sea level on the side of a mountain in China's Shennongjia Nature Reserve! These high hives imitate the insects' natural habitat, creating a sanctuary for the region's Asiatic honeybees, a species that has drastically diminished in recent years. To get to each hive, beekeepers have to climb on top of each box to reach the next one!

FIVE-YEAR TRAP Biso the cat spent five years trapped behind a wall in a subway station in Cairo, Egypt, and survived because an elderly man gave him food and water through a small hole every day. Biso apparently crawled into the hole when he was still a kitten but grew too big to get out again, and was only finally freed after a Facebook campaign.

DISCO CLAM In coral reefs off Indonesia, the mollusk *Ctenoides ales* reflects light through tiny bits of silica near the edge of its shell to create a dazzling marine light show. The display, which is designed to warn predators as well as lure prey, has earned it the nickname of "disco clam."

SCAREDY CATS After becoming trapped in the tiger enclosure in China's Fuyang Wildlife Park, a crane fought off impending attacks from two of the big cats by running around and spreading its wings threateningly. The timid tigers backed off, which allowed the brave bird to be rescued by zoo workers.

MIGHTY MITE A tiny Californian mite, *Paratarsotomus macropalpis*, can run 300 times its own body length in one second. By comparison, a cheetah can only manage 16 body lengths per second, which makes the mite one of the fastest recorded creatures on Earth.

HOT WATER The desert-dwelling pupfish can hold its breath for five hours. It lives in small pools in the Californian desert, where water temperatures can reach 95°F (35°C) and salinity levels are three times that of seawater. It has learned to survive without oxygen for long periods so that it can cope with its hostile environment.

COLOSSAL SQUID A female colossal squid the size of a minibus was hauled up from a mile (1.6 km) deep in Antarctica's Ross Sea by Captain John Bennett and his New Zealand crew in 2014. It weighed 770 lbs. (350 kg), had tentacles over 3.3 ft. (1 m) long that would have been double that length had they not been damaged, eyes the size of dinner plates, and was so heavy it had to be moved on land using a forklift truck.

Water Bear

This bizarre creature, which looks like something from a sci-fi film, is the tardigrade, also known as the water bear. A microscopic creature with eight legs, the tardigrade has the ability to survive in space—in 2007, scientists sent a group of tardigrades into orbit. Circling Earth strapped to a FOTON-M3 rocket for 10 days, 68 percent of the critters returned home alive, the only animals capable of doing so. These survivors can tolerate pressures six times that of the deepest oceans, can endure hundreds of times the radiation fatal to humans, and can easily withstand temperatures over 300° F (148° C)!

POOP SQUIRTER The baby hoopoe bird, which is native to Europe, Asia, and Africa, squirts its poop at its enemy's face if it feels threatened.

HOT TUB After finding a barely breathing newborn calf in a snow bank on his farm near Cutler, Indiana, Dean Gangwer saved the animal's life by jumping—fully dressed—into a hot tub with the shivering animal so that it could get warm quickly. He then dried the calf, took it indoors, and wrapped it in electric blankets. The calf, named Leroy, made a full recovery.

DRUNK SQUIRREL A drunk gray squirrel went on an overnight rampage at a club in Worcestershire, England, causing hundreds of dollars of damage. The intruder knocked over glasses and bottles after managing to turn on a beer tap and empty an entire barrel onto the floor. When the mayhem was discovered, the squirrel staggered around so aimlessly that it took the club secretary and two customers an hour to catch it.

BIG APPETITE A Bengal tiger can eat 60 lbs. (27 kg) of meat in a night—equal to 120 eight-ounce steaks. Its roar can often be heard at a distance of more than 1.2 miles (2 km) at night.

HUMAN ALLERGY Adam, a black Labrador mix owned by Beth Weber of Indianapolis, Indiana, used to be allergic to humans, as a result of which he would scratch and bite at his body, causing his skin to crack and his fur to fall out. Since his diagnosis, however, he has taken daily medication that helps him to live a normal, happy life.

MUSICAL CHIMP Holly, a chimpanzee at Rockhampton Zoo, Queensland, Australia, can play the ukulele. One of the keepers played his ukulele to her, and she was so fascinated by his fingers plucking the strings that he bought her one. She immediately held the instrument correctly and strummed away for around four hours.

Ripley's — **Believe It or Not!**
www.ripleys.com/books
Animals

Snub-Nosed MONKEY

It is rare that a new mammal species is discovered, especially large mammals, but within recent years, several members of a snub-nosed monkey species have been spotted across remote areas of China's Yunnan Province and the Eastern Himalayas. Nicknamed by scientists as "Snubby," these monkeys are actually quite easy to find—especially when it's raining! Their noses are so upturned that raindrops cause snub-nosed monkeys to sneeze!

PAMPERED PET Brajesh and Shabista Srivastava from Uttar Pradesh, India, are planning to leave all their money to their pet monkey, Chunmun. The childless couple has set up a trust fund for the long-tailed macaque, who already lives in style in his own air-conditioned room with a diet of Chinese food and tea. He also has a mate, Bitti, and each year their "wedding anniversary" is celebrated with a party to which hundreds of people are invited.

WONDER WOMBAT Patrick, a wombat at Ballarat Wildlife Park, Victoria, Australia, is 30 years old—more than twice the average lifespan of the species—and weighs a mighty 79 lbs. (36 kg), at least 22 lbs. (10 g) heavier than most adult wombats. Male wombats need to be aggressive toward the female, but Patrick is naturally placid, so his handlers have turned to Tinder in the hope of finding him a mate.

PARTY GUEST A 400 lb. (182 kg) black bear gatecrashed a student party at Lehigh University, Bethlehem, Pennsylvania. Summoned by the students, police officers chased the bear up a tree and then spent nearly two hours trying to coax it down again before the animal was finally able to be tranquilized.

PAW PRINTS Van Gogh, a one-eared cat who lives at an animal rescue center in London, England, paints pictures with her paws and has created her own versions of her famous namesake's works *Sunflowers* and *Starry Night*. To protect her paws, she uses fruit juice instead of real paint.

GOLDFISH BOOM After someone dumped three or four goldfish in Teller Lake, Boulder, Colorado, in 2013, their numbers have multiplied at such a rate that there are now as many as 4,000.

Blowing air through its blood to create a foam of toxic chemicals, the African Foam Grasshopper, scientifically referred to as *Dictyophorus cuisinieri*, defends itself from predators in its Guinea, West Africa environment.

FOAMY FOE

METAL MENAGERIE

Beak Bangin'

HATEBEAK

Believe it or not, avian death metal is a genre and it was pioneered by the Baltimore, Maryland, three-piece studio project Hatebeak in 2013—fronted by Waldo, a 22-year-old African Grey Parrot!

Waldo's vocals, accompanied by crushing riffs and bass from Blake Harrison and Mark Sloan, have been featured on four albums—in release date pecking order—*Beak of Putrefaction*, *Bird Seeds of Vengeance*, *The Thing That Should Not Beak*, and *The Number of the Beak*.

Since he was a fledgling, Waldo has always been quite talkative and responsive to music, and when he's happy he stands on one leg and becomes very hyper. The band claims that his excitement after an extended listening period makes it the perfect time to record Waldo's vocals. His best squawks and screams are then tracked with the rest of the music. Polly want a head bang?

Ripley's Asks

Band member Blake Harrison gives us the beaking news scoop on what Waldo is like backstage, and how it all started...

Q When was Waldo's talent discovered?

A It was kind of by accident, Mark and I were looking for a parrot after we had the idea, and we stumbled across a buddy of ours who owns Waldo, and we just went from there!

Q What is it like to collaborate with a parrot?

A The old showbiz adage of "never work with kids or animals" applies here. Fortunately, we don't do too many recordings, so it's not that bad, but he can be a bit of a diva at times. He pretty much does things on his own schedule and works when he wants to work. We ply him with dehydrated banana chips though.

Q Has putting out four records and gaining a bit of fame changed Waldo?

A We like to keep him sheltered so he doesn't get "lead singers disease." If he were aware of what he was doing, possibly, but at this time his reading comprehension skills leave a little to be desired.

THE DARK SIDE

Melanin is a pigment found in the skin, hair, and feathers of all animals. When an animal produces too much of this pigment it is considered melanistic—the opposite of albino, in which there is a lack of pigment. Although both melanism and albinism are genetic mutations, melanism works to the advantage of some species and becomes quite common. But, in other species, it is much more rare.

This pup, named Liquorice, is actually a young male grey seal. Male grey seals are commonly darker than females, but Liquorice's coat is an unusual jet black!

Melanism is extremely rare in penguins, but in this case, documented at Fortuna Bay on the sub-Antarctic island of South Georgia, this penguin is donning an all black tuxedo! Only one in every quarter million penguins show evidence of at least partial melanism.

This melanistic fawn was spotted by Richard Buquoi in a specific area near Austin, Texas, which hosts a large concentration of black "white-tailed" deer. Researchers have been unable to find any documentation of melanistic deer prior to 1929. It is very possible that this new mutation in the species offers camouflage in the region's dark brush and thickets.

Spotted at the Akrotiri Environmental Center in Cyprus, this is possibly the world's only black flamingo. A peculiar black-plumed flamingo was previously documented in Israel in 2013, but scientists believe it is the same bird, as flamingos can migrate very long distances.

73

Surly Sheep

Russian farmer Blasius Lavrentiev waited patiently for his prized ewe to give birth. When the time finally came, he was shocked to see a lamb resembling an angry old man staring back at him! The human-looking lamb became the talk of the village of Chirka, near the Republic of Dagestan, and Lavrentiev was even offered ten times the going rate for it! Likely due to too much Vitamin A, this abnormality isn't a heath concern—which means this strange sheep should live a full and, hopefully, not so grumpy life.

STOMACH ARSENAL Benno, a four-year-old Belgian Malinois dog owned by Larry Brassfield of Mountain Home, Arkansas, underwent surgery after swallowing a bag of 23 live .308 caliber rifle rounds. After the dog safely vomited four bullets, a veterinarian carefully removed 17 more from the dog's stomach, leaving two in his esophagus, which Benno "discharged" himself.

WALKING SHARK The epaulette shark from Australia and Indonesia can walk on land using its fins. To survive being out of water, it can live without oxygen for 60 times longer than humans.

FIVE LEGS A lamb on a farm in Powys, Wales, was spared from the dinner table because he was born with five legs. Jake is able to run and jump like the other lambs, but thanks to his rare deformity he's been kept on as a family pet by farmer Bethan Lloyd-Davies instead of being fattened up in readiness for sale to a slaughterhouse.

CARTWHEELING SPIDER A new species of spider discovered in Morocco, *Cebrennus rechenbergi*, moves across the sand by performing cartwheels. This enables the spider to scuttle around at a speed of over 6.5 ft. (2 m) per second—twice as fast as it would move if it were walking—which allows it to escape predators more easily.

DIETING DACHSHUND Since being adopted by Brooke Burton of Columbus, Ohio, in 2013, Dennis the miniature dachshund has lost more than 75 percent of his body weight—going from an obese 56 lb. (25 kg) to a svelte 12 lb. (5.4 kg). He used to be the size of four or five miniature dachshunds and was unable to take more than a few steps without being out of breath. Brooke put him on a strict diet, and now he is able to chase squirrels. He lost so much weight that at first he was tripping over his folds of excess skin.

FELINE THERAPY Ferray Corporation, an Internet solutions business in Tokyo, Japan, has introduced nine rescue cats into its offices to help employees unwind and improve productivity.

AIRBORNE ATTACK A peregrine falcon attacked several model gliders after they ventured too close to her nest in South Bay, near Los Angeles, California. The protective bird, which can fly at speeds of up to 200 mph (320 km/h), grabbed the gliders in her talons and forced them to land.

POOP RECYCLED Three-toed sloths recycle their own poop. Their poop attracts dung-eating moth larvae, which then colonize the sloth fur in a process that eventually results in the growth of green algae—which the sloths eat.

AGILE PIG Amy, a mini pig owned by Lori Stock, is one of the star performers at the Family Dog Training Center in Kent, Washington. By the age of five months, Amy had already graduated from the puppy manners class and had moved on to obedience and agility classes, where she jumps through hoops, balances on a teeter-totter, retrieves a dumbbell, and runs through a play tunnel.

BURNT ALIVE The Spoor spider of the Namib Desert of southern Africa kills its ant prey by pinning the ant's body to the hot sand, where it burns alive in less than a minute.

Ripley's — Believe It or Not!
www.ripleys.com/books
Animals

DEEP BREATH The spout of air and mucus expelled from a blue whale's blowhole can rise 50 ft. (15 m) above the surface of the water—the height of a five-story building. With a single breath, a blue whale could inflate 1,250 balloons.

HEROIC MOTHER Brave Diwalinen Vankar saved her 19-year-old daughter Kanta from the jaws of a 13 ft. (4 m) long crocodile by repeatedly hitting it over the head with a wooden washing paddle for 10 minutes until the reptile finally let go. The mother and daughter had gone to wash clothes in the Vishwamitri River in west India when the mugger crocodile suddenly grabbed Kanta by the leg and tried to drag her underwater.

BACK HOME Four years after Kelly Booker's Shih Tzu dog Lilly vanished from her home in Denver, Colorado, she was reunited with the family, having been found wandering the streets of Elgin, Illinois, 900 miles (1,450 km) away.

Walking Tall

Instead of crowing at the crack of dawn or pecking around a farmyard, this rooster struts his stuff a different way—walking upright! Purchased by his former owner on a business trip to eastern China for 10,000 yuan ($1,521), this bizarre bird now calls Jinhua, China's local zoo home. His strange stance and humanlike walk were not taught, but are rather the result of his suffering from a cartilage disease when he was young. After learning to adapt, this rooster is now cock-of-the-walk!

CAT'S REVENGE Searching for his missing cat, Tiger, Francis Bakvis ventured into the yard of his house in Clifton Beach, Queensland, Australia, and found a dead scrub python with a sinister bulge in its stomach. When he pulled the dead reptile onto the lawn, its body split open to reveal that Tiger was its last dinner. It appears the 16-year-old black and gray striped cat had proved too much for the 11.5 ft. (3.5 m) long snake to swallow, and he had caused a fatal rupture as his revenge.

Riding Horseback

At a quick glance, this seems to be a horse within a horse! It may look like an optical illusion, but the white fur pattern on the horse's chestnut coat perfectly resembles another horse! Named Da Vinci, this foal was born in May 2015 at the Fyling Hall School in Robin Hood's Bay, North Yorkshire.

Oink Oink

This little piggy, found outside a Buddhist temple in Tianjin, China, has two heads, two mouths, four eyes, but only three ears! Sadly, its little legs are too weak to support the weight of its two heads, but passer-by Yang Jinliang took it upon himself to care for the animal, bottle-feeding the piglet baby formula—using both mouths!

RARE SIGHTING There are only about 50 Sierra Nevada red foxes left in North America—and in December 2014, one was spotted inside California's Yosemite National Park for the first time since 1916.

MONKEY ARTIST German artist Jan Schekauski encouraged a monkey to daub paint on his naked back and then had the animal's artwork made into a permanent body tattoo.

BABOON JOCKEYS Baboons were once trained to tend herds of goats in Namibia, protecting them during the day and returning them to their pens at night— sometimes riding the biggest ones.

TONG TWISTER Winston the python had to undergo surgery after swallowing a pair of barbecue tongs. His owner, Aaron Rouse of Adelaide, Australia, was feeding him a rat with the metal tongs when the snake seized the implement and refused to let go. He left the tongs with the python but was horrified when he later returned and saw that the snake had swallowed them. They were about one-third as long as the snake and had moved halfway along his body. Winston had been unable to regurgitate them. To add to his discomfort, the tongs were trying to expand all the time they were inside him.

ROLE REVERSAL At the Lehe Ledu Wildlife Zoo in Chongqing, China, people pay to be locked in a caged truck while lions and tigers roam free around them. Lumps of meat are tied to the bars of the cage on the outside so that visitors can get a scarily close view of the big cats.

MISPLACED HEART On Tom Leech's farm in Amwell Township, Pennsylvania, a calf was born with its heart in its neck—only the third recorded case in history. The calf is believed to have been born with a defect that kept its breast bone from developing properly, allowing the heart to flop out into the neck, where it could be seen beating while making a sloshing sound because it was surrounded by fluid.

SNAKE SNACK A 10 ft. (3 m) long python managed to swallow a whole adult goat in the village of Garkhuta, West Bengal, India. It took the python over four hours to devour the goat, after which it slithered slowly back into the bushes with a full stomach.

BEETLE DIET The male great bustard of Europe and Asia eats poisonous blister beetles to attract a mate. The beetle diet rids the bird of parasites and so makes it look healthier and more desirable.

Bottle-Fed FISH

Bottle-feeding fish is a strange sight, and at China's Xiaoyaojin Park, it's an attraction! This Hefei city park created unique feeding devices for their koi fish by attaching baby bottles to the ends of long poles and filling them with fish food dissolved in water. When guests lower their bottles toward the water, some of the park's fish even poke their heads above the water's surface in their eagerness to eat!

STOPPED VEHICLE A dog stolen in a burglary at a house in the West Midlands, England, was reunited with his owner, Kirsty Mitton, after flagging down a van from the Royal Society for the Prevention of Cruelty to Animals 100 miles (160 km) from home. Alfie, a seven-year-old Yorkshire terrier, forced RSPC inspector Stephanie Law to stop on a deserted road in Buckinghamshire by barking in front of her vehicle. When she braked and opened her door to investigate, Alfie jumped in.

LABRADOR PARAMEDIC When Alan Spencer collapsed in the hallway of his home in Yorkshire, England, after choking on a pickled onion, his 18-month-old Labrador, Lexi, saved his life by performing the Heimlich maneuver. Lexi jumped with all four paws on the center of her owner's back and her prompt action successfully dislodged the blockage.

SHRINKING FROG The paradoxical frog from South America shrinks as it grows. It starts off as a 10 in. (25 cm) tadpole but ends up as an adult frog about a quarter of its original size. When the species was first discovered, scientists mistakenly thought the adults were the babies and that they somehow grew into giant tadpoles.

FAMILY FEUDS When Elaine and Don Sigmon of Maiden, North Carolina, adopted Peaches the cockatoo, they were shocked to hear the bird loudly repeating arguments she had heard between her first owners.

An over 1,300-year-old Japanese tradition, now protected by the Japanese government, ukai fishing uses seabirds called cormorants to catch trout. Ukai fishing takes place during the twilight hours, illuminated only by pine torches lit on long wooden boats. The fishermen are followed into the water, particularly the Nagara River in Gifu Prefecture, by about a dozen cormorants they have lived with and trained to help them in their work. When the birds spy their prey, they dive underwater, propelling themselves with their wings and feet, and catch the fish. A snare tied near the base of the bird's throat prevents anything but small fish to be swallowed. This allows larger catches to be retrieved from the cormorant's mouth by the ukai fisherman. Each cormorant can hold up to six fish in its throat at a time!

Ukai Fishing

77

HOSPITAL VISITOR When Nancy Franck was admitted to a hospital in Cedar Rapids, Iowa, she received a surprise visitor—her miniature Schnauzer, Sissy! The dog left home alone and made her way 20 blocks into the lobby of the Mercy Medical Center. Finding the dog's details on her collar, hospital staff allowed her to be taken up in the elevator to see her owner for a few minutes. Nancy's husband Dale said Sissy sometimes joined him in the car when he drove to collect his wife from work next door to the center, but they had never walked the route.

PROSTHETIC SHELL Suffering from a painful metabolic bone disease that had caused her shell to wear away leaving her susceptible to infections, Cleopatra, a leopard tortoise at Canyon Critters Reptile Rescue in Golden, Colorado, was fitted with a 3D printed prosthetic shell. Designed by Colorado Technical University student Roger Henry, the lightweight shell attaches to Cleopatra's own shell using Velcro®, and only needs to be worn when she is near other tortoises. Her own shell should regrow in a couple of years now that she is on a healthy diet.

GIANT LOBSTER A 480-million-year-old lobster, *Aegirocassis benmoulae*, was one of the largest animals alive at the time, measuring 7 ft. (2.1 m) long—almost as long as a lion.

SIZE DIFFERENCE At an animal rescue center in Hertfordshire, England, Digby, a Chihuahua puppy weighing less than 1 lb. (0.45 kg), became best friends with Nero, a Neapolitan mastiff weighing 130 lbs. (59 kg). Nero eats the weight of four Digbys every day.

PITCHING SPIDER *Mastophora dizzydeani* is a species of spider named after former baseball pitcher Dizzy Dean because it catches its prey by "pitching" a sticky blob ball attached to a thread.

EXTRA PASSENGER A stray dog emerged uninjured after being hit by a car and traveling 248 miles (397 km) while lodged in the vehicle's front grill. Following the collision in Hunan Province, China, the driver, Zhang Chou, thought it would be too dangerous to try and remove the dog himself, so he drove all the way to a veterinarian clinic with the animal still wedged in place. There, the pair formed such a bond that Zhang decided to adopt the mixed breed puppy.

FUGITIVE COW Matylda, a cow who escaped from Leszek Zasada's farm in Zloty Stok, Poland, in 2013, was finally recaptured after two years on the run. She spent the time living in a nearby forest, occasionally venturing out to damage crops, but nobody had been able to catch her.

SWIMMING LESSONS Charlotte, a baby king penguin at a bird park in Gloucestershire, England, was so scared of the water that she had to be given swimming lessons. Her keeper, Alistair Keen, donned a snorkel and climbed into the water with her to show her what to do.

CHIMNEY TRAUMA Chloe the cat survived being stuck up a chimney for six weeks without food or water after escaping from her outdoor pet kennel in Dorset, England, where she was being cared for while her owner, Marion Wood, was on vacation in Vietnam.

FREE RIDE Unable to travel far by themselves, some tiny species of worm "hitch rides" inside slugs to reach new locations and potential new sources of food. The slugs inadvertently swallow the worms while eating decomposing plants, but instead of being digested, the worms live in the slug's intestines until they are eventually pooped out, often some distance from where they were eaten.

DUMBO DOG When Remy, a two-year-old Basset hound, jumped more than 30 ft. (9 m) out of a third-floor window in East Sussex, England, after spotting a cat on the ground below, he survived the fall because his huge ears slowed his descent. Although he landed face first onto concrete, he suffered only minor injuries.

Alien Eyes

Matilda, a two-year-old tabby cat from Canada, has huge, glassy, alien-like eyes as a result of a condition called spontaneous lens luxation, a genetic disorder in which the lens of the eye completely dislocates from its usual position. A normal-looking kitten, her pupils started to become enlarged after her first birthday and now make it difficult for her to see. Her distinctive appearance has earned her over 105,000 followers on Instagram!

Alpaca Wedding

Hotel Epinard Nasu in Tochigi, Japan, offers one of the world's most unique wedding experiences. Upon request, couples can have an alpaca be their witness and pose with them in their wedding photos! This furry guest's primping process even rivals the bride's—before each ceremony the alpaca is carefully washed, groomed, and styled! Newlyweds, a word of warning: alpacas, closely related to llamas, have a tendency to spit—watch out!

SWAN CENSUS

In a tradition dating back to the 12th century, when swans were destined for the royal dining table, the Queen of England owns all the mute swans in Britain. Today, the Queen only exercises her ownership on certain stretches of the Thames, where a five-day census, the annual Swan Upping, occurs during the third week of July.

Her Majesty has only attended the Swan Upping once in her 64-year reign, in 2009. This duty is delegated to the current Swan Marker, David Barber, and Swan Warden, Chris Perrins. Dressed in scarlet coats, the team travels the 79 mile (127 km) long stretch in wooden rowing skiffs, and juvenile swans, called cygnets, are counted, weighed, checked for injury or illness, and then released. According to the 2015 report from the Queen's Swan Marker, 2,014 swans were counted, including 83 cygnets and 34 breeding pairs.

ICE RESCUE When Derik Hodgson of Elgin, Ontario, Canada, slipped and fell on a frozen lake, breaking his leg in two places and rupturing a tendon, his 11-year-old Labrador-Rottweiler mix named Badger dragged him off the ice and over 1,312 ft. (400 m) uphill to the safety of his cabin. Exposed to temperatures below minus 4°F (−20°C), Hodgson was drifting in and out of consciousness and was on the brink of suffering severe hypothermia.

SPIKED DRINK? In the early hours of the morning of May 31, 2015, a hedgehog was found curled up asleep at the side of a street in Arnhem, the Netherlands, after drinking from a broken bottle of the Dutch liqueur Advocaat, which had been left in the gutter. He was taken to a nearby animal rescue center to recover from his hangover.

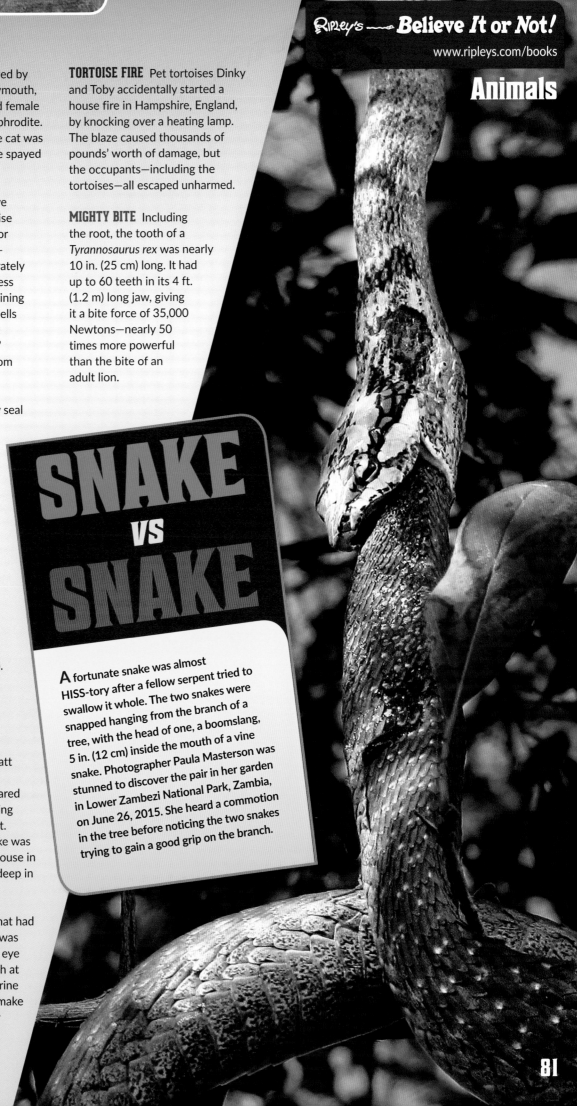

CONFUSED CAT Marbles, a cat owned by Tom Minns and Claire Gidley of Plymouth, Devon, England, has both male and female sex organs, making it a rare hermaphrodite. The couple had always thought the cat was female, but when they took it to be spayed they were told it was half-male.

SHELL SHOCK In an attempt to save the endangered ploughshare tortoise of Madagascar—an animal prized for its distinctive gold and black shell—conservationists have been deliberately defacing the shells to make them less desirable. The estimated 500 remaining tortoises on the island had their shells permanently engraved with a large serial number and the letters "MG" (for Madagascar) to stop people from stealing them.

WRONG DIRECTION A juvenile grey seal was found 20 miles (32 km) inland in the middle of a fenced-off field in Lancashire, England, after swimming in the wrong direction. Instead of heading out to sea, it had mistakenly swum into the estuary of the River Mersey and then up a series of small brooks before climbing into the field.

RAGING BULL Toystory, a bull raised by Mitch Breunig in central Wisconsin, sired an estimated 500,000 offspring in more than 50 countries. He weighed 2,700 lb. (1,225 kg) and his neck measured 57 in. (142 cm) around, making it nearly four times thicker than the average human neck.

SNAKE SUICIDE? Snake catcher Matt Hagan from Cairns, Queensland, Australia, found a snake that appeared to have committed suicide by sinking its fangs into its own neck. The 5 ft. (1.5 m) long venomous brown snake was found dead on the doorstep of a house in Earlville with its fangs embedded deep in its neck.

GLASS EYE A yellowtail rockfish that had developed cataracts in its left eye was fitted with a realistic-looking glass eye to stop it being bullied by other fish at Canada's Vancouver Aquarium Marine Science Center. Losing an eye can make fish appear weak, prompting other fish to attack it.

TORTOISE FIRE Pet tortoises Dinky and Toby accidentally started a house fire in Hampshire, England, by knocking over a heating lamp. The blaze caused thousands of pounds' worth of damage, but the occupants—including the tortoises—all escaped unharmed.

MIGHTY BITE Including the root, the tooth of a *Tyrannosaurus rex* was nearly 10 in. (25 cm) long. It had up to 60 teeth in its 4 ft. (1.2 m) long jaw, giving it a bite force of 35,000 Newtons—nearly 50 times more powerful than the bite of an adult lion.

SNAKE VS SNAKE

A fortunate snake was almost HISS-tory after a fellow serpent tried to swallow it whole. The two snakes were snapped hanging from the branch of a tree, with the head of one, a boomslang, 5 in. (12 cm) inside the mouth of a vine snake. Photographer Paula Masterson was stunned to discover the pair in her garden in Lower Zambezi National Park, Zambia, on June 26, 2015. She heard a commotion in the tree before noticing the two snakes trying to gain a good grip on the branch.

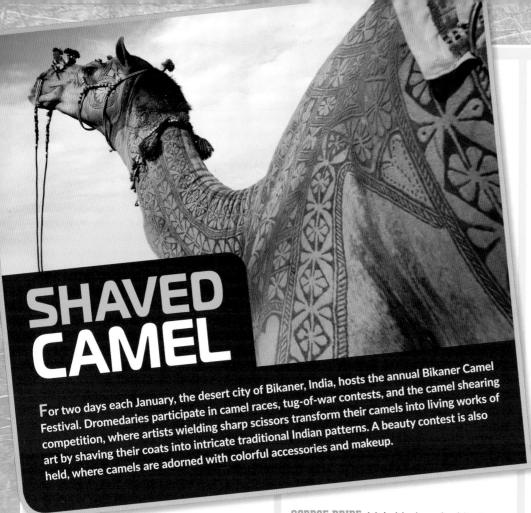

SHAVED CAMEL

For two days each January, the desert city of Bikaner, India, hosts the annual Bikaner Camel Festival. Dromedaries participate in camel races, tug-of-war contests, and the camel shearing competition, where artists wielding sharp scissors transform their camels into living works of art by shaving their coats into intricate traditional Indian patterns. A beauty contest is also held, where camels are adorned with colorful accessories and makeup.

VAN GOAT Bodie, a goat at the ABQ BioPark Botanical Garden in Albuquerque, New Mexico, has been dubbed "Van Goat" because of his ability to hold a brush in his mouth and paint. He has created more than 30 paintings, each of which sells for up to $40 (£27).

CANINE HELPER Glenn, a blind Jack Russell terrier from County Durham, England, has his own seeing-eye dog, a Staffordshire bull terrier named Buzz.

FAST HOPPER Rocket the Chihuahua has only two legs, but has learned to hop around like a kangaroo. He is a strong swimmer and can run so fast that his owner, Krissy Koller of Columbus, Georgia, is unable to keep up with him.

SELF-AMPUTATION Oarfish swim vertically and sometimes "self-amputate" by biting off their own tails. They can grow up to 36 ft. (11 m) long and have previously been mistaken for sea serpents.

NOT EXTINCT Two species of amphibians believed to be extinct—the Malatgan River caecilian and the Palawan toadlet—have been rediscovered after 40 years. They were last seen in the mountain forests of the Philippines.

CORPSE BRIDE Male black-and-white tegu lizards from South America sometimes court and try to mate with a dead female.

NEW TEETH A shark replaces its teeth every two weeks and can go through more than 30,000 teeth in its lifetime.

WONDER WEB An estimated 107 million orb-weaving spiders built a four-acre web in a water treatment plant in Baltimore, Maryland—equivalent to more than 35,000 spiders per cubic meter of space. The vast web covered 95 percent of certain sections of the building, and some of the webbing was so dense it had pulled 8 ft. (2.4 m) long fluorescent light fixtures out of place.

HIDDEN HIVE A colony of more than 40,000 bees was found beneath floorboards in the bedroom of Mary Jean Dyczko's house in Queens, New York. It took over two hours to remove the bees safely, and honey dripped off the massive honeycomb as it was pulled out piece by piece.

BUGGY WHEELS After his Labrador puppy Poppy was left with paralyzed back legs and unable to ever walk again, Peter Austin of West Yorkshire, England, helped her to become mobile by fitting her with a set of baby buggy wheels—and soon she could walk up to one mile (1.6 km) on them.

WRONG CAT Two weeks after London, England's John and Margaret Ross thought they had cremated their pet cat Amigo, the 19-year-old white, black, and tan Maine coon turned up alive and well. They had found an animal that looked identical to Amigo lying dead in the road, but they realized they had cremated a different cat.

TINY EGG A chicken kept by Shannon Hayes on her family's farm in Carmarthenshire, Wales, laid an egg measuring just 1.8 cm (0.71 in) long—about the size of a US dime.

MIRACLE DOG Bailey the dog fell 200 ft. (60 m) down an open mine shaft near Denver, Colorado, and not only survived, she did not even break a single bone. After a three-hour rescue operation winched the animal slowly up to the surface, owner Liza Martinez called Bailey "the miracle dog."

HUSKY BLING Keke the husky wears $40,000 (£26,415) worth of Apple® watches on his front legs. The dog is owned by Wang Sicong, the son of one of China's wealthiest property moguls.

⌃ YOUR UPLOADS

This unusual egg photo was sent to Ripley's by Charlotte Porter of Monrovia, California. The egg was laid by a hen belonging to Charlotte's friend, Karlene Briese of Montello, Wisconsin, on May 5, 2015. Shown here next to an ordinary chicken egg, the strange-looking specimen is an example of a conjoined egg—a series of contractions forced the egg back up the hen's oviduct, where it became attached to a second egg.

Animals

LAST RHINO STANDING

Sudan is the last male northern white rhino on the planet.

Armed guards protect Sudan the white rhino around the clock in Kenya's Ol Pejeta Conservancy. Sudan is shielded from poachers who kill rhinos and hack off their horns to sell them on the Asian medicine market—despite the fact that he has had his horn cut off to deter them.

Although there are still two females of this species in the world, Sudan is now 42 years old, and breeding efforts with the females so far have failed. Researchers have preserved some of Sudan's semen, as well as some from Angalifu, a male northern white rhino who died in captivity in 2014, in the hope that the species may be saved through artificial insemination, but the process has proven difficult with rhinos.

Watch Dog

Nearly 1 lb. (0.5 kg) of leather was found in Mocha's stomach!

Mocha the Doberman made it to Boston, Massachusetts's Angell Animal Medical Center in the nick of time after consuming three wristwatches and some leather jewelry! After noticing her odd behavior, owner Jeff Courcelle rushed Mocha to the vet, where they performed a three-hour endoscopy to search the contents of her belly. This wasn't Mocha's first time in the ER—she is a repeat offender. In 2014, Mocha had 20 in. (51 cm) of intestine removed after a piece of plastic perforated her digestive organ.

Mocha's X-ray shows her time-consuming meal, a belly full of metal and leather.

The contents of Mocha's stomach!

Weasel-Pecker

While we'd like to imagine this woodpecker is taking his friend, the weasel, on a magical ride, the truth is the woodpecker is being attacked. Martin Le-May spotted the scuffle while strolling through Hornchurch Country Park in East London, England, and managed to snap this photo. After a brief flight, the woodpecker landed on the ground, stunning the weasel. Seizing the opportunity, the woodpecker flew away with its life—while the weasel disappeared into the brush, still hungry.

GUARD DOG When 16-year-old Joseph Phillips-Garcia was seriously injured after his vehicle rolled more than 330 ft. (100 m) into the woods outside Lytton, British Columbia, Canada, his black King German shepherd dog Sako faithfully guarded him for 40 hours, fighting off bears and cougars until help arrived. With Joseph unable to move, Sako kept him warm at night by lying next to him and also fetched pieces of wood so that the boy could make a fire with the lighter he had in his pocket.

ANT TOILETS Black garden ants keep specially designated "toilets" in their nests. The clever ants deliberately pile their waste in certain corners of their underground nests, probably to keep the colony healthy.

PRESERVED PUPPY A 12,000-year-old mummified dog was found by archaeologists in Yakutia, a remote area of Russia. Preserved in permafrost, the puppy was in "perfect condition," with its hair, teeth and paws all intact.

AWKWARD NESTS In March 2015, telecommunications company Vodafone warned cell phone users in London, England, to expect poor signals for two months because at least three pairs of peregrine falcons were nesting on the company's phone masts around the capital. Under UK law, it is illegal to disturb the birds of prey while they are nesting.

LACE BALL When Garry, a two-year-old cat owned by Ana Barbosa of Hove, Sussex, England, went for an annual vaccine, veterinarians found a large mass in his stomach, which turned out to be a ball of tangled shoelaces and hair bands that he had swallowed.

PARROT DENTIST Fourteen-year-old Anton Androshchuk from Ferndale, Washington, had five of his baby teeth extracted by letting his pet parrot Gosha pull them from his mouth. Androshchuk simply opened his mouth wide and let the bird poke its head in to pull out the loose teeth.

FAMOUS FLY *Campsicnemus charliechaplini* is a species of fly native to Hawaii that gets its name because of its tendency to die with its midlegs in a bandy-legged position—like the signature stance of Charlie Chaplin.

LOUD PURR Merlin, a black and white cat owned by Tracy Westwood of Torquay, Devon, England, has a purr of 67.8 decibels, nearly three times louder than the purr of an average cat, and noisier than a washing machine.

CANINE MAYOR A Chihuahua-mix called Frida was named mayor of San Francisco, California, for the day on November 18, 2014, as part of a campaign to support the city's Animal Care and Control Department. She spent the day touring local landmarks as well as City Hall, and was then presented with a retirement package that included a doggy bed and gift basket. Her short term of office was made possible by a $5,000 (£3,525) bid by her owner, Dean Clark, during a gala fundraiser.

ELEPHANT PROP An 18-wheeler truck that became stuck in mud and had begun to tilt after pulling off the side of a Louisiana highway was prevented from toppling over by two of its passengers—a pair of five-ton circus elephants! They used their weight to prop up the vehicle until Natchitoches Parish sheriff's deputies arrived. The helpers were two of three Asian elephants being transported from New Orleans to a circus in Dallas, Texas, but when the truck got into difficulties, a trainer had the idea of enlisting the pachyderms to hold it upright.

CHEWED LEG Elsa, a five-month-old terrier puppy, gnawed off her own leg to free herself after becoming tangled in a curtain cord at her home in Milwaukee, Wisconsin. Although she chewed off her left hind leg, she is able to get around well on her remaining three legs.

STOWAWAY CHIHUAHUA When a suitcase triggered a luggage screening alert at New York's LaGuardia Airport, Transportation Security Administration officers looked inside and found a beige and tan Chihuahua. The dog's owner had no idea that it had crawled into her suitcase while she was packing for a flight to Los Angeles.

ANIMAL ANOMALY

Vamizi Island, off the coast of Mozambique, welcomed four rare albino green sea turtles on May 25, 2015, a first since the sea turtle monitoring program began in 2003. The hatchlings' red eyes indicate that they are true albinos!

Trees to Skis

Twiggy the Water-Skiing Squirrel made a splash in 2005 in Ripley's *Planet Eccentric*, which detailed her journey from rescue to recovery—and her first ride on a remote control toy boat. At speeds up to 6 mph (10 km/h), Twiggy stole the show once again at the 2015 Summer X Games in Austin, Texas. Trainer Lou Ann Best said the keys to training Twiggy are patience and plenty of nuts!

FIVE MOUTHS A mutant calf with five mouths was born on a dairy farm in Narnaul, India. The baby cow's ten lips all opened when he was sucking at his mother's udders, although he could only drink through two of his mouths. Hindu worshippers came from afar to visit the strange animal, whose eyes—one blue, the other black—were positioned in such a way on his distorted head that he could only see objects on his left and right side and not directly in front of him.

TICK BITE A bite from the tiny lone star tick, which is widespread over the eastern half of the United States, can stop someone from enjoying burgers, bacon, and steak. The tick—*Amblyomma americanum*—carries a substance called alpha-gal that makes people allergic to red meat.

CATERPILLAR TRAIN The pine processionary moth of Europe and Asia is so called because when the caterpillars emerge from their cocoons they form a straight train that can contain hundreds of caterpillars crawling head-to-tail.

LUCKY LUCY Lucy, a four-year-old miniature dachshund, was rescued by firefighters after spending 13 days trapped beneath a concrete slab at her Derby, Kansas, home. Ten days after Lucy had gone missing, one of owner Rebecca Felix's other dogs, Thor, started to take an interest in the spot where she was buried. Felix's husband then used an app on his phone to play a high-pitched dog whistle, prompting Lucy to bark back. When he dug under the concrete, he was able to see Lucy's nose and one closed eye. When he called her name, she opened the eye.

TRAP SURPRISE Justin Casey set a fox trap near his home in the Black Hills National Forest, South Dakota, but ended up catching a mountain lion instead. He released the lioness back into the forest unharmed.

SHAPE SHIFTER Ecuador's mutable rainfrog (*Pristimantis mutabilis*) can change its skin texture from smooth to spiky and back again in minutes, earning it the nickname "the punk rock frog." Researchers believe it does so to camouflage itself from predators.

FLYING POODLE

Thousands of new insects are discovered each year in the rainforests of South America—but with its bulging eyes and cotton-like coat, the Poodle Moth is really beyond belief. When zoologist Dr. Arthur Anker of Brazil's Federal University of Ceará posted this bizarre bug on Flickr, many were skeptical that it was genuine. But the fluffy Poodle Moth is native to the Gran Sabana region of Venezuela's Canaima National Park.

DONG TAO CHICKENS

With awkward-looking, bulky legs about the size of a human wrist, Dong Tao chickens aren't your average bird. This rare and highly prized Vietnamese breed hails from the Dong Tao commune in Khoai Chau, and was once bred exclusively to serve to royals. Now, exotic eaters can dine on this delicacy, too, if they are willing to pay an arm and a [Dong Tao-sized] leg. A pair of Dong Tao chickens can fetch $2,500 (£1,620)!

TWO HEADS In 2015, a two-headed bull called "Two Face" sold at auction in Mareeba, Queensland, Australia, for over $400 (£256)—or $200 (£128) a head. The 968 lb. (440 kg) animal was in excellent condition despite having a second head—containing one eye, a single tooth, and functioning nostrils—mounted on top of its first.

URGENT VOMIT If turkey vultures are threatened by a predator but have eaten too much to be able to fly, they vomit to empty their stomachs so that they can take off safely. Turkey vultures also wash their legs with their own urine, which acts as a sanitizer to clean and cool them.

HOCKEY WASP A new species of wasp discovered in Kenya has been named *Thaumatodryinus tuukkaraski* in honor of the Boston Bruins NHL® team's Finnish goaltender, Tuukka Rask, partly because its distinctive yellow-and-black coloring resembles a Bruins jersey. Robert Copeland, one of the researchers who discovered the wasp, also happens to be an avid Boston sports fan.

SMALL BOAR Due to the shortage of food on the small Japanese islands where it lives, the Ryukyu wild boar has shrunk to half the size of its cousins in mainland Asia as well as on the larger Japanese islands.

PROSTHETIC LEGS Born with abnormally small front legs and no front paws, which left him unable to walk or run, New Hampshire rescue dog Derby was given a new lease on life by being fitted with a pair of prosthetic front legs made with a 3D printer. Thanks to his new legs, he now runs up to 3 miles (4.8 km) a day with his new owners, Sherry and Dom Portanova.

CROWDED BATH Zoologist Chris Humfrey, from Macedon, Victoria, Australia, regularly shares a bath with Snappy Tom, a four-year-old saltwater crocodile, and Casper, a huge black-headed python.

4 Body

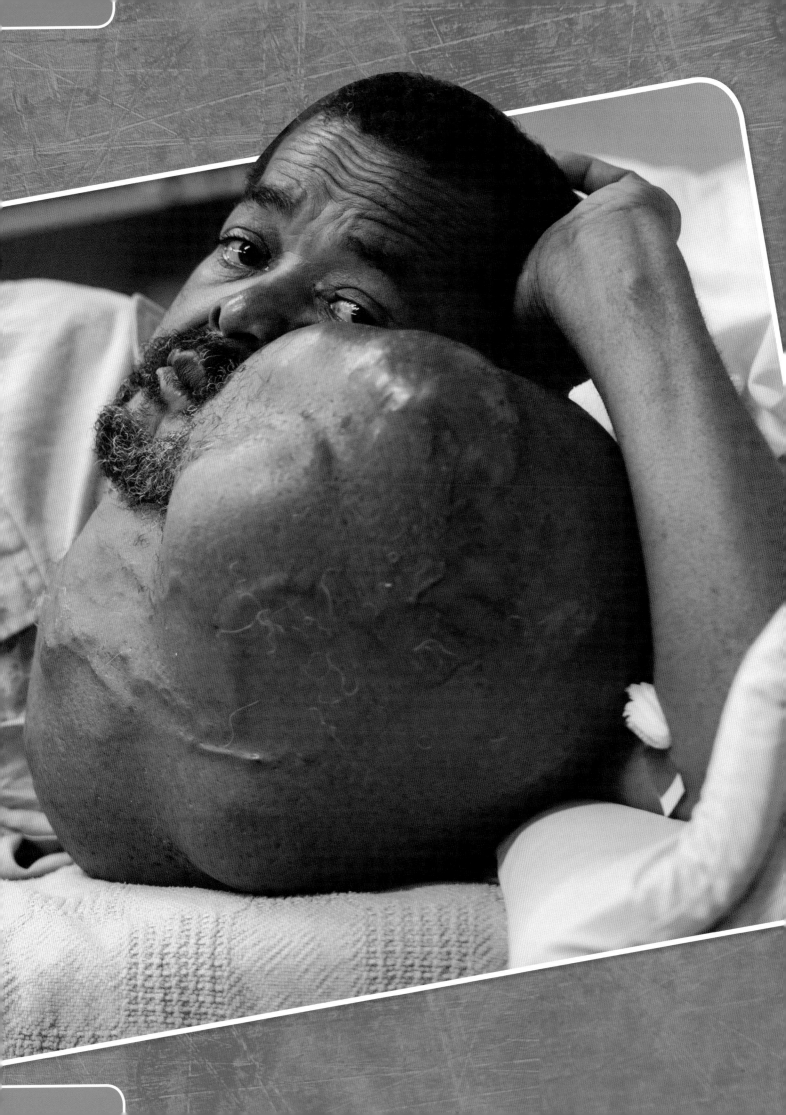

BABY FACE Christian Sechrist of Houston, Texas, had a massive tattoo of his baby son Perseus inked on the left side of his face. He already had several other tattoos—including one of a human skull—on the other side of his head.

HUMAN BARBECUE In an attempt to kill off cancerous cells in his body, impoverished leukemia sufferer Jia Binhui from Yunnan Province, China, roasted himself naked on a spit-like barbecue over hot coals. After learning from medical experts that temperatures higher than 107°F (42°C) may kill cancer cells, he lay for several days in his garden on two logs mounted on piles of bricks above the burning fire.

HEAVY LOAD After a 440 lb. (200 kg) man suffered a heart attack on Haiyang Island, China, it took 10 men and a large fishing net to carry him to the helicopter that transported him to a hospital.

GIANT CENTIPEDE Fourteen-year-old Grant Botti of Saline County, Arkansas, woke up with excruciating pain in his left ear. When he poked around to find out what was causing the discomfort, he pulled out a giant 4 in. (10 cm) long centipede. His mother put the insect in a bag and drove Grant to a hospital, where he was treated for abrasions to his eardrum and ear canal.

BRAIN TWIN Surgeons in Los Angeles, California, operating to extract what they believed was a tumor from the brain of 26-year-old Indiana University student Yamini Karanam, were shocked to discover that the growth was actually a teratoma—an embryonic twin, complete with bone, hair, and teeth—that had been lodged in her head since birth.

STRANGE REACTION People with the brain condition pain asymbolia do not react normally to pain—it makes them laugh instead.

10,000 Trees in 10 Years

In northern China's Hebei province, Jia Haixa, a blind man, and Jia Wenqi, a double amputee, have worked together to plant more than 10,000 trees over the last 10 years. Born with congenital cataracts that blinded his left eye, Haixa also lost sight in his right eye after a work-related accident, while Wenqi lost both his arms in an accident when he was three years old. After they were unable to secure jobs due to their impairments, the pair teamed up to plant trees on a 20 acre (8 hectare) stretch of riverbank—trees that would benefit the environment and future generations by protecting the nearby village from flooding.

Armed with only a hammer and an iron rod, Haixa and Wenqi start work early each morning with Wenqi carrying the blind Haixa across a fast-moving river. Without money to buy saplings, they collect cuttings, which involves Haixa scaling large trees and Wenqi guiding his blind friend from below.

NO PULSE Ruby Graupera-Cassimiro of Deerfield Beach, Florida, survived despite being without a pulse for 45 minutes after giving birth. Doctors at Boca Raton Regional Hospital spent three hours trying to revive the 40-year-old and were just about to pronounce her dead when she was suddenly resuscitated, and a blip on a monitor indicated a heartbeat.

WEIGHT LOSS Since 2011, Mayra Rosales of La Joya, Texas, has lost over 800 lb. (363 kg) in weight—equivalent to nearly five times the body weight of an average adult. She used to weigh 1,034 lb. (470 kg) and was confined to bed for years.

SNEEZING SYNDROME Autosomal dominant Compelling Helio-Ophthalmic Outburst (ACHOO) syndrome is a tendency to start sneezing when suddenly exposed to bright light—for example, when coming out of a dark movie theater into daylight.

HEROIC EFFORT In 2015, 71-year-old Gunhild Swanson, of Spokane, Washington, became the first woman over the age of 70 to finish the punishing 100 mile (160 km) Western States 100 Ultramarathon. She completed the California course just six seconds before the 30-hour cut-off time but had run an extra 3 miles (4.8 km) in the middle of the race after taking a wrong turn.

ALWAYS SEASICK Grandmother Diane Morley of Kent, England, still suffers from seasickness over three years after enduring rough seas while caught in a bad storm on a cruise to Norway. She feels as though she is swaying constantly, struggles with her balance, and experiences frequent nausea. She has been diagnosed with the rare Mal de Debarquement Syndrome, for which there is no known cure.

KNIFE RIDER Juacelo Nunes rode his motorbike 60 miles (96 km) to a hospital with a knife sticking out of his head after being stabbed at a party in Agua Branca, Brazil. The 12 in. (30 cm) long blade narrowly missed his left eye and went through his mouth into the right side of his jaw. He somehow completed the two-hour journey despite also suffering knife wounds to his throat, shoulder, and chest.

Bullfighting Protest

In a campaign to have bullfighting banned in her native Colombia, Fanny Pachon had her body pierced with a world-record-shattering 2,500 needles.

After years of trying unsuccessfully to raise awareness and gain exposure for their cause, Pachon and her colleagues held the "needle protest" in front of a city hall where a petition calling for a ban on bullfighting had failed. In bullfighting, the matador impales the bull with a sword or spear, so Pachon decided to pierce herself in a symbolic gesture of unity with the tortured animals. She also had a semi-permanent tattoo of a bloodied head of a bull inked onto her arm.

2,500 needles!

Ripley's caught up with Mike to ask about his new creation and career.

Q *How old is the oldest person using your product? The youngest?*

A It's funny—just the other day I got a call from a 73-year-old so he could go downhill skiing. Man, 73—that's getting pretty old to go down a mountain! I've got a guy in Canada who's gotta be almost 60 using the equipment for horseback riding and snowmobiling. And I know I've got a kid who's 16 using it.

Q *What extreme sports do you see your prosthetics being used for in the future?*

A Well, I also just started a company called Moto Sport Adaptive (MSA). It's an adaptive motocross championship series for upper- and lower-limb amputees and paraplegics. A lot of the competitors are gonna be wearing the BioDapt equipment and riding dirt bikes.

Q *What is the most rewarding part of starting BioDapt?*

A Originally I thought the most rewarding part was allowing myself to be back in action. But after teaching people to use my equipment and seeing their faces, their smiles, and excitement—it's priceless, and it keeps me motivated to design better things. Some of the most rewarding moments are working with military personnel whose lives are turned upside down after getting injured in the war. Seeing people get back to what they were doing before— that's where it's at, that's why I love doing this.

MOTO KNEE

"Monster" Mike Schultz from Minnesota has won six ESPN® X Games gold medals—all while using a prosthetic leg he constructed himself from a now-patented linkage system and FOX® mountain bike shocks.

When a December 2008 snowmobile race ended in disaster, his left leg was amputated above the knee. Schultz was soon fitted with a prosthesis but quickly discovered his new leg wasn't adaptable enough for the extreme sports he loved. To participate in a new adaptive motocross race in the summer 2009 X Games, he decided to build a leg that could withstand high-impact activity—and within seven months, he won a silver medal at the Games. What could have been a career-ending injury turned into a runaway success and even birthed Schultz's business, BioDapt, Inc., which manufactures a variety of action sport prosthetics available to amputees across North America.

NON-STOP CPR Found with no pulse after falling into an icy creek and drifting downstream, 22-month-old Gardell Martin of West Buffalo Township, Pennsylvania, was miraculously brought back to life by 101 minutes of non-stop resuscitation in an ambulance, at a community hospital, aboard a medical helicopter, and finally in the pediatric wing of Geisinger Medical Center in Danville.

PREMATURE AGING In June 2015, Ana Rochelle Pondare, from the Philippines, celebrated her 18th birthday—but her body age was 144. She suffers from the rare genetic condition *progeria*, which causes the body to age up to 10 times faster than normal. People with the condition do not usually live beyond age 14.

BLINKING POETRY Born with cerebral palsy that left him paralyzed and unable to speak, Adam Bojelian from Edinburgh, Scotland, composed poems one letter at a time by blinking. His mother, Zoe, would go through the alphabet and he indicated to her the letter he wanted by blinking.

GOLF MASSAGE At the Four Seasons Resort in Scottsdale, Arizona, masseurs relieve guests' tension by rolling warmed golf balls along the muscles either side of the spine and down the neck.

HEART RESTS If you added up all the rests a person's heart takes between beats, you would find that the heart does not beat for about 12 years of the average lifetime.

BUG FEAST In an attempt to find a remedy for bedbugs, Regine Gries, a biologist at Simon Fraser University in British Columbia, Canada, has allowed herself to be bitten by the insects more than 100,000 times. Once a month for over nine years, she has let up to 1,000 bedbugs at a time feast on her arms for about 10 minutes—but her sacrifice has paid off because she and husband Gerhard have finally perfected a chemical that can lure the bugs away from mattresses.

PROTECTIVE BRA When a robber opened fire and hit Ivete Medeiros of Belém, Brazil, her life was saved because the bullet became lodged in her bra instead of entering her heart.

FAMOUS BACK Kevin J. McCarthy of Frederick, Maryland, has a list of the first 20 Washington Redskins in the NFL® Hall of Fame tattooed down his back. The burgundy inking took 16 hours and is arranged like a football card, showing the jersey number, position, name, nickname, and year inducted.

YOUR UPLOADS

Tiffanie Bullard, 29, from Columbus, Georgia, thought she was going in for a routine wisdom tooth extraction but was shocked to learn the tooth was actually a fang! Instead of being a fully formed molar, the tooth simply had one singular point, much like a canine tooth. The tooth also took her dentist by surprise, who'd never seen a wisdom tooth so oddly shaped.

GUITAR HERO

Musician Mark Goffeney from San Diego, California, taught himself how to play the guitar and bass guitar at an early age—despite being born without arms. The 46-year-old uses a special technique, first placing the instrument flat on the ground and then strumming with his left foot while making chords with his right. Today, Goffeney and his band Big Toe appear nationwide, and Goffeney often performs solo all over the world.

BRAINS AND BEAUTY

While on a fishing trip with her husband in Hell's Canyon, Idaho, former beauty pageant winner Jamie Hilton slipped and fell 12 ft. (4 m). The severe swelling in her brain prompted doctors to remove 25 percent of her skull—and store it under the skin in her abdomen. The procedure, called a hemicraniectomy, helped reduce the pressure inside her head while keeping the removed bone sterile and nourished inside her body. Hilton's skull was kept in her abdomen for six weeks before the successful surgery to reattach her skull. Since then, the former Mrs. Idaho has made a miraculous recovery.

>Skull under her skin!

Ripley's Asks

Jamie spoke with Ripley's about her skull surgery.

Q *What did it feel like to have a piece of skull in your abdomen?*

A *The majority of the time I couldn't really feel the skull in my stomach. The edge would occasionally rub and migrate up under my rib, which caused discomfort—similar to a fatigued muscle, or a cramp. But when they put the skull back in, immediately I felt an aligning in my body—it was whole again.*

Q *Tell us the hardest part of your recovery.*

A *The fatigue was difficult, but while I was in the middle of my ordeal, it wasn't difficult for me, as they had me on good pain meds. It's been more difficult dealing with the trauma emotionally and mentally—overcoming my fears. Because I was doing such a safe activity (fishing), I feared many "safe" things like walking into my shower or walking on a road without a sidewalk.*

NIGHT VISION

In 2015, a group of California biohackers called Science for the Masses successfully gave biochemistry researcher Gabriel Licina temporary night vision. By having a chemical mixture found in some deep-sea fish injected directly onto his eyes, Licina was able to see more than 160 ft. (49 m) in the dark, accurately identifying moving objects and recognizing symbols against different backgrounds. He described the procedure as a "quick, greenish-black blue across my vision," but the concoction eventually dissolved into his retina, restoring his previous vision.

EYEBALL HORROR County sheriff's officials said Colin Corkhill of Scottsdale, Arizona, used his fingers to pull his right eyeball out of its socket while he was being held as a prisoner at Pinal County Jail near Phoenix. Doctors were unable to save his eye.

CUSTOMIZED WHEELCHAIR University of Central Florida engineering student and cosplay enthusiast Ben Carpenter, who was born with spinal muscular atrophy, gave his wheelchair a macabre makeover based on the postapocalyptic movie *Mad Max: Fury Road*. He rigged the upright wheelchair so that it could be attached to a chained chariot, and then dressed to mimic Max Rockatansky's look as a mobile blood bank.

SLEEP ADVENTURES Extreme sleepwalker Daniel Toft of East Yorkshire, England, wanders so far in the middle of the night that he has injured himself climbing over a garden wall, been found sleeping in a shop doorway, and once ran down the road screaming that spiders were crawling all over his body.

TINY WAIST To obtain her tiny 20 in. (50 cm) waist, Venezuelan model Aleira Avendano has worn a tight corset 23 hours a day every day for over six years. She sleeps in the restricting garment, only removing it for an hour a day so that she can wash herself.

BEARD SELFIES Starting in June 2014, Justin Basl of Las Vegas, Nevada, went an entire year without shaving and took a selfie every day for 365 days to create a time-lapse video showing the steady growth of his beard.

▶▶ AFTER SUFFERING FROM HEADACHES AND SEIZURES, A WOMAN IN CHINA HAD A 3.15 IN. (8 CM) PARASITE REMOVED FROM HER BRAIN, WHICH WAS CAUSED BY EATING LIVE FROGS.

LIFESAVER Five-year-old Lexi Shymanski of Prince George, British Columbia, Canada, saved the lives of her family by climbing barefoot up a cliff in Alberta after a car crash left her mother Angela and younger brother Peter unconscious. Her mom passed out at the wheel and crashed the car into a tree before it plunged down a 40 ft. (12 m) embankment, but Lexi managed to unclip the five-point harness on her car seat, clamber out of the vehicle, and crawl up the cliff to flag down a passing driver.

RED WOMEN The Himba women of northern Namibia appear bright red in color because they cover their hair and skin in *otjize*—a paste made of butterfat and red ochre (a natural earth pigment containing iron oxide)—to protect themselves from the sun.

SKIN AID Dr. Zoe Waller, a pharmacy lecturer at the University of East Anglia in Norfolk, England, uses her unusual skin condition as a teaching aid. She suffers from dermatographia, where a raised red rash appears on her skin after even the slightest pressure, but she puts it to good use by drawing pictures of molecules on her arm with a blunt pencil or cocktail stick. Her students are required to learn 100 drugs for their course, so each day she draws the chemical composition of a new one on her skin.

DICTATOR DOUBLE Wang Lei of Nanjing, China, has undergone cosmetic surgery to make himself look like North Korean leader Kim Jong-un. Said to be a fan of the dictator, Wang also wears Kim's trademark gray suit and styles his hair identically.

LAUGHTER RISK For over 15 years, Claris Diaz of Cardiff, Wales, suffered from a rare brain disease that put her life in danger every time she laughed. Moyamoya syndrome, a one-in-two-million occurrence, causes an irreversible blockage of the main blood vessels to the brain and can be triggered by any physical activity that raises the breathing rate. It first affected her at age 10, but following two major brain operations she can now laugh without being scared—and has even managed to run half marathons.

Parasitic Twin

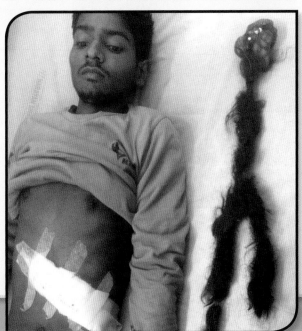

After suffering stomach pain, weight loss, and vomiting fits, an 18-year-old from Uttar Pradesh, India, discovered his symptoms were caused by his unborn parasitic twin. In January 2016, doctors removed the 7.8 in. (20 cm), 5.5 lb. (2.5 kg) mass of bone, hair, teeth, and yellowish amniotic-like fluid from his abdomen. The extremely rare condition is a developmental abnormality called "fetus in fetu," where one twin fetus envelops the other and the enveloped twin lives off the nutrients of its sibling's blood supply.

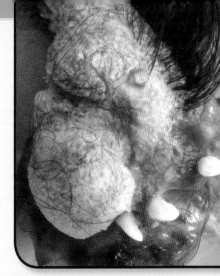

The OLDEST Bonded Brothers

> Inseparable since 1951!

In 2014, Ronnie and Donnie Galyon celebrated not only their 63rd birthday, but also their new achievement as the world's oldest conjoined twins—beating the previous record held by twins Giacomo and Giovanni Battista Tocci from Italy. The twins are joined at the waist and face each other. With four arms, four legs, and separate hearts and stomachs, they share a lower digestive tract, a groin, genitalia, and a rectum. The Galyon twins were born healthy in Dayton, Ohio, in October 1951, and they've stayed as one ever since.

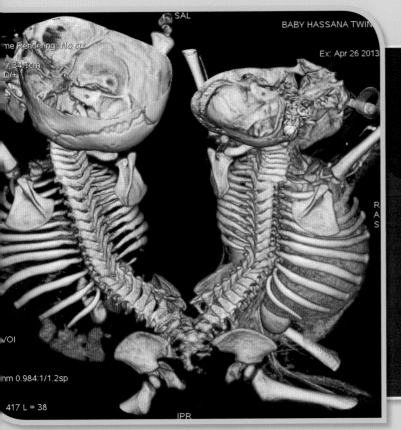

Eight-Limbed Baby

In the small town of Dumri-Isri, India, thousands of Hindi worshippers gathered to celebrate the birth of a baby born with eight limbs. The baby boy was born with four legs and four arms, which was thought to be the result of an underdeveloped conjoined twin. The worshippers believe the baby is a reincarnation of the Hindu god Ganesha.

Ripley's Research

Occurring **once every 200,000 live births**, conjoined twins are genetically identical and always the same sex. Female siblings have a **better chance of survival** than male siblings. There are two theories for how conjoined twins develop. One says that when an embryo splits, separation stops before the process is complete. The other suggests that two separate embryos fuse together during development.

SAL

BABY HASSANA TWIN

me Rendering No cut

Ex: Apr 26 2013

V 34.1cm
D/+

R
A
S

VOI

nm 0.984:1/1.2sp

417 L = 38

IPR

SEPARATED AFTER BIRTH

This high-definition body scan shows the spinal fusion of conjoined twins Hussaina and Hassana Badaru from Kano, Nigeria, before their separation surgery in August 2013. Born with a condition called pygopagus, the twins were joined at the hip and shared spinal cords, a lower gastrointestinal passage, and genitalia. The one-year-old sisters were separated at BLK Super Speciality Hospital in New Delhi in a difficult 18-hour operation involving 40 doctors. Only the fourth such operation in the world, the two-part procedure—which cost an estimated $99,580 (£64,000) and was paid for by a Nigerian philanthropist—was so risky, doctors were forced to practice on dummies before attempting it.

FROZEN STIFF

Every day is a bad hair day at the International Hair Freezing Contest at the Takhini Hot Springs in Whitehorse, Yukon, Canada, where competitors bathe in air temperatures of minus 22°F (−30°C) to create crazy frozen hairstyles. They put their hair underwater in the 104°F (40°C) hot springs, then dip it in snow, let it freeze, and sculpt it. In such icy temperatures, wet hair can freeze in less than a minute.

HEAD KICKER Puskar Nepal, a Nepalese teenager, can kick himself in the head 134 times in a minute. He practiced for nine months to make his body flexible and has become so adept that he is even able to alternate his kicking feet.

MIRACLE BABY Seriously injured in a car crash when she was pregnant, Sharista Giles of Sweetwater, Tennessee, only learned she had given birth to a baby boy when she awoke from a coma four months later.

THIN SKIN The skin on people's feet is more than 30 times thicker than the skin on their eyelids. Human skin is at least 0.06 in. (1.5 mm) deep on the soles of the feet but only 0.00196 in. (0.05 mm) on the eyelids.

DRASTIC CURE To cure stuttering, doctors in the 18th and 19th centuries often cut off half of the stutterer's tongue.

BUTTERFLY CHILD Born with an extremely rare condition called *epidermolysis bullosa*, which causes his skin to fall off in his sleep, Song Liuchen of Henan Province, China, was not expected to live long, but eight years later he has defied the odds and is at the top of his class at school. Even so, his mother, Wang, has to change his bed sheets every day because they are always covered in blood and liquid from the wounds to his fragile, butterfly-like skin.

CRAWLING SKIN Noticing itchy blotches on his body after returning home from a six-month visit to Africa, Mr. Ma of Guangzhou, China, went to see a dermatologist, who discovered the sores were caused by live maggots nestling under his skin. Ma had surgery to remove 20 maggots of the tumbu fly, a blowfly whose larvae feed on human tissue.

NOSE WRITER Cerebral palsy sufferer Richard Hopley of Liverpool, England, spent a year writing a book of poems on an iPad® using his nose to activate the letters.

FISH DRESSING Some fish are more effective than bandages for dressing wounds. Scientists at Shanghai University in China have discovered that collagen-rich fibers from the tilapia fish boost skin growth on wounds faster than normal dressings.

ELECTRIC ALLERGY Peter Lloyd of Cardiff, Wales, has a severe allergy to electricity, making him unable to heat or light his home or use electrical gadgets such as TVs or cell phones. He suffers from a rare debilitating illness, electromagnetic hypersensitivity, which leaves him in pain whenever he comes into contact with anything electrical. He is even afraid to leave his house for fear of encountering a power drill or someone with a phone.

HEIGHT DIFFERENCE Joelison Fernandes da Silva, who developed gigantism as a child and now stands 7 ft. 8 in. (2.3 m) tall, is married to Evem Medeiros, who, at 5 ft. (1.5 m), is nearly 3 ft. (0.9 m) shorter and only comes up to his waist. When they are standing up, she has to climb on a chair to kiss him. The gentle giant, from Paraiba, Brazil, was 6 ft. 4 in. (1.9 m) tall by age 14, and wears specially made size 23 shoes.

NAIL CLIPPINGS Jerry Robertson of Manning, South Carolina, has collected his finger and toenail clippings since 1969.

TOILET BIRTH A woman named Manu gave birth on a train toilet in Rajasthan, India, only to have her baby fall through the waste drainage system and end up on the tracks. Although Manu had lost consciousness, luckily a nearby guard heard the baby's cries and alerted railway bosses, who stopped the train and rescued the child.

SHORT MEMORY Since suffering severe brain injuries in a car accident when he was seventeen, 26-year-old Chen Hongzhi of Beipu, Taiwan, has been left with a memory span of just five minutes. He has to write every detail of his life—such as who his friends are—in a notebook so that he does not forget them. He also uses the notebook to record everything he does each day—from people he meets to the weather—because every morning he has to start again from scratch with his mother reminding him he is no longer 17.

STOMACH HAIRBALL Surgeons in Delhi, India, removed a huge 4 ft. (1.2 m) hairball from the stomach of four-year-old Sivam Kumar. He had been eating his own hair for nine months—a condition known as *trichophagia* or Rapunzel Syndrome—and had consumed so much that he could no longer swallow food, only water. His parents now shave his head to prevent a recurrence.

TRUE PATRIOT New England Patriots fan Victor Thompson of New Hampshire has an image of NFL® quarterback Tom Brady's football helmet tattooed right across his head. The tattoo includes the team logo, Brady's number—"12," a Super Bowl trophy, and replica signatures of famous Patriots players.

FAMILY FEAR People with *syngenesophobia* have a morbid and persistent fear of all their living relatives.

TOILET TRAP A woman who got her foot stuck in her toilet in Guangxi Province, China, had to be dug out by firefighters with a spoon. She slipped while taking a shower, and her foot became wedged in the small porcelain toilet bowl, which was set into the floor. When fire crews arrived, they smashed the bowl but still could not extract her foot from the fixture, so they dug away the surrounding rubble with a spoon until she was able to lift her foot free.

BEAN TATTOOS Barry Kirk, an eccentric Welshman who officially changed his name to "Captain Beany" because he loves baked beans, celebrated his 60th birthday by having 60 images of baked beans tattooed onto his bald head.

Ripley's —— Believe It or Not!
www.ripleys.com/books
Body

Gentleman's Request

Jonas Acevedo Monroy, 32, was enjoying himself at a Chihuahua, Mexico, bar when an angry patron plunged a pair of scissors into the upper-left side of Monroy's skull, hitting his parietal brain lobe and nearly killing him. The assailant fled, and a friend helped the blood-soaked but still alert Monroy to a nearby hospital, where he allegedly pointed to the scissors saying he had a "small problem," politely asked for assistance, and fainted. Monroy was rushed into surgery where they successfully removed the scissors, while Mexican police nabbed and charged his attacker.

Ripley's Research

Now used everywhere from hospitals to airport security, **X-rays** were discovered by accident! German scientist Wilhelm Conrad Roentgen (1845–1923) was experimenting with vacuum tubes when he noticed a glow coming from a nearby chemically coated screen, which he dubbed "X-ray." **When he took the first X-ray in history of his wife's hand in 1895**, she declared, "I have seen my death!"

DEEP SLEEP Georgia Green of Adelaide, South Australia, suffers from Kleine-Levin Syndrome, a rare neurological disorder that makes her sleep without waking properly for up to 10 days at a time—and there is no known cure.

UNLUCKY DAY Fourteen-year-old Brock Leach fell 100 ft. (30 m) down a cliff in Cornwall, England, and while climbing to safety before the tide came in, was bitten by an adder, Britain's only venomous snake. He suffered a fractured pelvis and severe bruising from the fall, and his arm swelled to three times its normal size following the snake bite, but he recovered after being flown to a hospital, where he was given antivenom treatment.

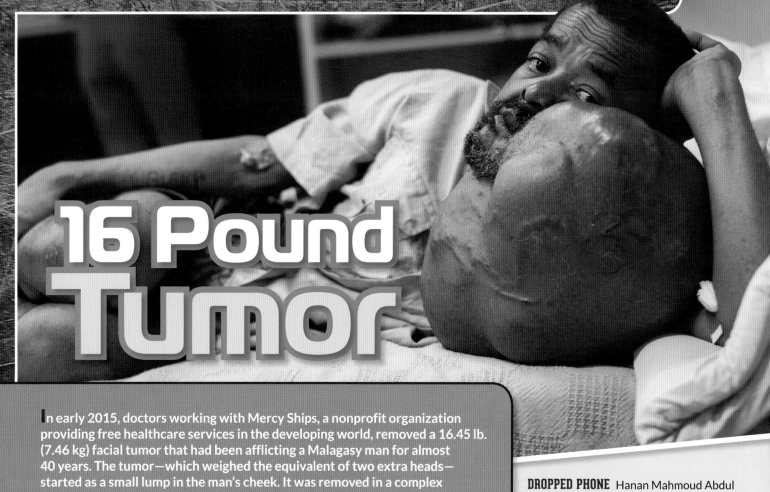

16 Pound Tumor

In early 2015, doctors working with Mercy Ships, a nonprofit organization providing free healthcare services in the developing world, removed a 16.45 lb. (7.46 kg) facial tumor that had been afflicting a Malagasy man for almost 40 years. The tumor—which weighed the equivalent of two extra heads—started as a small lump in the man's cheek. It was removed in a complex 12-hour operation that required blood transfusions from 17 Mercy Ships volunteer crewmembers, who also act as a living blood bank for patients. After his recovery, six of the ship's crew hiked for five days through remote areas of Madagascar to bring the patient back to his rural village.

DROPPED PHONE Hanan Mahmoud Abdul Karim claims her gynecologist's cell phone was left inside her stomach following the birth of her child—but that she only realized hours later when it started vibrating inside her. She had been admitted to a private hospital in Amman, Jordan, for a Cesarean section, and after giving birth to a baby boy, she was sent home, where her family noticed that she was in pain and that her abdomen appeared to be vibrating. She was then rushed to another hospital where she says X-rays revealed a foreign object, and the phone was surgically removed.

SAVIOR SIRI Trapped beneath nearly 5,000 lbs. (2,270 kg) of metal after his truck fell on him while he was trying to repair it, 18-year-old Sam Ray of Waterhill, Tennessee, owes his life to Siri, the voice recognition service on his iPhone®. As he struggled to free himself, he heard the feature's familiar voice activate and told it: "Call 911." Siri immediately called the emergency dispatcher—who initially thought it was a mistaken pocket-dial until she heard Ray's screams for help—and was able to identify his location using his cell phone signal.

LONG TONGUE Eighteen-year-old Adrianne Lewis of Twin Lake, Michigan, has a 4 in. (10 cm) long tongue, with which she can touch her nose, chin, and elbow. She can even touch her eyeball if she uses a finger to give her tongue a little additional elevation.

DNA STRETCH If uncoiled, the DNA in all the cells in the human body would stretch for 67 billion miles (108 billion km)—equal to about 150,000 round trips to the Moon.

Buzz Barter

On August 8, 2015, to help prepare students for the upcoming school year, Courtney Holmes, a barber in Dubuque, Iowa, gave free haircuts to children in his neighborhood who read their favorite books to him!

The patient meets one of his blood donors before the surgery.

Mercy Ships staffer Allison Heermance changes his bandages while he looks at his new reflection.

While recovering from his life-changing surgery, the patient poses with 14 of his volunteer blood donors.

RECYCLED URINE The drug penicillin was once so rare that it was recycled from the urine of treated patients.

LUNG LIFE After being plagued with a bronchial condition, Phil Lyndon of London, England, suddenly coughed up a wriggling 5 mm (0.2 in.) long brown insect. It is thought he ingested the mayfly nymph in his sleep and it had been living in his lungs.

NIGHT WALK Somerset, England sleepwalker Marie Lord wandered out of her house in the middle of the night. She'd walked half a mile before climbing down steps and into the sea, where she was suddenly awakened by the taste of salt and grit in her mouth as waves crashed around her. She managed to stagger back up the beach and clung to some rocks until her cries alerted a hotel porter who came to her rescue.

EAR GRAFTS Born without any ears, nine-year-old Kieran Sorkin from Hertfordshire, England, had a pair created by doctors from cartilage taken from his ribs. The ears were grafted onto his head under pockets of skin. While it was a strictly cosmetic procedure, they were shaped so successfully that a year later he was able to wear sunglasses for the first time.

SKYDIVER RESCUE Before having a chance to deploy his parachute, 22-year-old skydiver Christopher Jones of Perth, Western Australia, suffered a seizure, lost consciousness, and rolled onto his back 9,000 ft. (2,743 m) above ground in Pinjarra. Fortunately his instructor, Sheldon McFarlane, managed to grab hold of Jones in free fall and pull his rip cord. Jones soon regained consciousness and was able to land unaided.

BEAR WEIGHT Eddie "The Beast" Hall from Stoke-on-Trent, Staffordshire, England, can deadlift a weight of 463 kg (1,020 lb.)— the equivalent of a full-grown polar bear. Hall himself weighs 172 kg (380 lb.), so he is able to lift nearly three times his own body weight.

DUBIOUS HONOR In 1993, a basketball-loving doctor named a newly discovered strain of bacteria Salmonella mjordan after NBA® star Michael Jordan.

HELPING HAND While covering the 2015 Nepal earthquake, CNN's chief medical correspondent Dr. Sanjay Gupta found himself performing surgery with a saw on an 14-year-old girl. He was asked by a Nepalese medical team to assist with a craniotomy on Selena Dohal, whose skull was fractured when the roof of a house in Panchkhal collapsed on her head.

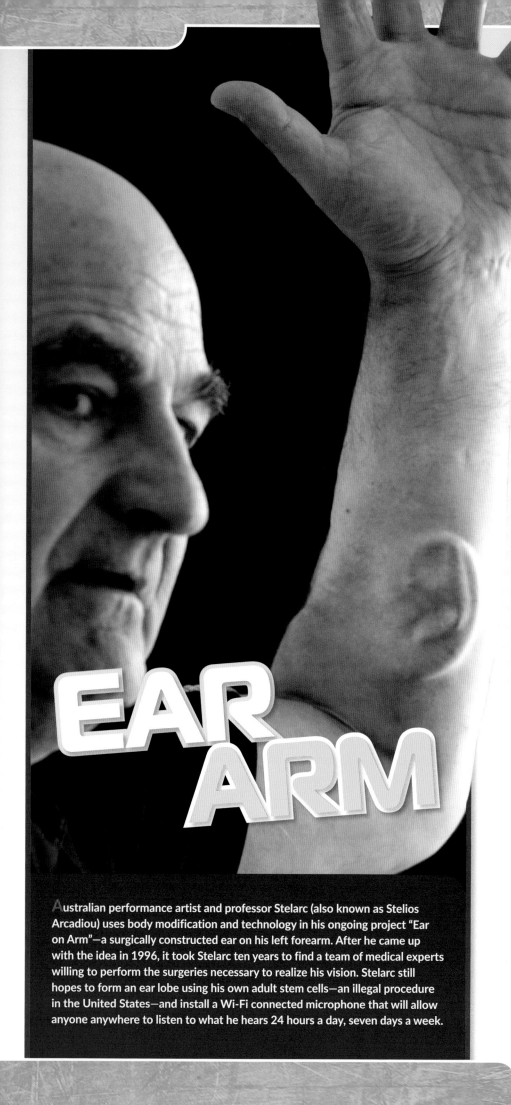

EAR ARM

Australian performance artist and professor Stelarc (also known as Stelios Arcadiou) uses body modification and technology in his ongoing project "Ear on Arm"—a surgically constructed ear on his left forearm. After he came up with the idea in 1996, it took Stelarc ten years to find a team of medical experts willing to perform the surgeries necessary to realize his vision. Stelarc still hopes to form an ear lobe using his own adult stem cells—an illegal procedure in the United States—and install a Wi-Fi connected microphone that will allow anyone anywhere to listen to what he hears 24 hours a day, seven days a week.

TITANIC TONSILS When Patrick Kelleher of Murray, Utah, had his tonsils removed, they were so big that the surgery took twice as long as usual and, instead of both tonsils fitting in a single specimen jar, each needed a jar of its own. His left tonsil measured 2.4 in. (6 cm) long, 1.4 in. (3.5 cm) wide, 1.2 in. (3 cm) thick, and weighed 28 grams—almost the size of a tennis ball—while his right tonsil was 2 in. (5 cm) long, 1.4 in. (3.5 cm) wide, 1 in. (2.5 cm) thick, and weighed 0.8 oz (25 g) —slightly larger than a golf ball.

▶▶ STARTING IN EARLY 2007, A 23-YEAR-OLD BRITISH STUDENT EXPERIENCED ATTACKS OF PERSISTENT AND INTENSE DÉJÀ VU FOR EIGHT YEARS.

STONE SURGERY After 49-year-old Mousumi Dam of Kolkata, India, complained of stomach pains, doctors removed 360 gallstones from her gallbladder.

FOOD ALLERGY Alex Visker of Lehi, Utah, is allergic to all food—and for more than four years, since he was 15, he has had to rely on a feeding tube to receive sufficient nutrition. After being sick for much of his childhood, he discovered that he has a rare, unnamed condition that makes him allergic to the proteins in food and that he will never be able to eat properly again. Even one bite is enough to leave him with stomach pain, fatigue, a headache, and extreme nausea.

STRAY BULLET A baby was born safely in Bangladesh despite being hit by a bullet while still in the womb. The bullet went through the shoulder of baby Suraiya and damaged her eye when her mother, Najma, was accidentally shot in the abdomen during a 2015 political rally in Magura. Luckily the bullet did no permanent damage to the unborn child, and she was born after a three-hour emergency Caesarean operation.

LUCKY TREE Dutch honeymooner Mamitho Lendas became the first person to survive plunging off the World's End, a 4,000 ft. (1,200 m) high cliff in Sri Lanka, when a tree miraculously broke his fall. He had been taking a picture of his new bride when he stepped back too far and tumbled over the edge. He was trapped in the tree for three and a half hours before being rescued.

DENTAL TERROR Angie Barlow, a mother from Manchester, England, was so terrified of going to the dentist that for more than 10 years whenever her teeth fell out, she glued them back into her mouth. However, the toxic chemicals in the glue eventually caused her to lose 90 percent of the bone supporting her teeth in the upper jaw. This forced her to go to the dentist to have titanium pins inserted into her mouth so that false teeth could be screwed on to restore her smile.

SHARED PAIN Dr. Joel Salinas, a neurologist at Massachusetts General Hospital in Boston, suffers from a rare condition called mirror-touch synesthesia, which allows him to experience the same physical sensations that he observes in other people, including his patients. While watching an amputation in medical school, he felt as if his own arm was being cut off.

PEE POWER Peeing over certain cut flowers—including roses, gerberas, and daffodils—can make them last twice as long. The urea in urine, combined with other acids, prevents stems submerged in water from being contaminated with bacteria that would otherwise kill the blooms.

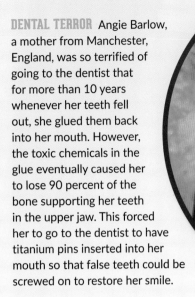

Long Lashes

Valery Smagliy from Kiev, Ukraine, grew incredibly long eyelashes at around 3 cm (1.2 in) long and credits the amazing growth to a special food—a secret he closely guards. Although the 58-year-old enjoyed the extra attention from women, he ultimately decided to trim his lashes because they weighed down his eyelids and were a huge distraction to anyone speaking with him face-to-face.

BODY MARKS Ciera Swaringen of Rockwell, North Carolina, has learned to love the hundreds of dark-colored birthmarks that cover more than two-thirds of her face and body, the largest one stretching from her navel to her lower thighs. She was born with a rare skin condition—giant congenital melanocytic nevus—that caused the oversized mole-like marks.

THREE STRIKES A middle-aged man in Kunshan, China, survived being hit by three cars in the same accident. Mr. Li was trying to cross a busy road when he was struck by two cars within seconds. As passers-by rushed to his aid in the middle of the road, a third car braked sharply to avoid him, but was then rammed from behind by another vehicle and slowly ran over the hapless Li. He suffered leg and rib fractures but soon recovered.

ROBO SPINE After three decades of living in pain with a 130-degree-shaped spine, Deirdre McDonnell from Drogheda, County Louth, Ireland, became the world's first adult to receive a revolutionary "robo spine." She had remote-controlled magnetic rods inserted into her back to correct the curvature and straighten her spine.

ICE BATH After Bulent Sonmez collapsed from a massive heart attack and all attempts to revive him had failed, doctors in Ankara, Turkey, brought him back to life by dropping him into an ice bath, which shocked his heart into beating again.

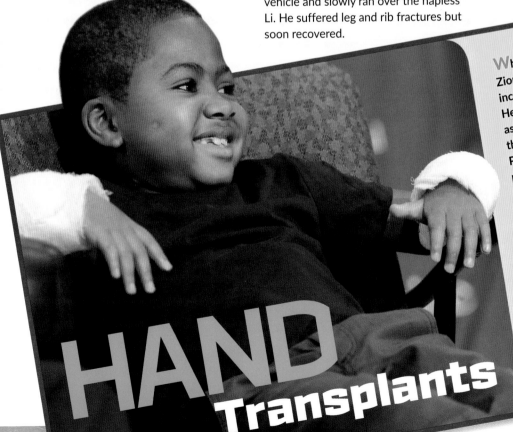

When he was 8 years old, Zion Harvey received an incredible gift—two new hands! He had lost his hands and feet as a toddler, but in July 2015, the Children's Hospital of Philadelphia performed the first pediatric bilateral hand transplant. Surgeons attached Zion's new hands and forearms in a complex 10-hour surgery where they connected bone, blood vessels, muscles, tendons, and skin. Zion now looks forward to swinging on the monkey bars and holding his little sister with his new hands!

HAND Transplants

SCARFLAKE

Traditionally practiced in African societies as a form of cultural identification, scarification—where a design is cut or scratched into human skin to create a permanent scar—has become a popular body modification option. In August 2014, tattoo artist Ulises Jacome of Quito, Ecuador, cut pieces of skin from Andres Ramos's arm to create a scarification tattoo in the shape of a snowflake.

STONE BODY Joey Suchanek of Poughkeepsie, New York, is slowly turning to stone. He has a rare genetic disorder—*fibrodysplasia ossificans progressiva*—which causes muscles, ligaments, and tendons in his body to turn to solid bone, making it increasingly difficult for him to move around. He is one of only 800 people in the world with the condition, for which there is no known cure.

MOUSE CURE A popular cure for warts in 16th-century England was to cut a mouse in half and apply it to the growths.

BROKEN NEEDLE Xu Long of Jiangxi Province, China, had an acupuncture needle lodged in his intestines for 40 years. He had been given acupuncture in 1974, but eventually began to feel worsening chest and back pains. Doctors dismissed them as symptoms of old age until an X-ray revealed the presence of a broken 1.2 in. (3 cm) needle inside his body.

SNOW CRAWL After abandoning his car in a severe blizzard in New Glasgow, Nova Scotia, Canada, in February 2015, 73-year-old Gerald Whitman crawled through the snow for more than an hour before finally being rescued by a Good Samaritan who mistook him for a seal. Charlie Parker had been shoveling snow near his home when he spotted the long, dark shape about 330 ft. (100 m) away, and thought it was a seal until on closer inspection he discovered it was his former banker.

LOOSE TOOTH Eleven-year-old Alexis Davidson from Aurora, Colorado, tied her loose tooth to a sling bow and fired it out of her mouth!

METAL BAR Adam Armitage walked into a gas station in Tauranga, New Zealand, with an iron rod impaled in his head after being attacked while sitting in his car. Even though the metal bar was embedded in his skull and blood was streaming down the side of his head, he waited patiently in line behind other customers before asking for help.

LEGLESS BRICKLAYER Although he was deaf and had both legs amputated below the knee after being run over by a railroad train, William Boular (1869–1953) of Atchison, Kansas, was an accomplished bricklayer who once laid 46,000 bricks in an eight-hour day. He refused to wear prosthetic legs, preferring to walk on his stumps wearing a pair of specially made boots.

BIONIC PILOT Despite losing his right arm in a 1982 motorcycle accident, Steven Robinson of Leeds, West Yorkshire, England, was determined to fulfill his dream of becoming a pilot, but his prosthetic arm kept falling off at the controls. He built his own bionic arm, and in 2015 it was signed off by an aviation medical examiner, finally allowing him to fly a plane solo.

HAIR LOSS Nineteen-year-old Tiarne Menzies from Sydney, Australia, pulled all her hair out in her sleep one night and woke up bald with clumps of long, dark hair on her pillow. She was diagnosed with *trichotillomania*, an incurable impulsive disorder where sufferers feel compelled to pull out their hair.

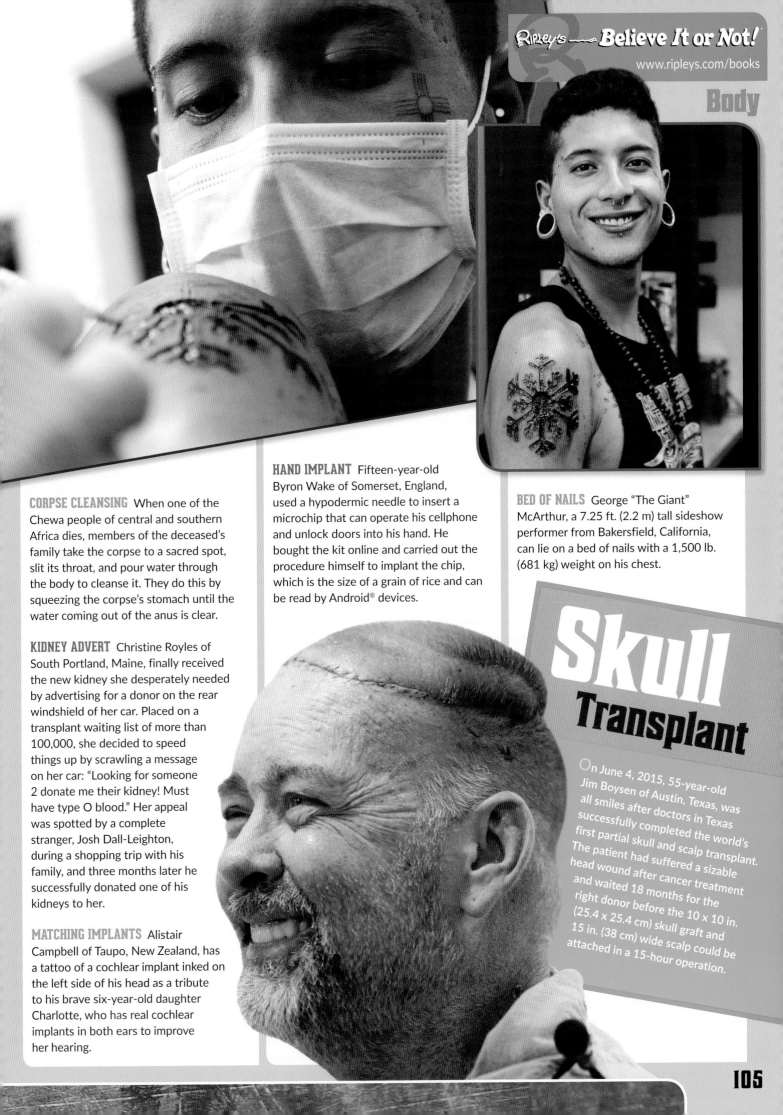

Ripley's — Believe It or Not!
www.ripleys.com/books
Body

CORPSE CLEANSING When one of the Chewa people of central and southern Africa dies, members of the deceased's family take the corpse to a sacred spot, slit its throat, and pour water through the body to cleanse it. They do this by squeezing the corpse's stomach until the water coming out of the anus is clear.

KIDNEY ADVERT Christine Royles of South Portland, Maine, finally received the new kidney she desperately needed by advertising for a donor on the rear windshield of her car. Placed on a transplant waiting list of more than 100,000, she decided to speed things up by scrawling a message on her car: "Looking for someone 2 donate me their kidney! Must have type O blood." Her appeal was spotted by a complete stranger, Josh Dall-Leighton, during a shopping trip with his family, and three months later he successfully donated one of his kidneys to her.

MATCHING IMPLANTS Alistair Campbell of Taupo, New Zealand, has a tattoo of a cochlear implant inked on the left side of his head as a tribute to his brave six-year-old daughter Charlotte, who has real cochlear implants in both ears to improve her hearing.

HAND IMPLANT Fifteen-year-old Byron Wake of Somerset, England, used a hypodermic needle to insert a microchip that can operate his cellphone and unlock doors into his hand. He bought the kit online and carried out the procedure himself to implant the chip, which is the size of a grain of rice and can be read by Android® devices.

BED OF NAILS George "The Giant" McArthur, a 7.25 ft. (2.2 m) tall sideshow performer from Bakersfield, California, can lie on a bed of nails with a 1,500 lb. (681 kg) weight on his chest.

Skull Transplant

On June 4, 2015, 55-year-old Jim Boysen of Austin, Texas, was all smiles after doctors in Texas successfully completed the world's first partial skull and scalp transplant. The patient had suffered a sizable head wound after cancer treatment and waited 18 months for the right donor before the 10 x 10 in. (25.4 x 25.4 cm) skull graft and 15 in. (38 cm) wide scalp could be attached in a 15-hour operation.

FIERCE PIERCER

In Vancouver, Canada, Matthew Menczyk set a new world record for "most surgical needle piercings in one session" by having 4,500 needles inserted into his arms and back over eight hours. Menczyk endured the painful ordeal to raise money for a Canadian youth charity. The most painful part, according to Menczyk, was removing the needles one handful at a time.

STRANGE BIRTHMARK

Jacob Puritz has a large birthmark on his hand and arm that resembles a map of a world that doesn't exist. Tracing the edges in pen to better highlight the continents, he plans to name his imaginary world with the help of a linguist or cartographer.

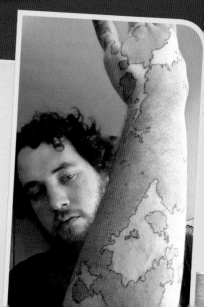

MOUNTAIN PLUNGE Fourteen-year-old Jack Fox from Southport, England, survived falling 2,500 ft. (762 m) down an Austrian mountain. He lost his footing after stepping back to take a photo but escaped with only ice burns to his arms despite bouncing off rocks on the way down.

NO LAUGHING MATTER Jodie Kelly from Dublin, Ireland, suffers from a rare medical condition that causes her to fall to the floor every time she laughs, cries, or becomes angry—up to 10 times a day. She has cataplexy, a neurological disorder that results in a sudden loss of muscle control when she experiences strong emotions. Although she has learned to control her falls so that she does not hurt herself, she tries to avoid watching sad or funny movies.

SEVERED HAND While carrying out home improvements, Edryd Jones from Ferndale, Wales, did not realize that he had cut off his left hand with a power saw. He only became aware of what had happened when he went to pick up a piece of wood but noticed that his hand was not in its usual place—it was on the floor. Luckily, quick-thinking neighbors plunged the severed limb into a bowl of ice, and after a nine-hour operation doctors managed to reattach the 69-year-old grandfather's hand.

BODY TWIST Leilani Franco, a 29-year-old contortionist from London, England, can fold her body into a small, carry-on suitcase. She is also able to brush her teeth with her feet.

CLIP ART Nariko, a barber based near Sao Paulo, Brazil, etches images of famous people, including Snoop Dogg and Brazilian soccer star Neymar, onto the back of his customers' heads. He uses hair clippers to cut the outline of the portrait, then picks up a razor blade to trim in the fine detail, sometimes adding color.

WALKING DEAD For three years, Alabama teen Haley Smith believed she was one of the walking dead—because of a rare condition called Cotard's or Walking Corpse Syndrome. The delusional disorder, which convinces living people that they are really dead, made her fantasize about having picnics in graveyards and being with zombies, but she was eventually brought back to life by a combination of therapy and Disney® movies, which gave her a warm, comforted feeling.

BLOOD DRINK Eighteenth-century European doctors encouraged epileptics to drink the blood of executed criminals to treat their condition.

NARROW ESCAPE Construction worker Xie Mo was accidentally impaled through the neck by six long metal bars while building a bridge in Xiangyang, China, but the poles missed vital arteries in his neck and windpipe by inches, and he survived.

AUTO DENTIST Professional wrestler Robert Abercrombie—known as Rob Venomous in the ring—pulled out his eight-year-old son James's loose front tooth by tying it to the back of his Chevrolet Camaro automobile and hitting the gas pedal. James had been begging his father for days to perform the unorthodox extraction.

EYEBALLS EATEN After failing to take out her disposable contact lenses for six months, Taiwanese student Lian Kao was blinded because microorganisms had eaten away at her eyeballs. Acanthamoeba bugs do not feed directly on human tissue but eat bacteria, and when bacterial infections became established in her corneas, the amoebas burrowed into her eyes to get at them.

OPTICAL ILLUSION Paddy Buckley has a clever geometrical tattoo that makes it look as if he has a hole going right through his arm. The optical illusion ink work was performed by artist Paul O'Rourke of Limerick, Ireland.

Maggot Head

Doctors at Hanoi's Viet Duc Hospital in Vietnam removed more than a dozen maggots from laborer Pham Quang Lanh's skull. After an iron bar fell off a building and struck him in the head, Lanh had a titanium plate inserted over his skull. He then suffered from occasional headaches, but it was not until Lahn had his family inspect his infected, swollen wound that they rushed him to the hospital—they saw maggots crawling under his skin! In a bizarre twist, the maggots did not eat any of his brain, which was protected behind the metal plate, but managed to keep Lanh alive by eating the dead tissue that might have made the infection spread more quickly.

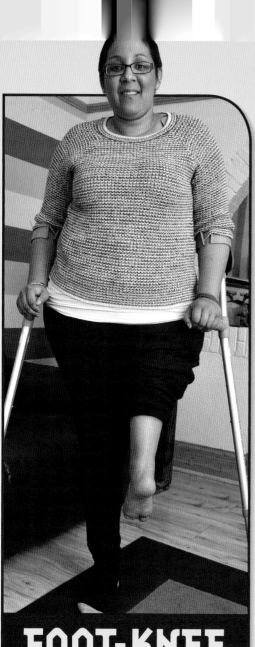

FOOT-KNEE

When 22-year-old Jordon Moody was diagnosed with bone cancer, she never imagined that she'd lose part of her leg, let alone receive a new knee joint made from reattaching her foot backward. Moody, from East Yorkshire, England, underwent chemotherapy and eventually had to have her left thigh amputated. Doctors then moved her lower leg up to replace her thigh and rotated it 180 degrees, leaving her heel facing forward—providing a natural angle similar to how a normal knee bends. Moody hopes to be fitted with a new artificial lower limb, which will be attached to the joint created with her foot.

EYEBALL PARASITE Jessica Greaney, a student at the University of Nottingham, England, had to stay awake for a whole week to stop a parasite from burrowing into her eyeball. Eye drops were administered every 10 minutes for seven days after doctors found a small wormlike creature in her left eye. The parasite, which was eating away at her cornea from the inside, got there after tap water splashed on her contact lens and caused her eye to swell up like a huge red golf ball.

PICKLED EARLOBES Body modification enthusiast Torz Reynolds from London, England, has had her earlobes removed and pickled. She keeps them in a jar in her home.

SUCKED VENOM When her four-year-old son Vinny was bitten by a baby rattlesnake, heavily pregnant Jaclyn Caramazza from Folsom, California, risked her life by sucking the venom out of his leg. When she noticed his ankle quickly swelling and turning purple, she took off his shoes and saw two small puncture marks. Luckily the venom she sucked out did not infect her or her unborn child, and Vinny soon recovered.

SWALLOWED LEECH After 11-year-old schoolboy Xiabo Chien, from Sichuan Province, China, complained of a sore throat and dizzy spells, doctors found a 2.8 in. (7 cm) long, bloodsucking leech growing inside his throat. The leech had blocked his airway, causing him to drift in and out of consciousness. The parasite entered his body when he accidentally swallowed it while drinking from a roadside pond.

STINK JARS To combat the Black Death in 14th-century Europe, doctors encouraged people to store their farts in jars. Whenever the killer plague struck locally, they were told to open the jars and take a sniff of their gas. The plague was believed to be caused by deadly vapors, so medics hoped that the stink would keep it at bay.

HUMAN BILLBOARD Jason George of Mumbai, India, has turned himself into a human billboard by having over 200 logos of his favorite international companies—including fast-food chains, cell phone networks, TV channels, and social networking sites—tattooed all over his body. He had 144 company logos tattooed in just one month.

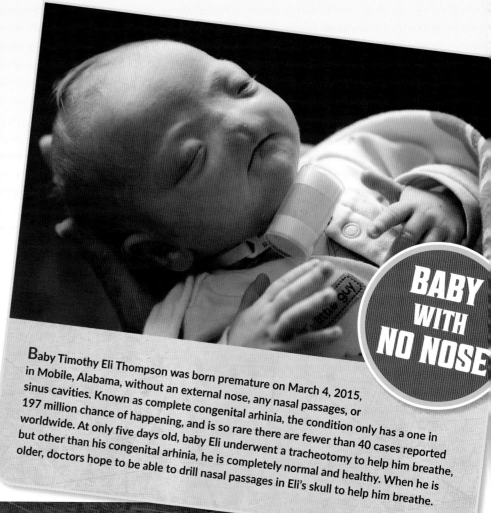

BABY WITH NO NOSE

Baby Timothy Eli Thompson was born premature on March 4, 2015, in Mobile, Alabama, without an external nose, any nasal passages, or sinus cavities. Known as complete congenital arhinia, the condition only has a one in 197 million chance of happening, and is so rare there are fewer than 40 cases reported worldwide. At only five days old, baby Eli underwent a tracheotomy to help him breathe, but other than his congenital arhinia, he is completely normal and healthy. When he is older, doctors hope to be able to drill nasal passages in Eli's skull to help him breathe.

CLINICALLY DEAD Sara Brautigam of Doncaster, England, suffers from a rare heart condition that causes her to "die" up to 36 times a year. She suffers from Postural Orthostatic Tachycardia Syndrome, which, when combined with other symptoms, causes her heart to stop beating and her blood pressure to plummet to the point where she is considered clinically dead. Each attack can last for up to 30 minutes until her heart starts beating properly again.

SWALLOWED COINS Over a three-year period, Rajpal Singh, from Bathinda, India, swallowed 140 coins, 150 needles, and a handful of bolts, nuts, batteries, nails, screws, and magnets. He underwent 240 endoscopy procedures to remove the items from his body.

VIOLENT SNEEZE Toronto Blue Jays outfielder Kevin Pillar was sidelined for 10 days in March 2015 after he strained an abdominal muscle while sneezing.

MIRROR IMAGE Schoolgirls Taylin and Katelin Michael of Swansea, Wales, are "mirror image" twins who do everything— from parting their hair to holding a fork— on the precisely opposite side of their bodies. The identical twins always wave to their mother with opposite hands, and Taylin always stands to the left of her sister in photographs, which allows mom Traci to tell them apart. When they lost their first teeth, Taylin lost the bottom left tooth and Katelin the bottom right. Researchers believe the phenomenon of asymmetrical twins is caused by the embryo splitting several days later than with ordinary identical twins.

LOVING GESTURE To make their young daughter Honey-Rae feel better about the large, strawberry-red birthmark that covers her right leg, Tanya and Adam Phillips, of Grimsby, England, had similar blemishes tattooed all over their own legs.

GRUESOME DISCOVERY A 65-year-old man went to a hospital in Sao, Paulo, Brazil, after suffering persistent nosebleeds for a week—and when doctors examined him they found more than 100 flesh-eating maggots living in his nose.

In 2011, a Chinese woman had a mysterious large horn growing on the left side of her head. The deaf and dumb woman from Henan province in central China sought treatment for her unusal ailment at Beijing Military General Hospital.

Despite having a fingernail-sized growth removed from her forehead in 2008, the object grew again in the same position and reached a size of almost 8 in. (20 cm) when surgeons successfully removed it.

Horned Growth

EXPENSIVE LENSES In the 1920s and 1930s, contact lenses cost as much as a new car, and customers were instructed to lubricate them with their own spit.

FAMILY BOND Heather Penticoff and her daughter, Destinee Martin, not only found out they were pregnant on the same day, they also went on to give birth on the same day—November 11, 2014—at the very same hospital in Fort Myers, Florida.

TIGHT SPOT Trying to avoid arrest on a probation violation, Steven Shuler squeezed down a narrow hole in the attic floor next to the chimney in his home in Monrovia, Indiana, only to discover that he had become wedged in. Unable to climb out, he had to remain in his 16 in. (40 cm) wide hiding place for more than a day until a visiting friend found him and called firefighters to rescue him.

WHEELCHAIR ROBBER A man in a wheelchair robbed a New York City bank of over $1,200 (£791) in cash after handing the teller a note. He then fled down the street—still in his wheelchair—at such a speed that he was out of sight by the time the police were able to send helicopters.

FIRST GIRL When Hannah and Mark Lawrie of Maidstone, Kent, England, had daughter Myla in 2014, she was the first girl born into the family since 1809. The sequence of boys had lasted for five generations spanning over 200 years.

PEACE MISSION Whenever he has an argument with his girlfriend, He Ganhui of Foshan, China, cools off by going on long bike rides. He once cycled all the way to Africa—a distance of over 7,000 miles (11,200 km)—and was away for six months.

IDENTICAL RESULTS Identical twin sisters Claire and Laura Newing from Cornwall, England, achieved identical exam grades—A in psychology and B in biology—allowing them to study the same course—speech and language therapy—at the same university.

SHOCK DISCOVERY William Wilson thought he was getting a great deal when he bought a home in Cape Coral, Florida, for $96,000 (£61,524) at an auction in 2014—but when he went to inspect his purchase the next day he discovered a human corpse on the floor of the master bedroom.

ADULT DIAPERS Facing a portable toilet shortage, Manila's 2,000 traffic enforcers wore adult diapers during Pope Francis's January 2015 visit to the Philippines.

RUSH WEDDING When eight months' pregnant Stephanie Tallent went into labor early while having an ultrasound scan at a Houston, Texas hospital, her fiancé, Jason Nese, arranged a wedding in less than an hour so that they could be married before the birth. They had picked up their marriage license the day before, so Nese fetched it from the car, along with a dress for the bride, called a chaplain, and assembled a group of doctors and nurses from the Texas Children's Pavilion for Women. A few hours after the impromptu ceremony, the newly married Tallent gave birth to daughter Sophia.

FLEX ABILITY

Fifteen-year-old Jaspreet Singh Kalra of Punjab, India, can rotate his head 180 degrees, his arms 360 degrees, and bend backward so far that he can look through his own legs. Kalra discovered his ability four years ago when he started practicing yoga and says he feels no discomfort or pain when he contorts his body.

Ripley's —— Believe It or Not!
www.ripleys.com/books
Body

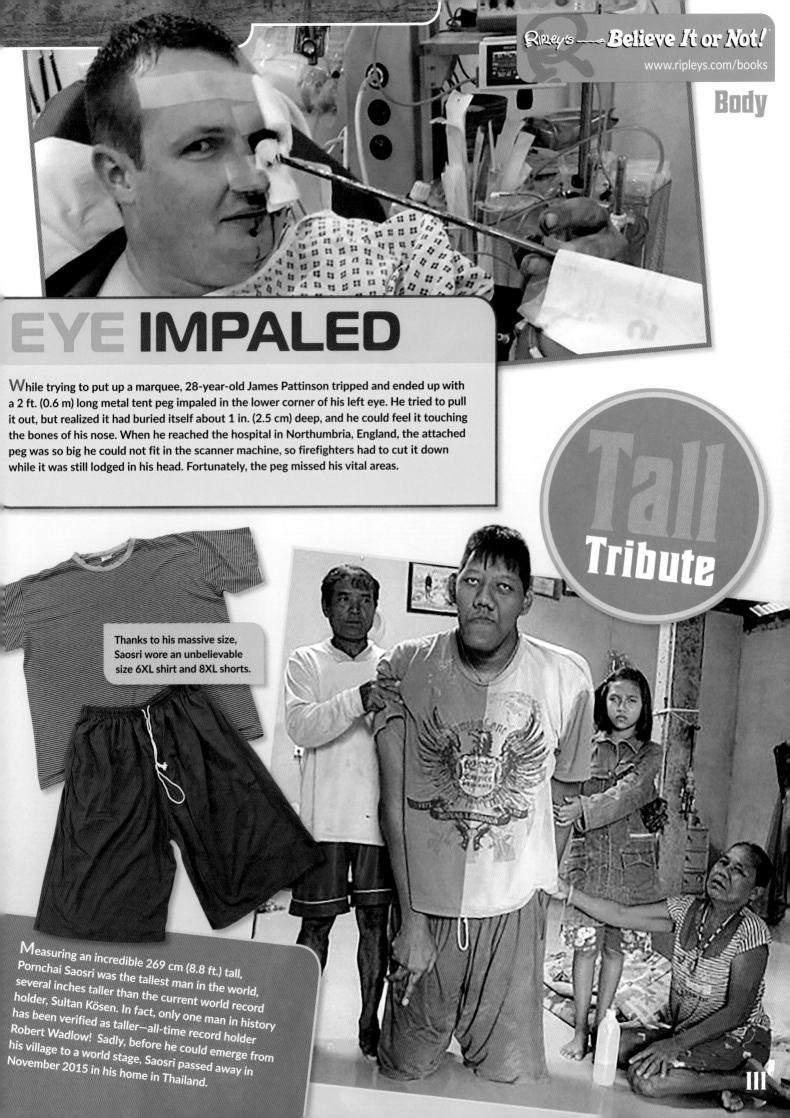

EYE IMPALED

While trying to put up a marquee, 28-year-old James Pattinson tripped and ended up with a 2 ft. (0.6 m) long metal tent peg impaled in the lower corner of his left eye. He tried to pull it out, but realized it had buried itself about 1 in. (2.5 cm) deep, and he could feel it touching the bones of his nose. When he reached the hospital in Northumbria, England, the attached peg was so big he could not fit in the scanner machine, so firefighters had to cut it down while it was still lodged in his head. Fortunately, the peg missed his vital areas.

Tall Tribute

Thanks to his massive size, Saosri wore an unbelievable size 6XL shirt and 8XL shorts.

Measuring an incredible 269 cm (8.8 ft.) tall, Pornchai Saosri was the tallest man in the world, several inches taller than the current world record holder, Sultan Kösen. In fact, only one man in history has been verified as taller—all-time record holder Robert Wadlow! Sadly, before he could emerge from his village to a world stage, Saosri passed away in November 2015 in his home in Thailand.

UNBORN TWIN When doctors examined Jenny Kavanagh from London, England, they found an unborn twin that had been inside her for 45 years. The 4 in. (10 cm) mass discovered in her left ovary was her undeveloped twin that had grown inside her from birth—complete with a face, an eye, a tooth, and long black hair like hers.

TATTOO TAX People in Arkansas have to pay a six percent state tax on any body piercings or tattoos.

HOLDING HANDS Twins Jenna and Jillian Thistlethwaite of Orrville, Ohio, were born holding hands. Although not conjoined, they shared an amniotic sac and placenta, a condition known as monoamniotic, or "mono mono," a birth that occurs in only one in 50,000 pregnancies and in just one percent of twins. Despite fears for their survival, the twins have grown up to be healthy, and celebrated their first birthdays in May 2015—having only recently stopped holding hands.

BIRD MAN

Retired shoe factory worker Ted Richards of Bristol, England, adores his four parrots so much that he's had his face and eyeballs tattooed to look like them—and even had his ears removed in a risky six-hour operation. As well as sharing his home with his parrots, 56-year-old Ted lives with his South American green iguana, Iggy, and pit bull terrier, Candy. Despite his incredible body modifications so far—110 tattoos, 50 piercings, and a split tongue—Ted still wants to turn his nose into a beak!

STRANGE REACTION A 94-year-old Chinese woman, Liu Jieyu, awoke from a coma two weeks after suffering a stroke to find that she could only speak English. The former teacher from Changsha had not spoken English for more than 30 years, but suddenly could no longer speak or understand her native language.

KIDNEY ROMANCE After donating her kidney to a total stranger, Ashley McIntyre of Louisville, Kentucky, became engaged to him, too. She gave her kidney to Danny Robinson in April 2014, they began dating soon after—and on Christmas Day he asked her to marry him.

NAVEL OPERATION Venezuelan body modification enthusiast Emilio Gonzalez has had his navel surgically removed. It was skinned down to its base and then sealed up with a combination of internal and external sutures. He also has multiple facial tattoos, horn-like piercings in his forehead, and "tunnel" holes in his ears and lower lip.

HELPING HAND For more than three years, 18-year-old Xie Xu has carried his disabled friend, 19-year-old Zhang Chi, to and from Daxu High School in China's Jiangsu Province. Although he suffers from muscular dystrophy, Zhang has never missed a class—because Xie gives him a daily piggyback from their dorms to school and also carries him from class to class.

RIHANNA TATTOOS Rihanna fan Sarah Ridge, 23, from Wiltshire, England, has 14 tattoos related to the pop star inked all over her body. She has seven tattoos of the singer's face, as well as copies of seven tattoos actually worn by her idol.

CARDBOARD HUSBAND As part of an art project, Lauren Adkins of Las Vegas, Nevada, wore a white wedding gown and an elegant ring to marry a life-sized cardboard cutout of actor Robert Pattinson in a $3,000 (£1,946) ceremony attended by 50 guests at the Viva Las Vegas Wedding Chapel. She paid $20 (£13) for the cutout, which is of Pattinson as vampire Edward Cullen in the *Twilight* series, and later took it on a honeymoon in Los Angeles.

YELLOW FEAR People with xanthophobia have an intense fear of the color yellow, and sometimes even the word "yellow."

LUNG POWER Brian Jackson of Muskogee, Oklahoma, lifted a 4,387 lb. (1,991 kg) SUV off the floor by using nothing more than his breath to inflate two bags that had been placed under the vehicle. It took him just over 36 minutes.

STRONG STOMACH As a performance stunt, Asha Rani had 40 motorbikes drive over her stomach in one minute in her village of Rampur Attari in Punjab, India, in July 2014.

TWIN RUSH Out of 11 babies born in Montana's Bozeman Deaconess Hospital on July 22, 2015, more than half were made up of three sets of twins.

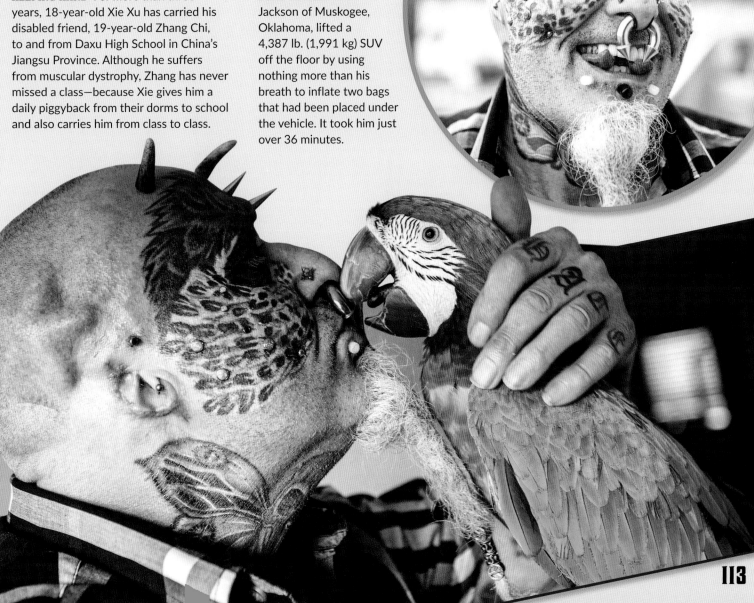

5 Pop Culture

All Nippon Airways (ANA) introduced the first passenger aircraft to feature a *Star Wars* character, as part of an agreement with The Walt Disney Company (Japan) Ltd. The largest airline in Japan, ANA hopes its 787-9 Dreamliner with R2-D2 painted on the fuselage will thrill international and galactic passengers and fans of the popular *Star Wars* franchise.

FLIGHT-SABER

Ripley's Asks ?

Crummy Gummy told Ripley's about the Force behind his face mask.

Q How long did it take to make?

A This took me about two months to create, but the last week of its creation was the craziest. I was trying to make a deadline so it could be exhibited at Wyn317 gallery for Art Basel. It was pretty much just energy drinks and late, late nights every day for that week.

Q How much does it weigh?

A Twelve pounds! You wouldn't think it, but those little bears start to get pretty heavy after you use over 1,000 of them.

Q How many gummies did you eat in proportion to the number of gummies you used?

A The piece used over 1,000 gummy bears. Now, if I ate that many, I'm pretty sure I would have gone into diabetic shock. But I did eat quite a few.

Q Was Star Wars your only inspiration for the piece?

A It was definitely part of it, but not the only thing. Don't get me wrong—I am a HUGE Star Wars nerd, but my art is also inspired by a lot of other things that I enjoyed in my childhood and even still do now as an adult.

DARTH GUMMY

The Force was with Orlando, Florida's Crummy Gummy when he created his 1:1 scale model of Darth Vader's infamous helmet made out of more than 1,000 orange and red gummy bears.

Rice Paddy, Far, Far Away

Ripley's ——— Believe It o
www.ripleys.c
Pop Cu

Japan's Aomori Prefecture paid tribute to *Star Wars* by meticulously planting 11 varieties of rice in seven different colors to "paint" the popular space droids into a rice paddy field. An example of Japanese "tanbo" rice paddy art, it featured BB-8 from *Star Wars Episode VII: The Force Awakens*, and longtime favorites C-3PO and R2-D2 surrounding the *Star Wars* logo.

Force Facts

Darth Vader's **INFAMOUS BREATHING** was recorded by putting a **MICROPHONE INSIDE A REGULATOR** on a scuba tank.

Coins featuring *Star Wars* characters are **LEGAL TENDER** on the South Pacific island of Niue!

In 2007, a **GENUINE LIGHTSABER** used in the film *Star Wars* **TRAVELED INTO SPACE** aboard the space shuttle *Discovery*.

There is a **STONE GARGOYLE** of *Star Wars* character Darth Vader on the northwest tower of the **NATIONAL CATHEDRAL IN WASHINGTON, DC.**

Believe it or not, an estimated **2.2 MILLION PEOPLE IN NORTH AMERICA MISSED WORK ON MAY 19, 1999,** to stand in line for tickets to the new *Star Wars* movie, **THE PHANTOM MENACE!**

The famous **"EWOK" CREATURES** from *Star Wars* are not actually named as such in any of the movies.

The phrase **"I HAVE A BAD FEELING ABOUT THIS"** is said in each film.

← Living on the Set

Many of the buildings constructed as part of Tatooine are still standing in Tunisia.

It took up to **SEVEN DIFFERENT PUPPETEERS** to be **JABBA THE HUTT.**

SCENE-TROOPER

David Eger of Milton, Ontario, Canada, has recreated movie posters, iconic paintings, album covers, and famous moments from history using *Star Wars* figures. His tribute to *The Wizard of Oz* features Chewbacca as the Cowardly Lion, Princess Leia as Dorothy, C-3PO as the Tin Man, and Han Solo as the Scarecrow. Eger has also substituted Princess Leia for the *Mona Lisa* and used stormtroopers for his version of da Vinci's *The Last Supper*. It can take him an entire day to set up and photograph a scene.

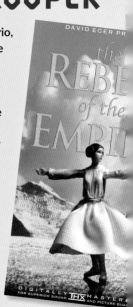

TAYLOR-MADE

JUNIOR DJ In 2014, Oratilwe Hlongwane from Johannesburg, South Africa, became one of his country's most popular DJs with more than 144,363 fans on Facebook—at age two. Even though he could barely speak and was still wearing diapers, he had learned how to DJ on his father's iPad® and soon mastered the console. Known as "DJ ARCH JR," he draws crowds whenever he performs at local shopping malls.

GUNS 'N' NOISES The members of Belgian experimental rock band Tat2noiseact play while inking themselves or each other with tattoos. The audience hears the noise of the tattoo guns, amplified by the sound systems into which they are plugged.

SCENTED SHIRTS Los Angeles–based T-shirt company Hiro Clark joined forces with New York perfumery Le Labo to create scented T-shirts that retain their scent for up to 12 washes.

EXCLUSIVE WEBSITE Justin Foley of Columbus, Ohio, has created a website that only one person can visit at a time. The deliberately pointless site, mostexclusivewebsite.com, consists of just a few lines of text and a counter. Visitors access it by requesting a "ticket" for a 60-second window and then wait patiently in line behind as many as 40,000 other hopefuls. Only around one in nine people actually make it inside the website—the rest give up before their number is called.

REPLICA BATSUIT Batman fan Jackson Gordon, a student of industrial design at Philadelphia University in Pennsylvania, has created a replica Batsuit that can withstand knife stabbings, punches, kicks, or blows from a baseball bat. The suit has strong plastic armored plates and weighs 25 lbs. (11.3 kg).

TWITTER CONTROL In 2014, Twitter users anywhere in the world were able to control the lights on a 9 ft. (2.7 m) tall Christmas tree and menorah at Oxford Communications in Lambertville, New Jersey. Different hashtags turned on different color lights.

PAY-PER-LAUGH The Teatreneu comedy club in Barcelona, Spain, charges customers based on the number of times they laugh. Admission to the club is free, but for each smile that registers on special facial-recognition software patrons are charged 38 cents (£0.27), up to a maximum charge of $30 (£19).

SPOCK CURRENCY

Canadians pay tribute to the late actor Leonard Nimoy by drawing his most famous character—Mr. Spock from *Star Trek*—on their money. Known as "Spocking," Canadians have been turning Sir Wilfrid Laurier, the country's first French-Canadian prime minister, into the Vulcan character for years, but the practice became more prevalent after Nimoy's death in February 2015. The Bank of Canada discourages the act, as banknotes are a symbol of the country and a source of national pride.

BOOTY DRUM The Booty Drum is a hi-tech musical instrument played with butt cheeks instead of hands. Players attach the drum to their butt and start twerking. The drum records the dancer's movements and uses software to translate them into sounds.

GOLD BUCKLE The Swiss-made Calibre R822 Predator belt buckle costs $550,000 (£352,316)—almost three times the price of an average house in the United States. The limited edition belt has 167 components, including self-cleaning mechanisms, and it is made of solid 18-karat white gold and titanium.

HEALTHY PROFIT An unopened Boba Fett toy, which originally sold for $2.50 (£1.50) when released in 1980 to promote the movie *The Empire Strikes Back*, fetched $27,000 (£18,000) at an auction in 2015. The rare figurine was put up for sale by London, England's Craig Stevens, who has a memorabilia collection of more than 10,000 *Star Wars* items.

KISSING AID Tokyo, Japan, eyewear company Blinc Vase has created a pair of eyeglasses that can be worn by two people simultaneously. The two-way eyeglasses consist of a single lens, and have two pairs of arms facing opposite ways so that people wearing them can kiss each other more easily.

Rockabilly Footwear

Ripley's collection of music memorabilia includes late Rock and Roll Hall of Famer Carl Perkins's personal pair of blue suede shoes. Made of Italian leather by designer Giorgio Brutini, the shoes were worn by Perkins for many years, according to his son Stan Perkins. Carl Perkins was inspired to write the 1956 classic song "Blue Suede Shoes" while playing at a high school dance where he overheard a man who kept telling friends not to step on his blue "suedes." Believe it or not, when Perkins sat down later that night to write the lyrics, he couldn't find any paper, so he wrote one of the world's most famous songs on a potato sack.

UNDERWATER MUSIC Evan Holm, an artist based in Oakland, California, has created a turntable that allows records to be played underwater with a waterproof needle.

BICYCLE INSTRUMENTS Linsey Pollak, Ric Halstead, and Brendan Hook formed the Cycologists, an Australian band who played musical instruments made entirely of bicycle parts—including strange clarinets and a bicycle pump panpipe.

HUGE HARP The Earth Harp, a giant harp created by US artist and musician William Close, has strings up to 1,000 ft. (300 m) long. The instrument, which he plays wearing special gloves coated in violin rosin, has been installed in various famous locations around the world. Its strings have been stretched across a canyon in Malibu, California, attached to the top of the Seattle Space Needle, and the Colosseum in Rome.

FIRST TWEET On October 24, 2014, at age 88, Queen Elizabeth II sent her first-ever tweet—to mark the opening of a new exhibition at London's Science Museum. Twitter accounts that have been followed by British Monarchy members include Bill Gates and the late Joan Rivers.

> ▶▶ EMIOTA, A FRENCH COMPANY, HAS CREATED THE WORLD'S FIRST SMART BELT—BELTY GOOD VIBES—WHICH LOOSENS WHEN YOU SIT AND TIGHTENS AGAIN WHEN YOU STAND.

NASA STAGE The Cyberdyne Systems factory in the movie *Terminator: Genisys* had to be shot on the NASA stage in New Orleans, where they built the space shuttle, because there was no other venue in Louisiana tall enough to hold the set.

FREE ROOMS In 2014, the social media-friendly Nordic Light Hotel in Stockholm, Sweden, offered seven nights' free accommodation to guests with at least 100,000 Instagram followers or 2,000 private Facebook friends.

ANTHEM BAN Cell phone users in Bangladesh are not allowed to use the country's national anthem as their ringtone.

DELAYED RELEASE When *Harry Potter and the Prisoner of Azkaban* was first released in the UK, the publisher asked stores not to sell the book until schools were closed for the day to prevent children skipping class.

LONG SENTENCE A single sentence in UK author Jonathan Coe's 2001 novel *The Rotters' Club* is 13,955 words long and covers 33 pages.

OPERA DEATH US baritone Leonard Warren died on stage at the Metropolitan Opera House in New York City on March 4, 1960, just as he had finished singing Giuseppe Verdi's recitative "Morir Tremenda Cosa," which translates as "To Die, A Momentous Thing."

GUINEA PIG Before he was famous, rock star Axl Rose used to earn $8 (£5.12) an hour for smoking cigarettes as part of a science experiment at UCLA.

In this vast, complicated, and ridiculous universe, one bar in Brooklyn, New York, stands out—The Way Station, also known as "The *Doctor Who* Bar." The music venue and pub features a life-sized replica of the iconic blue police box known as the TARDIS, and even serves a *Doctor Who*-themed cocktail menu. If you time travel on a Sunday, you could take part in a sci-fi movie screening or even watch the newest episodes of *Doctor Who*.

Since its 1982 release, Steven Spielberg's beloved film *E.T. the Extra-Terrestrial* has charmed its way into our hearts and minds—and now trees. At the Uig Hotel on the Isle of Skye, Scotland, owner Billy Harley noticed this out-of-this-world likeness inside a tree trunk he was chopping for firewood.

E.T.
THE EXTRA-TREE-ESTRIAL

SCARLETT DRESS When collector James Tumblin learned that a dress worn by Vivien Leigh as Scarlett O'Hara in the movie *Gone with the Wind* was going to be thrown out in the 1960s, he negotiated a deal to buy it for $20 (£13)—and in 2015, the dress sold at auction in Beverly Hills, California, for $137,000 (£87,764). Tumblin has a collection of over 300,000 items of *Gone with the Wind* memorabilia at his home in Portland, Oregon.

OUTLIVED OBITUARIST When comedian Bob Hope died in 2003, aged 100, his *New York Times* obituary had been sitting on the shelf for so long that the man who wrote it—movie critic Vincent Canby—had himself died of old age three years earlier.

RAP NEWS To get young people interested in current affairs, a Ugandan TV news program, *Newz Beat*, features "rap-orters" who rap the headlines to hip-hop music.

BART FAN Travis McNall of Wolcottville, Indiana, has built up a collection of more than 3,400 items of memorabilia from the television show *The Simpsons*. He collected his first piece, a Bart Simpson shirt in 1990, and is now so devoted to the show that his friends call him "Bart."

MISSED SHOW When 87-year-old WOND-AM radio host Pinky Kravitz of Atlantic City, New Jersey, called in sick on May 15, 2015, it was the first time he had missed his show in 56 years. He had previously done the show from a hospital without any of his listeners knowing.

TINY OSCAR

Measuring just 5.5 in. (14 cm) tall, this miniature Oscar® statue was produced by Columbia Pictures to celebrate the 1934 film *It Happened One Night*, which swept the Academy Awards®, winning Best Picture, Director, Actress, Actor, and Screenplay. Only a few of these solid metal mini Oscars were presented to studio executives.

CHARLES TRIPPY

Charles Trippy, bassist for the band We the Kings, holds the world record for the longest consecutive daily video blog, or vlog, making YouTube videos of every day in his life for the past seven years! He never misses a day of filming, even when he underwent brain surgery for a tumor in 2012. "I was going through something so crappy, and there's so many other people going through things way worse. I figured if I could give up a bit of my privacy to help someone, I was all for it," he explained.

His "Internet Killed Television" YouTube channel, which he hosts with his fiancée, Allie, gets 300,000 to 400,000 views a day. Guests have included actor Alex Winter (from Bill and Ted's Excellent Adventure), wrestler Hulk Hogan, musician Kenny G, and actor Danny Trejo.

Ripley's Asks?

Charles commented about his YouTube connection.

Q What prompted you to start the videos?

A I originally started doing the videos online as a bet with my college roommate to see who got the most viewers, but then I started loving it. It's been 10 years now—seven years of daily videos and 10 years on YouTube.

Q What would you say is your most unusual video?

A Filming my brain surgery, just because I actually got to film the whole thing. I held the camera until my arm went down—no tripod. Once my hand went down (I was awake the whole time) the surgeon grabbed the camera 'cause he knew how important it was for me to film, and he started asking me questions. He said my humor was still there and that I was still making fun of things. The fact that you can see me still talking, and then in the corner you can see my brain, makes this my most unusual video.

Q What would you tell people interested in starting a YouTube series?

A Some people think these daily videos are lies or fabricated, when in fact there's no producer. My friends, family, Allie, my dog—they're all real. It takes dedication, and it's a very stressful, unique type of work because YouTube is a community that's never consistent... anyone can do YouTube, but it's not for everyone.

YouTube CONGRATULATIONS
For Surpassing
One Million Subscribers

Ripley's — Believe It or Not!®
www.ripleys.com/books
Pop Culture

Helen Ruth Van Winkle, known as Baddie Winkle on social media, is another Internet innovator, boasting an impressive 1.7 million Instagram followers—and she's 87 years old! Baddie (the name is a combination of her persona as a "badass grandmother" and her last name, Van Winkle) captivated fans ever since her first Instagram post in April 2014, but her eccentric style evolved out of grief. After the passing of both her husband and son, Helen Van Winkle coped with her loss by dressing more adventurously and adopting her now popular Baddie Winkle persona. With the help of her granddaughter and great-granddaughter, Baddie Winkle has utilized social media to not only mend her broken heart, but also delight millions who find her not only charming, but also inspiring.

Baddie Winkle

Ripley's Asks ?

Baddie sat down and shared about all things social media.

Q How do you feel about today's Internet culture?

A I think if you want to survive and thrive in this world, you have to be connected to social media. Whether it's connecting with loved ones or friends on Facebook or Instagram or selling a product to the public, you have to know how to use social media to be a success.

Q What famous celebrities have you met?

A I have met quite a few celebrities: Nicole Richie, the cast of Orange Is the New Black, Drew Barrymore, Tyler Oakley, Becky G, Marnie the Dog, Jiff Pom the Dog, Gwen Stefani, Dada Life, Dr. Drew, Lindsey Sterling, the cast of The Doctors on CBS, and of course, my bestie Miley Cyrus!

Q What's the funniest outfit you've ever been sent?

A Oh, my goodness, I am sent some crazy stuff you would not believe. The one thing I will not wear is pasties, and it seems like everyone thinks I want to wear them 'cause they get sent a lot, but I never will. I have been sent some very skimpy stuff, but I do have my limits.

Q What's next for Baddie Winkle?

A I've got a lot of projects in the works—from an online clothing store, to shirts in retail outlets around the world, a music video being released by Vice Music, exciting commercials, and I'm even shooting a pilot for my own reality series!

Rainbow Ring

British jeweler Theo Fennell designed this "Over the Rainbow" ring, a one-of-a-kind piece inspired by the myth of a pot of gold being hidden at the end of a rainbow. Crafted from 18 karat yellow gold and set with pavé diamonds, the ring's crystal dome, which is carved with clouds, veils a hand-painted rainbow. Opening the top portion of the ring reveals a miniature pot of gold, and the "wooden" side doors open to reveal two fairy tale village scenes.

WAGON TRAIL To research his 2015 book, *The Oregon Trail: A New American Journey*, US author and journalist Rinker Buck became the first person to make the epic 2,100 mile (3,380 km) journey by covered wagon since 1909.

SMILE, PLEASE Street musicians in Oxford, England, must smile at all times while performing—or risk being fined $1,505 (£1,000) by the city council.

GROWING BOOK To teach children where paper comes from, Buenos Aires, Argentina publisher Pequeño Editor launched a picture book that grows into a tree once it has been read. The pages are lined with jacaranda seeds, so when the book, titled *My Father Was In the Jungle*, is planted in the ground after use, the seeds sprout and eventually form trees.

BEAR NECESSITY Austrian amateur photographer Christian Kneidinger has taken pictures of his teddy bear in more than 20 exotic locations around the world—including a glacier in Iceland, a waterfall in Mauritius, and a beach in Dubai—because his wife, Ranati, is too shy to pose.

PRESIDENT'S FOLLOWERS When President Barack Obama opened his own Twitter account in May 2015, he amassed one million followers in under five hours.

LONG WAIT In 2015, American author Harper Lee published her first novel in 55 years. *Go Set a Watchman* is the sequel to her only previous novel, the Pulitzer Prize-winning classic *To Kill a Mockingbird*—even though it was actually written first.

GROWTH SPURT During filming of the 1965 movie *The Sound of Music*, 13-year-old Nicholas Hammond, who played Friedrich, one of the von Trapp children, had a six-inch growth spurt, raising his height to 5.75 ft. (1.7 m). For later scenes together, Charmian Carr, who played his sister Liesl, had to stand on boxes in order to appear taller than her younger brother.

DRUM ROLL Musician Joshua Scott played the drums from Boston, Massachusetts, to his home city of San Francisco, California—a journey of 3,000 miles (4,800 km). Joined by filmmaker Joseph Lafond, Scott drove across the United States so that he could play Clyde Stubblefield and James Brown's "Funky Drummer" at various iconic locations along the way, including the Bonneville Salt Flats in Utah. They spent just 10 minutes at each location, and that included the time setting up the drum kit.

FESTIVE SONG The traditional Christmas song "Jingle Bells" was originally written for Thanksgiving. It was composed in 1850 by James Pierpont in a tavern in Medford, Massachusetts.

LAST SURVIVOR Leonardo DiCaprio and Kate Winslet, the stars of the 1997 movie *Titanic*, helped pay the nursing home fees for Millvina Dean, the last RMS *Titanic* survivor, so that she did not have to sell any more mementos of the disaster to raise cash. She died in 2009 at age 97.

LARA'S LAIR Gamer Rodrigo Martin Santos of Madrid, Spain, has more than 2,380 items of *Tomb Raider* memorabilia, including life-sized statues of Lara Croft. He began collecting the merchandise in 1996 when he was nine, and he owns the original costume worn by model Rhona Mitra in the video game *Tomb Raider 2*.

HIGH NOTES In December 2014, Britain's ACM Gospel Choir performed a 15-minute Christmas carol concert at an altitude of 39,000 ft. (11,887 m) on board a flight from London's Gatwick Airport to Geneva, Switzerland.

STAIRS

The entrance to a new underground shopping mall in Luoyang, China, features stairs painted as piano keys to recognize history's most renowned composers. The stairs also feature portraits of famous composers, including Mozart, Chopin, Beethoven, Liszt, and Tchaikovsky.

HELLO KITTY CAPSULE

rom April 29 through September 13, 2015, visitors to Manhattan's Dag Hammarskjold Plaza were able to pack personal objects into a translucent, 9 ft. (3 m) tall Hello Kitty. Part of Japanese artist Sebastian Masuda's newest installation, called "Time After Time Capsule," this multi-city, multi-Kitty project includes sculptures being filled in such places as Miami and Amsterdam. All of Masuda's Hello Kitty sculptures will be united in the famous cat's hometown of Tokyo to mark the 2020 Summer Olympics.

FACEBOOK APPEAL Manuel Parisseaux, who has Down syndrome, received more than 61,500 cards for his 30th birthday after his father, Lucien, posted an appeal on Facebook. There were so many cards that the mail service had to use a truck to deliver them to his home in Calais, France.

PIG PRIZE The winner of the UK's Bollinger Everyman Wodehouse Prize for comic literary fiction—created in honor of English humorist P. G. Wodehouse (1881–1975)—receives a bottle of champagne, a complete set of all 52 Wodehouse novels, and a live pig named after the winning novel.

UNDER AGE Bollywood star Sridevi played a stepmother in a 1976 Tamil movie called *Moondru Mudichu* when she was just 13 years old.

DAILY SCREENING Since its October 1995 release, the Bollywood comedy *The Brave-Hearted Will Take Away the Bride* has been screened almost every day at the Maratha Mandir Theater in Mumbai, India.

FRIENDS LIFESTYLE Du Xin of Beijing, China, is so obsessed with the TV series *Friends* that he has legally changed his name to Gunther and has modeled his home, job, and family after the hit sitcom. He decorated his apartment to be an exact replica of the one that Chandler and Joey shared, started his own coffee shop called Central Perk, married a woman named Rachel, and named their son Joey. He even has a pet named Smelly Cat in honor of Phoebe's famous song.

SOLAR ALBUM Singer-songwriter Jack Johnson's 2008 CD, *Sleep Through the Static*, was recorded entirely using solar energy at his Solar Powered Plastic Plant Studios.

CHILDREN'S PAPER *Balaknama*, or *Children's Voice*, is a quarterly Hindi-language newspaper written and run by children living in the slums of New Delhi, India—and it has a readership of tens of thousands.

IMITATING ART The actors who dub the voices of Homer and Marge in the French version of *The Simpsons*, Philippe Peythieu and Véronique Augereau, are married in real life. They met during auditions and wed a decade later.

RECORD HOARD Keith Sivyer from London, England, bought every release that entered the UK singles chart from its inception in 1952 right up until his death in 2015. Every week, he visited his local record store with a copy of *Music Week* magazine and bought the latest songs that had entered the top 40. His collection, filed in alphabetical order on specially built floor-to-ceiling shelves, consisted of around 27,000 7-inch vinyl singles, 8,000 12-inch singles, and more than 10,000 CD singles.

COSTNER CORPSE Kevin Costner's first major screen role, in *The Big Chill* (1983), was cut so heavily that in the final movie he appears only as a corpse.

Greetings from Coney Island

Brooklyn, New York, has changed quite a bit in recent years, and although Coney Island may currently seem like the borough's most bizarre pocket, don't let the wafting smell of Nathan's® Hot Dogs and the rumble of the Cyclone roller coaster fool you—this amusement park's past is even more strange.

From the 1880s through World War II, with easy access from New York City, Coney Island was a major vacation destination. Three major parks—Luna Park, Steeplechase Park, and Dreamland—all competed for visitors by taking advantage of the public's fascination with the unknown and unexplained, from distant lands to tragic disasters. In their heyday, nothing was too eccentric, big, or outlandish for Coney Island.

DREAMLAND.

CONEY ISLAND, N.Y.

CENTRAL DUMPS

CONKLIN   THEATRE

FOOLISH HOUSE

Pop Culture

One of Coney Island's most popular attractions also became one of its most influential. From 1903 to 1943, millions of people visited Dr. Martin Couney's "Baby Incubator," viewing what would soon become commonplace in hospitals around the world.

A German immigrant, Couney struggled to find a way to implement his technology, which was believed at the time to be too radical by the medical community. Couney turned to Coney Island to support his life-saving invention, charging visitors 25 cents to view "the world's tiniest babies."

Couney exhibited his incubators at both Luna Park and Dreamland in a pristine operation—one in which Couney trusted enough to display his own premature daughter, Hildegaae. During his 40-year run, Couney saved the lives of 6,500 children, and when the Coney Island exhibit closed in 1941, a preemie ward opened in Cornell's New York Hospital.

In 1901, Couney successfully exhibited the incubators at the Pan–American Exposition in Buffalo, New York. This encouraged him to settle in the United States and open a permanent exhibit.

Infant Incubators

Fighting Flames

Over 2,000 people were employed at Dreamland's "Fighting the Flames," where performers reenacted what it was like to be a firefighter—from hitching live horses to the fire engine to extinguishing a real fire. They also made dramatic rescues as trapped victims jumped from the blazing building's windows to the ground.

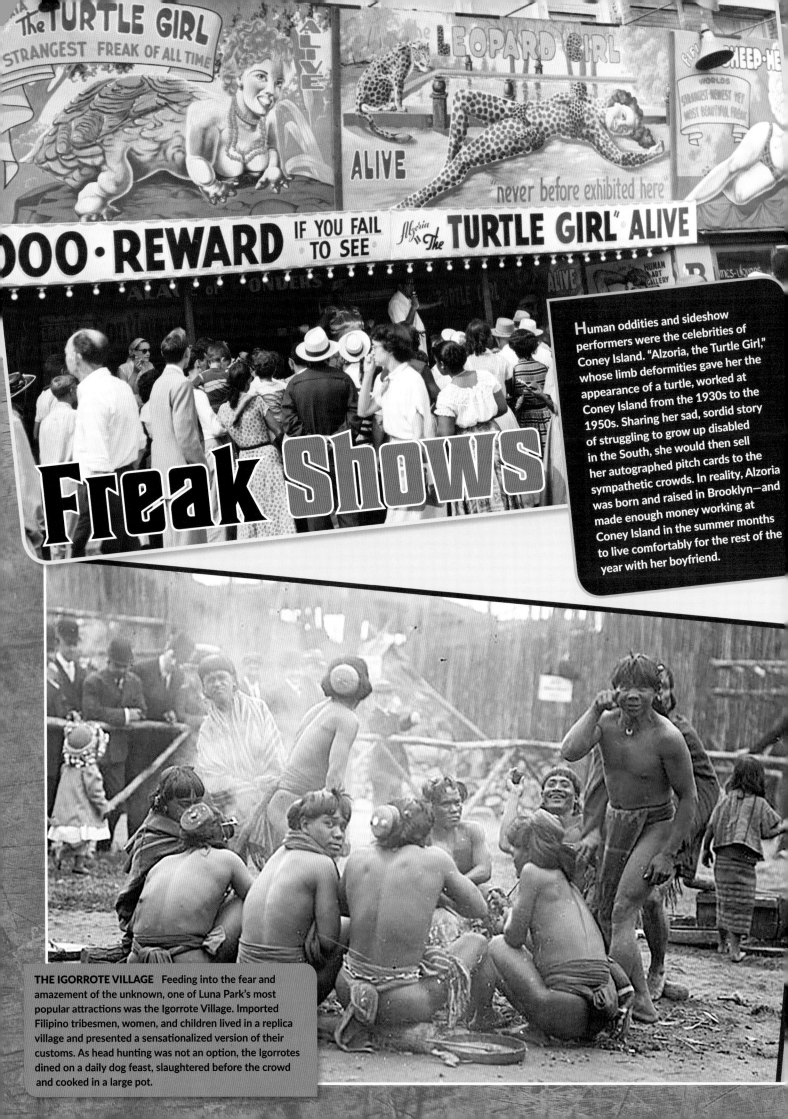

Freak Shows

Human oddities and sideshow performers were the celebrities of Coney Island. "Alzoria, the Turtle Girl," whose limb deformities gave her the appearance of a turtle, worked at Coney Island from the 1930s to the 1950s. Sharing her sad, sordid story of struggling to grow up disabled in the South, she would then sell her autographed pitch cards to the sympathetic crowds. In reality, Alzoria was born and raised in Brooklyn—and made enough money working at Coney Island in the summer months to live comfortably for the rest of the year with her boyfriend.

THE IGORROTE VILLAGE Feeding into the fear and amazement of the unknown, one of Luna Park's most popular attractions was the Igorrote Village. Imported Filipino tribesmen, women, and children lived in a replica village and presented a sensationalized version of their customs. As head hunting was not an option, the Igorrotes dined on a daily dog feast, slaughtered before the crowd and cooked in a large pot.

A HELLISH DEMISE This photo was taken at Dreamland's Trained Wild Animal Arena. Dreamland was short-lived. In 1911, just seven years after opening, it was burnt to the ground in a dramatic fire started by a ride called Hell Gate. All of the incubator babies were saved, but 60 of the wild trained animals perished.

DREAMLAND
TRAINED WILD ANIMAL
COL. JOS. G. FERA

RICARDO
and his
PERFORMING
LEOPARDS
and JAGUARS

BAMBOO
DOC. HAST
JUNGLE Co
Pon

Galveston Flood

On September 8, 1900, a Category 4 hurricane ripped through Galveston, Texas, killing more than 6,000 people and causing a 15 ft. (4.6 m) storm surge that flooded and destroyed the city. Only a few years later, a re-creation of the disaster drew crowds at Coney Island. A mechanical cyclorama dramatized the flood, destroying a replica of Galveston before the audience's eyes.

MIDGET CITY

Midget City, or the Lilliputian Village, was Dreamland's miniature town populated by over 300 little people. Villagers actually lived onsite and functioned as a community in their built-to-scale world. They had their own police and fire departments and even performed their own acts, such as the Tom Thumb Circus.

LITTLE MEN AND WOMEN
Midget City, Dreamland, Coney Island

Count Chocula, with Lemmy the spider!

Totally Sweet!

Detroit, Michigan, artist Eric Millikin would probably be the first person to ask you to trade some of your Halloween candy with him—especially since he needed over 1,000 miniature bags of M&Ms® to finish his picture of breakfast cereal favorite Count Chocula! His *Totally Sweet* series of portraits of spooky characters such as Freddy Krueger, Frankenstein's monster, and Jason from the *Friday the 13th* films are created using thousands of wrapped pieces of Halloween candy, and each features Millikin's pet spider, Lemmy, hidden in the picture.

Jack Skellington!

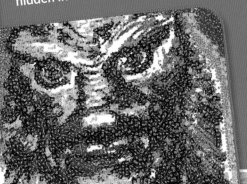

The Creature from the Black Lagoon!

Ripley's Asks ?

We asked Eric Millikin what inspired him to create his candy-covered canvases.

Q Why did you use "fun-sized" candy?

A Well, I was influenced by the very scary amount of candy I've eaten while watching so many monster movies! I like making something big out of a lot of little things. It's a reminder that in any part of your life, big, wonderful things can happen when a bunch of little things come together.

Q Which of the *Totally Sweet* pieces used the most candy—and how much?

A Probably Count Chocula, because I wanted to make him so dark and so colorful—and I was really, really hungry when I was making that portrait. You can find almost 10,000 candies in there.

Q Why did you feature Lemmy in all of the portraits?

A I wanted to include a surprise, sort of like the prize in the bottom of a cereal box, as a bonus for people who really look at these portraits. What would be more surprising to find in your bag of Halloween candy than a tarantula?

SHARK CRIB Movie fan Joseph Reginella of New York City made his two-month-old nephew, Michael Melaccio, a *Jaws*-inspired crib, designed to look like the baby sleeping in it is about to be devoured by a fearsome great white shark.

DYLAN LYRICS Bob Dylan's original draft of the lyrics for his 1965 song "Like a Rolling Stone" were written on four sheets of headed notepaper from the Roger Smith Hotel in Washington, DC—and the pages sold at a New York auction for $2 million (£1.3 million) in 2014.

EXPLOSIVE NOVEL Readers tackling *Private Vegas*, a 2015 novel by American thriller writer James Patterson, faced a race against time because the book self-destructed if they failed to finish it within 24 hours. One thousand e-books made available through the author's website had 24-hour digital timers, and once the clock ran out, the book vanished forever from the user's tablet.

SAME SUIT As an experiment to prove how women on TV are too often judged by their clothes, male presenter Karl Stefanovic, the cohost of Australia's *Today* program on Channel 9, wore the same blue suit on screen every day for a year—and not one viewer complained.

HOT LICKS Brian May of the UK rock band Queen has an electric guitar that he and his father, Harold, hand-carved over fifty years ago. Using wood from an old table for the body, and an oak 18th-century fireplace mantel to create the neck, it took two years to make—but the guitar, known as the "Red Special," has subsequently been played by May in concerts for 50 years.

ROYAL BOOK "The Adventures of Alice Laselles," a children's short story penned by Britain's Queen Victoria when she was a 10-year-old princess, was finally published in 2015—almost two centuries after it was written.

WEBCAM ALERT Finland's Ari Kivikangas has broadcast almost every minute of his life since 2010 via webcam. He suffers from epilepsy and spends most of his time at home. During a broadcast in 2014, one of his online followers saw how ill he looked and called paramedics, who gave him urgent CPR, saving his life.

FROZEN FAN Kirsty Taylor, 21, from Rotherham, South Yorkshire, England, has seen the movie *Frozen* more than 100 times and has spent $1,500 (£1,056) on Disney® merchandise from the movie. She has also bought a custom-made blue dress just like the one worn by Queen Elsa—and frequently asks her boyfriend, Jake Martin, to dress up as Kristoff.

SNEEZED OUT In 2015, 51-year-old Steve Easton from Surrey, England, gave a mighty sneeze—and blew out a toy dart that had been stuck up his left nostril for 44 years. He had suffered from a blocked nose and headaches for most of his life, but put it down to hay fever, unaware that he had accidentally inhaled the dart while playing with a toy gun when he was seven.

REGAL NAME More than 50 babies in the UK have been named Khaleesi, the word for "queen" in Dothraki, one of the fictional languages devised for the TV fantasy drama *Game of Thrones*.

POPULAR TRAILER The trailer for the 2015 movie *Avengers: Age of Ultron* was viewed 34 million times—equivalent to four times the population of New York City—on YouTube in the first 24 hours after its release.

HORROR MASK The scary mask worn by the character Michael Myers in the 1978 horror movie *Halloween* was actually a Captain Kirk death mask. The production budget on the movie was tight, so the designer picked up a *Star Trek* novelty mask for a couple of dollars and sprayed it white. When William Shatner found out, he was so amused that he went trick-or-treating with his daughters one Halloween wearing one!

Take a close look at this image and see if you can spot the two models, even if it's difficult to see where one begins and the other ends. Named *Chameleon*, this amazing bodypainting piece consists of two women and is created by South Tyrol, Italy, artist and musician Johannes Stötter, whose work has always been influenced by both spiritual and nature-related themes.

CHAMELEON PEOPLE

>Two people!

Harlem Pope-trotter

In May 2015, stars of the Harlem Globetrotters met with Pope Francis to name him the ninth Honorary Harlem Globetrotter in team history. The esteemed honor recognizes an individual of extraordinary character and achievement who has made an everlasting mark on the world. The ceremony took place at the Vatican, where the team presented the Pope with a framed number 90 Globetrotters' jersey with "Pope Francis" printed across the back. Other notable honorees include Whoopi Goldberg (1990), Nelson Mandela (1996), and Pope John Paul II, who was named the seventh honorary team player in 2000.

Flight Time Lang set a spinning basketball on the Pope's finger, which fell only a second later.

WRONG MOVIE In June 2015, the projectionist at a theater in Middletown, Ohio, accidentally screened a horror movie, *Insidious: Chapter 3*, to startled parents and young children instead of the advertised film, Disney's® *Inside Out*.

NO INSTRUMENTS It is against the law to show musical instruments being played on TV in Iran. Some Shia Muslim clerics say broadcasting music is against their faith, so the instruments are often replaced with pictures of flowers.

PLASTIC POP STAR

Adam Daniel, a 31-year-old from Los Angeles, California, has spent $75,000 (£48,467) on plastic surgery in order to look like his idol, Madonna. He first became obsessed with her music as a teenager—but has since had cheek implants, his jaw and brows surgically altered, and has had numerous fillers across his face. He now performs as a Madonna impersonator under the name Venus Delight and keeps his closet fully stocked with replicas of Madonna's most famous outfits.

TOUCHY SUBJECT Since September 24, 2003, Alberto Frigo, an Italian conceptual media artist who now lives in Stockholm, Sweden, has photographed every object his right hand has touched. Using his left hand to hold the camera, he photographs an average of 76 objects a day, and has taken more than 330,000 pictures. He plans to continue the project until the year 2040, when he will be 60—and will have taken around one million pictures.

ONE-LEGGED DANCER Clayton "Peg Leg" Bates (1907–1998) lost his left leg in an accident at age 12, but went on to become a famous dancer, appearing on *The Ed Sullivan Show* on 21 occasions. The signature move of the one-legged tap dancer from South Carolina was the "Imitation American Jet Plane," in which he would jump 5 ft. (1.5 m) in the air and land on his wooden leg, with his good leg sticking straight out behind him.

AUTOGRAPH COLLECTOR Over a period of 70 years, Jack Kuster of Rochester, New York, collected over 33,000 celebrity autographs, traveling to 19 different countries in his search for famous signatures. He began collecting at age 14 when he approached movie star Carmen Miranda for her autograph while she was visiting Rochester during World War II. He also took more than 17,000 never-published photographs of celebrities.

DIAMOND LOAFERS Beverly Hills, California, jewelry designer Jason Arasheben created an all-diamond pair of shoes worth $2 million (£1.3 million). The loafers contained more than 14,000 white diamonds set into white gold with a total weight of 340 karats.

TEEN INTERVIEWER In November 2014, 17-year-old celebrity journalist Pavlina Osta conducted 347 radio interviews in 24 hours in Port Orange, Florida. Each interview consisted of a minimum of five unique questions. She has a syndicated radio show, *Pavlina's Kidz Place*, and has interviewed more than 400 celebrities since she was 11.

LIGHTNING STRIKE After being struck by lightning in 1994, Chenango County, New York, orthopedic surgeon Tony Cicoria found that his head was suddenly flooded with piano music. Although he had no particular interest in music before the accident, he spent the next 12 years learning to play the piano so that he could perform the piece in his head, which he called the "Lightning Sonata."

HAND COPIES The manuscript for *War and Peace*, the 1,400-page epic by Russian novelist Leo Tolstoy, was painstakingly written out seven times by hand by his editor, and wife, Sophia.

ZEALOUS EDITOR Since 2007, software engineer Bryan Henderson of San Jose, California, has removed the same phrase—"comprised of"—over 47,000 times from Wikipedia pages.

DANGEROUS AUTHOR Scottish crime fiction writer Ian Rankin—creator of the Edinburgh-based *Inspector Rebus* novels—has sometimes been turned down for car insurance because his job was considered too dangerous.

Pop Culture

Ripley's Asks

Ripley's caught up with Greg to ask him about his custom-made collection.

Q *Do you have a favorite doll? If so, what makes it so special?*

A The thing I love about them is they are all 100 percent unique. Even though they were based on a pattern book, they each reflect the different artisan's skill level. There are few that are "anatomically correct." I like those just because I have to think, "What was the maker of the doll thinking?"

Q *Is your entire collection kept with you or kept elsewhere?*

A My entire collection is with me! I do not have them all out on display, as there are so many of them. But they do come out once in a while for photo shoots and exhibitions.

Q *Have you met Mr. T?*

A I never have! I know that he knows I exist, though. The first time I exhibited the dolls I was interviewed by the Washington Post. They interviewed Mr. T and told him about my collection. He said it touched his heart and he wanted to tell his momma about it. He also signed a bobblehead doll for me that the reporter gave me!

Q *What's next for your collection?*

A I recently moved to L.A., and I hope to exhibit the collection here soon. I have yet to show it in L.A. so I am very excited about that!

MR. T IN EFFIGY

New Yorker Greg Rivera has a collection of 250 handmade dolls of Lawrence Tureaud—otherwise known as Mr. T. The dolls look similar to the Cabbage Patch Kids® dolls popular during the 1980s, but Rivera's Mr. T dolls sport Mohawks, wear Mr. T's signature gold jewelry, and some even have tattoos. Rivera considers Mr. T his childhood hero and used to watch *The A Team* TV show with his dad when he was young. Rivera started seriously collecting when a friend decided to sell his Mr. T collection in 1998—Rivera bought all 50 items. Rivera's now massive collection has even been featured at art galleries as "I Pity the Dolls! A Collection of Contemporary and Vintage Mr. T Dolls."

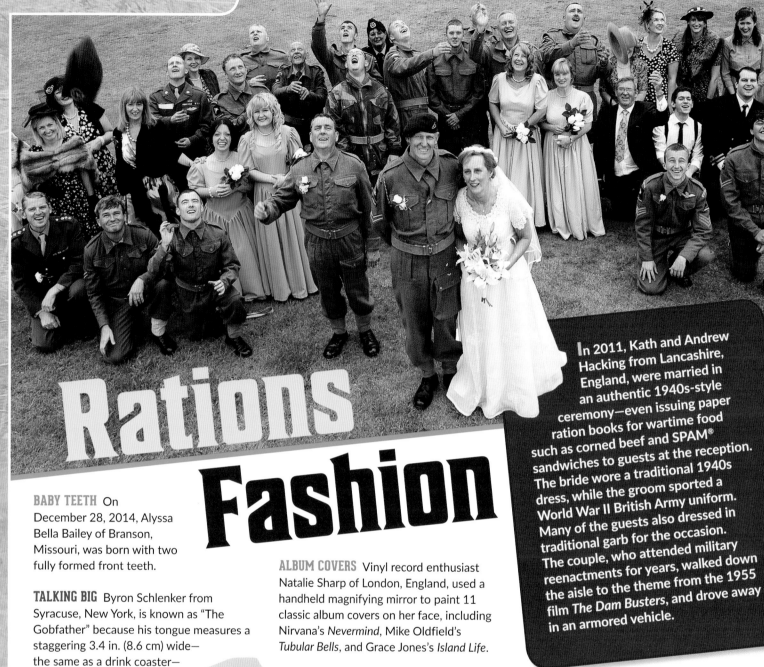

Rations Fashion

BABY TEETH On December 28, 2014, Alyssa Bella Bailey of Branson, Missouri, was born with two fully formed front teeth.

TALKING BIG Byron Schlenker from Syracuse, New York, is known as "The Gobfather" because his tongue measures a staggering 3.4 in. (8.6 cm) wide—the same as a drink coaster—and 2 cm wider than an iPhone® 6. Large tongues apparently run in the family, as his 14-year-old daughter Emily's is 2.9 in. (7.3 cm) wide.

ALBUM COVERS Vinyl record enthusiast Natalie Sharp of London, England, used a handheld magnifying mirror to paint 11 classic album covers on her face, including Nirvana's *Nevermind*, Mike Oldfield's *Tubular Bells*, and Grace Jones's *Island Life*.

SKIN TRIBUTE Tattoo artist Steve Pearce of Calgary, Alberta, Canada, inked large images of the faces of several of his wife Lindsay's favorite characters from the UK TV soap opera *Coronation Street* onto her leg.

QUICK WORK Musician Bryan Adams and his producer Mutt Lange took just 45 minutes to write the six-and-a-half-minute long hit, "(Everything I Do) I Do It For You," which went on to sell more than 15 million copies worldwide.

Atari Landfill

Many game enthusiasts had long speculated that unsold copies of the *E.T. the Extra-Terrestrial* video game for the Atari® 2600 console were systematically buried in 1983 in a New Mexico desert to conceal one of the biggest commercial failures in video game history, as well as one of the worst video games ever released. In April 2014, the urban legend was proven to be true, when hundreds of the unsold *E.T.* video game cartridges were excavated from a landfill in Alamogordo, New Mexico.

CANNIBAL CURE Members of Papua New Guinea's Fore tribe built up immunity to dementia and some other degenerative disorders by eating the brains of deceased relatives at funerals.

FOOT TYPIST Hu Huiyuan from Anhui Province, China, has written more than 60,000 words of a novel using only her left foot. The 21-year-old was diagnosed with cerebral palsy when she was 10 months old, and the condition has left her entire body permanently paralyzed except for her head and her left foot. Her body is fastened to a wheelchair, and by using her foot to type on a computer keyboard she is able to type 30 words a minute.

PIANO MAN Russian strong man Vatan Seitumerov can carry a full-size 660 lb. (300 kg) grand piano on his back—and can even play another piano while doing so.

GRAVE MISSION Walter Skold of Freeport, Maine, has traveled thousands of miles across North America visiting more than 500 poets' graves. He began his cemetery odyssey in 2009, partly inspired by the 1989 Robin Williams movie *Dead Poets Society*.

UNIQUE BROTHERS Only two people in the world have a debilitating neurological disorder called Arts Syndrome—teen brothers Thomas and Bradley Farrell from Sydney, Australia. The incurable genetic condition has deteriorated their hearing, sight, and muscle movement since birth.

SURGERY SERENADE Anthony Kulkamp Dias serenaded doctors by playing six songs on a guitar while he was undergoing major brain surgery. Doctors at the Nossa Senhora de Conceiçao Hospital in Santa Catarina, Brazil, wanted to keep the 33-year-old bank worker awake during the nine-hour operation to remove a tumor so that they could monitor his senses, movement, and speech and avoid hitting brain parts that would damage key functions. With the guitar balanced on his stomach, he played a selection of songs, including the Beatles's "Yesterday," even though his right hand was weaker than normal because that was the side on which they were operating.

GALLSTONE SALE In 2013, Anita Crawley, a 64-year-old grandmother from Hertfordshire, England, sold her removed gallstones on eBay for 99 pence ($1.50). She had originally intended to make the 42 gallstones, which were removed during surgery, into a necklace.

PARTY LIKE IT'S

1984

On June 25, 2015, Dutch artist duo Front404 celebrated what would have been author George Orwell's 110th birthday by decorating CCTV cameras in the city of Utrecht, the Netherlands, with colorful party hats. Orwell is best known for his novel *1984*, which is set in a dystopian future society where every citizen is under constant surveillance by the authorities, referred to as Big Brother. Front404 sought to draw attention to how many cameras are actually monitoring the city's residents—and to imply that Orwell's surveillance state is fast becoming a reality.

Polar Bear
ROBOT

To promote an upcoming Arctic crime drama TV series, a realistic-looking replica of a polar bear wandered the streets of London, surprising unsuspecting commuters. Made of semi-rigid foam with each hair individually placed, the robot bear creation was controlled by two puppeteers who spent hours learning real polar bear behavior and movements.

DEVIL'S NUMBER While working on UK heavy metal band Iron Maiden's 1982 album *The Number of the Beast*, producer Martin Birch was involved in a car accident—and when he got the vehicle back from the garage, the bill came to £666.66. Terrified by the significance of the so-called "devil's number," he insisted it be rounded up to £667.

CHEETO COLLECTION Andy Huot from Louisville, Kentucky, has over 40,000 followers on Instagram eager to see his pictures of oddly-shaped Cheetos®. Since starting in October 2013, he has opened hundreds of packets of the cheese snacks, but only eats about two-thirds, saving the interesting ones for his collection, which includes Cheetos in the shape of humans, a *Tyrannosaurus rex*, a hammerhead shark, a sea horse, and Bigfoot.

CICADA CHALLENGE On the Japanese TV game show *AKBingo!*, two contestants use a plastic tube to try and blow a cicada insect into each other's mouths.

Wearing a hat and bowtie, a dinosaur robot greets visitors to the Henn-na Hotel in Japan, along with a female humanoid robot and a friendly android. "The Weird Hotel," as it's called in English, opened in July 2015 and is one of the first to use facial recognition technology instead of swipe cards as room keys. Almost all the employees are robots, with human employees taking up the security and housekeeping positions. All rooms are kept at a comfortable temperature with technology that detects body heat, and guests are encouraged to tip when they order robotic room service.

DINO CONCIERGE

WEATHER REPORT Setting a world record, New York City meteorologist and host of NBC's *Today Show* Al Roker successfully completed a weather report that lasted for 34 hours. For the feat, dubbed #Rokerthon on social media, he started broadcasting at 10 pm on November 12, 2014, and finished at 8 am on November 14.

NAME CHANGE Jemma Rogers of London, England, legally changed her name to Jemmaroid Von Laalaa just so she could log in to Facebook. She decided to change her name to match her "stupid" Facebook pseudonym after suddenly being locked out of her online account.

WORLDWIDE AUDIENCE An episode of the long-running CBS crime drama *CSI* was simultaneously broadcast in 171 countries on March 4, 2015.

UNIQUE GUITAR Blind and homeless, Liberian reggae fan Wesseh Freeman has taught himself to compose and play music on a handmade guitar assembled from an old stick, a paint can, and three used strings. Although his frets are made from bicycle spokes or coat hangers, he manages to play perfectly in tune.

SOAP BIRTHDAY The Australian TV soap *Neighbours* celebrated its 30th anniversary in 2015—to watch all 7,083 episodes back-to-back would take 147 days.

INVISIBLE CELEBRITIES For shy celebrities, Los Angeles, California, DJ Chris Holmes has invented a range of anti-paparazzi clothes made from a reflective material that ruins flash photographs. The fabric is coated with glass nanospheres that reflect the bright lights back at the camera. This overexposes the photos and turns whoever wears the clothes into ghostly silhouettes.

BLIZZARD CHALLENGE When winter storm Juno hit the eastern United States in January 2015, teens all over Boston, Massachusetts, turned the conditions into a new social media craze called the Boston Blizzard Challenge by filming each other diving headfirst from upstairs windows into deep snowdrifts while wearing only their underwear. Some even jumped into 7 ft. (2.1 m) deep snowbanks from rooftops, performing backflips on the way down.

ANGRY BIRD Paul Lewis, a pianist with England's Royal Liverpool Philharmonic Orchestra, had to pull out of two 2015 concerts after he was attacked by a seagull, causing him to stumble and sprain a finger of his right hand.

GODZILLA HOTEL

In April 2015, Hotel Gracery Shinjuku, otherwise known as "The Godzilla Hotel," finally opened in Tokyo, Japan. Part of a new commercial complex, the hotel unveiled a massive 40 ft. (12 m) tall replica of Godzilla's head, based on the original 1954 film. Six Godzilla View Rooms have a direct view of the giant monster, while Godzilla-themed rooms contain an adult-sized Godzilla statue and a Godzilla claw looming over the beds.

6 Transport

Ripley's — Believe It or Not!
www.ripleys.com/books
Transport

Photo: XDubai

MEN
OVER DUBAI

In May 2015, Swiss daredevil Yves "Jetman" Rossy and his protégé, skydiver and BASE jumper Vince Reffet, soared through the skies above the deserts of Dubai using Rossy's latest custom-made jet packs. Reaching speeds of up to 186 miles per hour (300 km/h), the pair, known as Jetman Dubai, became the first to complete a twin human formation flight over landmarks that included the iconic Burj Khalifa, the Palm Jumeirah, and the Liwa Desert. Each jet pack weighed in at 120 lbs. (54 kg) and featured a 7 ft. (2.1 m) wingspan and four kerosene-powered jet engines.

Photo: XDubai

Roasted Road

During an intense heatwave that swept across south India in May 2015, road markings in New Delhi blistered, distorted, and ultimately melted in the sweltering sun. Weather officials said northwesterly dry and hot winds from the desert state of Rajasthan were responsible for temperatures that reached as high as 113°F (45°C).

STEERING PROBLEMS The S.S. *Bessemer*, built by English industrialist Henry Bessemer in 1875, was a ship designed to cure seasickness. It featured a pivoting deck that stayed flat as the ship rolled, but it was impossible to steer and crashed into a French pier on its maiden voyage.

HAPPY REUNION When Lynda Alsip's 1967 Ford Mustang was stolen in Salinas, California, in 1986, she gave up hope of ever seeing it again—but 28 years later she was reunited with her car after a local man tried to register it. In all the time it was missing, the vehicle had never left Salinas.

PRESIDENTIAL GIFT Passengers on the US presidential jet, Air Force One, receive a box of M&Ms® signed by the president after every flight.

DODGE ODYSSEY For seven years, Jonathan and Jennifer Riehl of Hancock, Michigan, drove their 1999 Dodge Intrepid on a 540,000 mile (864,000 km) journey across the US to visit all 3,108 counties in the lower 48 states. They completed their mission in March 2015 by boarding a ferry to the island of Nantucket, Massachusetts.

HIDDEN NUTS Mechanics in Gloucestershire, England, spent an hour sucking peanuts out of an automobile engine with a vacuum cleaner after a squirrel had hidden dozens in the vehicle's air filter. The owner had taken the car in for repairs because she was puzzled as to why it would not go over 40 mph (64 km/h).

SLEEPY IN SEATTLE An Alaska Airlines flight bound for Los Angeles was forced to turn back to Seattle-Tacoma International Airport shortly after it had taken off because a sleeping baggage handler was trapped in the cargo hold. The stowaway had woken up to find the plane was already airborne, and when crew and passengers heard frantic banging from below the cabin and flight deck, the pilot turned the plane around to make an emergency landing.

PENNY CAR Gayle Hoover and her husband Mike Morphy of Wendell, North Carolina, spent two years gluing more than 28,750 pennies to the bodywork of a 1996 Geo Metro car.

Steering Stiletto

A giant motorized stiletto is not what you'd expect to see cruising down the streets of Tehran, Iran, but it certainly gets attention—and business—for intrepid shoe-shine man Mohammad Ali Hassan Khani, 42, also known by his nickname "Aliwaxima." Fans of his red, three-wheeled high heel made of fiberglass follow him on his website, Instagram, and Facebook to have their shoes shined and take selfies with the car. Before building the stiletto, he drove around in a men's loafer.

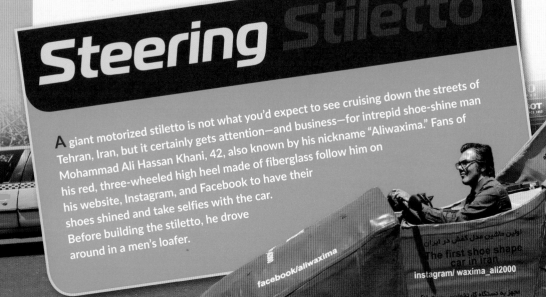

BLING BENZ

SUV SWALLOWED A 15 ft. (4.6 m) deep sinkhole swallowed a police SUV in Sheridan, Colorado. After the road beneath him suddenly gave way, Sgt. Greg Miller had to climb onto the roof of the SUV and haul himself out of the hole.

MAYFLY BLIZZARD A dense swarm of thousands of mayflies caused several motorcycle crashes and led to the closure of a bridge in Lancaster County, Pennsylvania, in June 2015. The mayflies swarmed around the lights on the bridge and then fell to the ground, forming slippery piles of dead bugs about 1 in. (2.5 cm) thick on the road.

CASH PURCHASE Mr. Gan bought a new car in Shenyang City, China, with 660,000 coins. He arrived to purchase the car in a truck laden with $106,000 (£68,773) worth of coins wrapped into 1,320 individual rolls, which weighed a total of around 4 tons—the weight of a small elephant.

TITANIC DECKCHAIR A deckchair from the *Titanic* sold at an auction in Wiltshire, England, for $150,000 (£97,320) in 2015. The Nantucket wooden chair, which had been on the first-class promenade deck when the liner sank in 1912 on its maiden voyage, was found bobbing on the surface of the Atlantic by the crew of the *Mackay-Bennett*, the ship sent from Halifax, Nova Scotia, to recover bodies from the shipwreck.

PAPER BOAT A 12 ft. (3.6 m) long boat built out of folded paper set sail on a lake in London, England, in January 2015. Weighing in at about 220 lb. (100 kg), the craft used 1,070 sq. ft. (100 sq. m) of water-resistant paper, 500 ft. (150 m) of sticky tape, and 2.2 gallons (8.3 liters) of glue. The only part of the vessel not made of paper was a stability keel constructed from wood and polystyrene.

WATER POWER Ricardo Azevedo of Sao Paulo, Brazil, has invented a motorbike that runs on water—and can travel 310 miles (496 km) on just 0.2 gallons (.76 liters). The bike utilizes an external car battery to produce the electricity that separates hydrogen from the water molecules. This process results in combustion, which creates the energy necessary to power the bike. It can even run on polluted river water.

FAST LADY Becci Ellis, a 46-year-old IT analyst and mother of two from Scunthorpe, Lincolnshire, England, became the fastest woman in the world on two wheels when she rode a 1300cc Suzuki motorbike at a speed of 264 mph (422 km/h) at a Yorkshire airfield in August 2014. She bought the bike secondhand, and it was modified by her husband, Mick, who developed a unique turbo system so that it could reach extreme speeds.

CHOPPER BIKE Dave Sims from Southport, Merseyside, England, spent 117 hours in the saddle riding the 1,600 mile (2,575 km) Tour de France route—including treacherous mountain passes—on a Raleigh Chopper bike, a popular children's bicycle from the 1970s.

DAREDEVIL GRANNY Hilda Jackson of Abergavenny, Wales, a great-grandmother and former nurse who is blind in one eye, celebrated her 101st birthday by driving an FV432 tank.

VETERAN PILOT Peter Weber Jr. of Cameron Park, California, has been a pilot for more than 70 years and still regularly flies at least twice a month—at age 95.

WEATHER SIMULATOR Arlanda Airport in Stockholm, Sweden, has a climate portal that uses wind and temperature simulations and up-to-date meteorological information so that people can actually feel what the weather is like in various cities around the world before they fly there.

Customizers and accessory aficionados Garson/D.A.D. showed off their twin Swarovski® crystal-studded Mercedes Benz® SL600s at the Tokyo Auto Salon in 2013. Each Benz is gold with silver accents, and features a total of 300,000 crystals.

FACTORIA CIRCULAR

In 2010, renowned Barcelona, Spain designer and musician César Alvarez Bayer created the Rodafonio—perhaps the weirdest music contraption in the world. The gigantic wheel is over 14 ft. (4 m) hig and barely 6 in. (15 cm) wide, yet it accommodates all five membe of the Catalan music band Factoria Circular. Each musician sits in a designated smaller circle that occasionally spins inside the gian wheel, while the other two members are actors who pedal the wheel into motion, bringing the huge mechanical device to life.

RED LIGHT A traffic light in Dresden, Germany, has been red since 1987—nearly 30 years. The signal has never lit up yellow or green, even though annual maintenance costs for the intersection include replacement yellow and green bulbs.

MOUSE ALERT A Qatar Airways flight from Madrid, Spain, to Doha was delayed for more than six hours in December 2014 after a live mouse was spotted in the cabin. The entire cabin had to be fumigated, and passengers then had to wait until the fumes had completely cleared before they were allowed to board the plane.

GOAL STOPS To celebrate the arrival of the 2015 Copa America soccer tournament, bus stops in Rancagua, Chile, were decorated to look like soccer goals with benches and artificial turf.

TIGHT PARKING In November 2014 in Chongqing, China, driver Han Yue parked his Mini in a gap that measured just 3 in. (8 cm) longer than his car.

TAXI HOTEL For just over $30 (£19) a night, visitors to New York City can sleep on a bed in a parked van with amazing views of the Manhattan skyline. Jonathan Powley, a stand-up comedian and former hotel concierge, rents out a fleet of stationary four-wheeled hotel rooms, including a yellow taxi, through the website Airbnb. Although there is no running water or bathroom, he changes the bedsheets every day, puts out fresh flowers, and arranges with neighborhood coffee shops for his guests to have free snacks and use of the restrooms.

TRAIN HOME German student Leonie Müller grew so disillusioned with landlords that in the spring of 2015 she gave up her rented property to live on a train instead. She carries all her possessions in a backpack, washes her hair in the train bathroom, studies on board with the help of her tablet computer, and hurtles around the country at 190 mph (300 km/h). Her nationwide season ticket is $75 (£49) cheaper per month than the rent on her last apartment!

LOBSTER SMASH A truck containing some 25,000 live lobsters slid off Interstate 95 north of Augusta, Maine, and landed on its side after swerving to avoid another vehicle. Although the truck was damaged beyond repair, its cargo of $300,000 (£194,640) worth of lobsters, which were being transported in seawater from Nova Scotia, Canada, to markets in New Hampshire and Rhode Island, survived! Luckily, they were loaded unharmed onto other trucks and completed their journey.

BEE SPILL A tractor-trailer containing 14 million honeybees worth $92,000 (£59,690) overturned on Interstate 5 near Lynnwood, Washington, in April 2015, scattering its load of 448 hives all over the highway. As the bees swarmed angrily, beekeepers wearing protective suits recovered as many of the insects as possible.

MOBILE HOME Guillaume Dutilh and Jenna Spesard quit their day jobs and set off from Los Angeles with their dog Salies to drive across the US and Canada, towing their self-built home behind them. It took them a year to build the 125 sq. ft. (11.6 sq. m) wooden house on wheels, which they hauled behind their 2006 Ford F-250 for more than 20,000 miles (32,000 km) through over 30 states and provinces.

TAXI FLEET There are over 100,000 taxicabs on the streets of Mexico City —more than seven times the number of yellow taxis in New York City.

REPLICA ARK In 2014, Dr. Irving Finkel of the British Museum, London, built a scaled-down replica of Noah's Ark to the specifications found on a 4,000-year-old Babylonian clay tablet. Although it was only about one-fifth of the size of the vessel described on the ancient tablet, Dr. Finkel's circular ark still weighed 35 tons and was seaworthy.

MOBILITY RACER David Anderson and Matthew Hine from the Isle of Man, UK, have custom-built a mobility scooter that can reach speeds of over 107 mph (171 km/h)—and it even has a shopping basket attached to the front.

HOMEMADE AIRPLANE Ethiopia's Asmelash Zerefu single-handedly built his own airplane by reading aviation books and watching YouTube tutorials. It cost him over $7,500 (£4,877) and took him 570 days to make his plane, which features the wheels from an old Suzuki motorcycle, as well as a handmade propeller, and is powered by a secondhand Volkswagen Beetle engine.

HUMAN POWERED

On September 19, 2015, a bullet-shaped bike blew past the competition in the World Human Powered Speed Challenge in Battle Mountain, Nevada, setting a new world record for fastest human-powered vehicle, reaching 86.65 mph (139.45 kph) using nothing but innovative design, aerodynamics, and human power. Known as the Eta speedbike, the 55 lb. (25 kg) vehicle is made of a carbon fiber frame enclosed in an aerodynamic, carbon-honeycomb shell. Toronto-based company Aerovelo designed the bike to allow the driver to lay in an almost horizontal position inches from the ground, where the driver uses a display powered by two small cameras to help steer.

TRAVELING CHAIR When Kalman Kallai drove 2,796 miles (4,500 km) across Canada from Borden, Ontario, to Comox, British Columbia, he made the nine-day journey more interesting by towing a 60 lb. (27 kg) green armchair behind him. The secondhand chair allowed him to stop and enjoy the spectacular scenery in comfort.

TATTOOED BIKE Polish tattoo artists Tomasz Lech and Krzysztof Krolak spent 250 hours inking a motorcycle. They customized the bike—called The Recidivist—with leather similar to the color of human skin, and used that as their canvas for tattooing the wheels, tank, seat, and rear fender.

TRUCK FLIP Mechanic Rick Sullivan, of Clinton, Illinois, has built up a street-legal automobile with eight wheels—four on the ground and four spinning in the air. He spent six months and $6,000 (£3,852) creating his "upside down" hybrid vehicle (whose license plate reads "FLIPOVR") from two pickup trucks—a 1991 Ford Ranger with a 1995 Ford F-150 flipped over on top of it.

STYLIN' SCOOTERS

Andrew Wylie, 40, and his father, Rick, 63, of North Tyneside, England, started a company that customizes mobility scooters to look like Jeeps®, Land Rovers®, and even Harley-Davidsons®. Wylie got the idea to redesign the vehicles—which are predominantly used by the elderly and the disabled and reach maximum speeds of just eight miles per hour (13 km/h)—when he drove a taxi for disabled children, saying, "We customize scooters for everyone. No one wants to feel disabled, and this way they don't have to." The pair also customized eight of the vehicles for pop stars Robbie Williams and Dizzee Rascal to ride in the music video for their single, "Going Crazy."

CLASSIC AUTOS A rare Ferrari 250 GT SWB California Spyder, which had been left rusting in a derelict French farmhouse for 40 years, sold for $18.5 million (£11.8 million) at an auction in 2015, making it the fifth most expensive automobile ever sold. One of only 36 ever made, and part of 60 classic cars, including a 1956 Maserati A6G 200 Berlinetta Grand Sport Frua—one of only three in the world—that sold for $2.2 million (£1.41 million), that had been collected by entrepreneur Roger Baillon but were abandoned before their chance discovery in 2014.

BUMPER CAR Tom Evans drives around Glasgow, Scotland, in a street-legal, converted fairground bumper car. The purple vehicle, which has the engine and three wheels of a Reliant Robin, runs on gasoline and has working lights, brakes, speedometer, turn signals, wing mirrors, and a top speed of 75 mph (120 km/h).

HOMEMADE SUB Tan Yong, a chicken farmer from Hubei Province, China, built his own fully functional submarine by welding sheets of scrap metal together and using parts from old cars. It took him five months to build the one-ton submarine, which dove to a depth of 33 ft. (10 m) on its maiden voyage in a local lake.

FIVE-RINGED RIDE

China native Meng Jie helped promote the 2008 Beijing Olympics by cycling around the city on a bike he designed using the five Olympic rings. Riders of the colorful bike can switch between riding the bike normally or using their arms and legs to generate speeds of more than 62 mph (100 km/h). Jie has quit his job as a mechanic to join a sports company in the hope his new employers will help him develop the bike.

SNOWMOBILE PARADE On February 12, 2015, 1,044 snowmobile riders formed a parade of more than 2.5 miles (4 km) through the downtown streets of Whitecourt, Alberta, Canada.

PERMANENT PASSENGER Florida widow Lee Wachtstetter pays $164,000 (£105,321) a year to live on a luxury cruise ship. She sold her home in Fort Lauderdale following the death of her husband Mason and has been living on the 1,070-passenger *Crystal Serenity* for more than seven years, rarely venturing ashore. During her lifetime she has completed over 200 cruises, including 15 round-the-world trips.

HELICOPTER HUNT Jerry Grayson, who carried out rescue missions for the British Royal Navy in the 1970s but now lives in Melbourne, Australia, flew 23,000 miles (37,015 km) to track down every helicopter he had ever flown. He traveled all over the UK and found that most had been turned into museum pieces while one, a Wessex Mark 1, had been customized with beds, curtains, and cushions and turned into luxury sleeping quarters for campers.

CRASH LANDING After the electrical systems failed on their single-engine plane in February 2015, a pilot and his wife used their iPads® to fly about 80 miles (129 km) in the dark and touch down safely without landing gear at Rapid City Regional Airport, South Dakota. The couple were flying from Wyoming to Wisconsin when all their instruments stopped working except the airspeed and altitude indicators, forcing them to use their iPads to navigate to the small airport runway for a crash landing.

DEATH ROAD As many as 300 people a year die on Bolivia's North Yungas Road, a single-lane dirt track with a rocky surface, tight hairpin bends, no guard rails, and steep falls into the canyons of the Coroico River Valley half a mile below. Known locally as the "Road of Death," it twists and turns for over 40 miles (64 km) between La Paz and Coroico.

SOLITARY SIGN There is only one stop sign in the entire city of Paris, France. Drivers approaching an intersection from the right automatically have priority.

LONG JOURNEY On December 9, 2014, the first freight train in history to link China directly to Spain completed a continuous 21-day journey of over 8,100 miles (13,000 km). It set off from Yiwu on November 18 and passed through Kazakhstan, Russia, Belarus, Poland, Germany, and France before reaching its destination of Madrid.

REVERSING CHAOS A 92-year-old man crashed into no fewer than 10 vehicles while trying to back out of a shopping center parking lot in Mayville, Wisconsin. The driver accidentally lurched forward and backward into several automobiles before driving off and hitting a pickup truck. No one was seriously injured.

POTATO FIX Mario Papademetriou, an automotive breakdown mechanic in Essex, England, fixed a faulty condenser on a 1960s vintage Land Rover using a potato.

CRAFTY WATERCRAFT

A Slovenian company has created the Quadrofoil, a futuristic electric speedboat that allows passengers to FLY across water.

Priced at $28,144 (£17,586), its C-shaped legs, or hydrofoils, lift the boat above the water's surface, giving the sensation of flying at a top speed of 25 mph (40 km/h) for up to 62 miles (100 km) on a single charge while producing marginal noise pollution, zero emissions, and creating only the tiniest of waves.

FAST BREAK

J oe Fiscella of Huntington Beach, California, has made it possible to play pool on the go—by building a full-sized regulation pool table on the back of a Chevrolet. This billiards-mobile took 30 days to build on the body of a 2000 Monte Carlo and can travel up to 100 mph (161 kph). It features a television, refrigerator, and state-of-the-art sound system. Fiscella recruited professional car builder Vini "Big Daddy" Bergeman to help him create his dream car.

MOWED MESSAGE Farmer Ruston Smith asked his girlfriend Kobi Sliva to marry him by mowing his proposal into a field near Portland, Texas. She saw the message after Smith persuaded a pilot friend to fly them over the field.

KLINGON REPLY When UK politician Darren Millar wrote to the Welsh government about the number of alien spaceships reportedly sighted near Cardiff Airport, he received an official email reply in Klingon. He then had to find a translator to decode the alien *Star Trek* language into English.

MISSING BACON Shaneka Torres of Grand Rapids, Michigan, was sentenced to three to seven years in prison for shooting at a McDonald's® restaurant drive-through because workers twice failed to put bacon on her cheeseburgers. No one was injured in the shooting.

ICE WHEELIE Just a year after recovering from a Superbike crash that put him temporarily in a wheelchair, Swedish racer Robert Gull performed a 114 mph (183 km/h) motorcycle wheelie on ice over a distance of 330 ft. (100 m) at Lake Kakel, Sweden.

FLYING CAT Romain Jantot was flying a light airplane hundreds of feet in the air above Kourou, French Guinea, when a cat suddenly poked its head into the cockpit. The cat must have been sitting on the wing at takeoff and had somehow clung on throughout the steep ascent. The shocked pilot landed the plane as quickly as possible, allowing the unharmed stowaway to jump down safely onto the runway.

LAST MENU A menu for the last lunch served on board the *Titanic* before it sank in 1912 sold at an auction in New York in 2015 for $88,000 (£57,817). The menu was saved by first-class passenger Abraham Lincoln Salomon, who escaped on a lifeboat as the luxury liner went down.

TWEETING POTHOLES To highlight the poor condition of roads in Panama City, local TV news show *Telemetro Reporta* installed motion-sensitive devices in potholes across the city that sent a complaint tweet directly to the Twitter account of the Department of Public Works every time they were run over by a vehicle.

BAREFOOT RUNNER Taking an indirect route, Aleks Kashefi of Derbyshire, England, ran 1,160 miles (1,856 km) barefoot from Land's End, Cornwall, to John O'Groats, Scotland, in 38 days. He injured his foot on the second day after being blown into a large rock by howling gales, and had to use a walking stick for the next 40 miles (64 km).

DOGGY DRIVER While his owner Tom Hamilton tended lambs on his farm in Lanarkshire, Scotland, his four-year-old collie Don leaped into a farm vehicle, leaned on the controls, and, with the hand brake off, shot away down a steep field. With Don at the wheel, the tractor smashed through a fence and across the busy M74 motorway before crashing into the barrier on the median strip. Shocked drivers managed to avoid Don, who was unhurt following his adventure.

Transport

FALSE LEG A flamingo at Sorocaba Zoo in Brazil, was fitted with a lightweight carbon fiber prosthetic leg after infection caused its own leg to be amputated. Although flamingos are famous for being able to stand on one leg, veterinarians said the bird would not have survived with just a single limb.

MAD MAX MUSEUM Adrian Bennett, of Silverton, Australia, runs a museum dedicated to the 1981 Mel Gibson movie *Mad Max 2: The Road Warrior*, and has seen the movie more than 200 times.

PRISON COSTUME James Lowe of Barnet, Vermont, found a novel way of avoiding jury duty—he turned up at court wearing a prison costume of a black-and-white striped jumpsuit and matching hat, and was promptly dismissed by the judge.

TURBO HEARSE Arne Toman of Chicago, Illinois, has built a hearse that can go from 0 to 60 mph (96 km/h) in just 2.26 seconds. He fitted the 1996 Chevrolet Caprice hearse with a 6 liter turbocharged engine, giving it 1,300 hp— yet there is still room in the back for a coffin.

UNDERGROUND and UNBELIEVABLE

The Louisville Mega Cavern spans 17 miles (27 km) beneath the city of Louisville, Kentucky. This man-made, monster-sized facility offers activities ranging from a geological tram tour to zip lining, but the most unbelievable is the world's only underground bike park! As if being 100 ft. (30 m) below Earth's surface wasn't impressive enough, the park covers 8 acres (3 hectares), making it the largest indoor bike park in the world, boasting 45 trails that include BMX®, cross country, and jump tracks!

BEER TRUCK Firefighters from the Feldhausen Volunteer Fire Service in Germany built a replica fire truck measuring 50 ft. (15 m) long and 16 ft. (5 m) tall from nearly 5,000 beer crates. They used a cherry picker and cranes to lift the crates into position.

LATE TRAIN The Guwahati-Trivandrum Express is India's most unreliable train, running 11 hours late on average and sometimes being delayed for a whole day.

SUNKEN VOLVOS There are 30 Volvo cars resting on the floor of the Bedford Basin near Halifax, Nova Scotia, Canada. They sank in 1969 after the container ship that was transporting them sustained severe water damage in the Atlantic Ocean.

PLANE PUSH When an airplane froze to the ground in temperatures of minus 61°F (−52°C) at Russia's Igarka Airport, 100 miles (161 km) north of the Arctic Circle, the 70 passengers disembarked and helped to push-start it. The oil in the airplane's chassis had iced up, causing the brakes to seize.

Wheelchair TANK

Shropshire, England, war hero Eddie Shaw, 96, loves nothing more than getting out and about and taking trips to the seaside. When his son Peter, 60, found it increasingly difficult to push his father's wheelchair across the sand, he replaced it with a custom-made one that is modeled on an all-terrain tank.

FRY SPILL A six-vehicle pileup on Interstate 90 near Salem, South Dakota, on January 8, 2015, left the road covered with 500 lb. (227 kg) of McDonald's® French fries that had fallen from one of the trucks involved.

STEAM MOTORCYCLE René van Tuil from Eck en Wiel, the Netherlands, spent eight months building a steam-powered motorcycle with a top speed of just 5 mph (8 km/h). The "Black Pearl," which looks like a cross between a steam locomotive and a motorbike, is powered by a steam engine, and its rear wheel is driven by a large crankshaft.

SOFA SURFER Alexander Shapovalov rode through the icy streets of Krasnoyarsk, Russia, sitting on an old armchair that was being towed by a Subaru Forester at dangerously high speeds. He had intended to take the chair to the dump, but when it would not fit inside his car, he tied it to the rear fender and filmed his white-knuckle ride while one of his friends drove.

Snow Walls

From mid-April to late May each year, nearly a million people travel to view the 63 ft. (19 m) tall "snow walls" along the Tateyama Kurobe Alpine Route near Murodo-daira, Tateyama, Japan. The snow walls are created with the 23 ft. (7 m) of heavy snowfall that's been cleared away from the roads along the mountain sightseeing route during the winter season. The route is about 56 miles (90 km) long, and goes across the nearly 10,000 ft. (3,000 m) high North Alpine mountains, the so-called "roof of Japan."

CABLE CROSSING For the 2015 launch of Jaguar's XF car in London, England, stuntman Jim Dowdall drove it high above the River Thames on parallel cables just over 1 in. (34 mm) thick. The Thames crossing involved a journey of 790 ft. (240 m) on cables suspended 60 ft. (18 m) above the river.

ON TIME Japanese bullet trains are among the world's most punctual—their average delay is just 18 seconds.

FREE RIDE For one day in 2014, the Siberian city of Novosibirsk offered free subway rides to any passenger who could recite at least two verses from any work by Alexander Pushkin, one of Russia's greatest poets.

LOST PROPERTY Items left behind by passengers on trains in northern England in 2015 included 2,000 cell phones, 1,300 wallets and purses, 600 umbrellas, 529 keys, 237 lanyards, 120 shopping bags, eight sets of false teeth, a wooden casket containing ashes, a Barry Manilow CD, a hamster, and a 6 ft. (1.8 m) tall inflatable dinosaur.

KITT CAR Scott Bainbridge, a mailman from Newcastle upon Tyne, England, spent 10 years transforming an old Pontiac Firebird Trans Am into a replica of KITT, the automobile from the TV series *Knight Rider*. He bought the Pontiac for $3,000 (£1,919) in 2004 and spent more than $25,500 (£18,000) refurbishing it with an electronic display dashboard, new doors, wings, wheels, and a 5.7-liter V8 engine. He even recorded the car's voice from the show so that his replica could talk to him.

GLOBE TROTTERS Since 1997, Peter and Ellen Crichton from Leicestershire, England, have traveled more than 200,000 miles (320,000 km) around the world in their 1991 Land Rover Discovery, which they named Rabia. They have visited the world's most northerly point that is accessible to vehicles in Scandinavia, and the most southerly near Cape Horn, Chile.

SAME SHIP Between 2003 and 2015, Lakeland, Florida's Bernard and Janice Caffary sailed on 100 cruises on the same ship, the *Carnival Sensation*.

TOILET RESCUE When passenger Steven Staples became trapped in a train toilet in London, England, and no one came to rescue him, he sent bosses at the Southeastern Rail Company an SOS message on Twitter. After establishing which train he was on and his precise location, they alerted the train's driver so that Staples could be freed.

SUBWAY SQUATS In Moscow, Russia, subway ticket machines dispense free rides to passengers who can do 30 squats within two minutes.

GENEROUS TIP In January 2015, a generous passenger gave Philadelphia, Pennsylvania, taxi driver Oumar Maiga a tip of nearly $1,000 (£640) on a $4.31 (£2.76) fare.

RIDEABLE COOLER A New Orleans, Louisiana, company has invented a foldable electric scooter called the Kreweser, where the rider sits on a large cooler that can accommodate 96 drink cans plus ice. Perfect for tailgating and picnics, it reaches a top speed of 18 mph (29 km/h), and its fully charged battery provides enough power for a 16 mile (26 km) journey. The motorized cooler can also be fitted with a Bluetooth® music system.

TANK RUN Nick Mead of Northamptonshire, England, owns a collection of 130 military vehicles worth over $3 million (£1.9 million)—and regularly drives his sons to school in a street-legal tank.

Robot Horse

Inventor Su Daocheng rides a 5 ft. (1.5 m) tall gasoline-powered robotic horse through the streets of Shiyan, China. It took him two months to build the mechanical metal horse, which weighs 551 lb. (250 kg) and has spring-loaded legs and a recycled go-kart engine.

Stained Glass SLEEPER CAR

At the 2015 London Design Festival, UK artist Dominic Wilcox revealed his vision for the future of transport—a stained glass–covered, driverless car with a bed. The hand-cut, stained glass shell was constructed using the same technique used to make Tiffany lamps, and opens to reveal only a bed inside, where the passenger can sleep while the car takes them to their destination. Wilcox believes that by 2059, it will be "statistically proven" that computer-controlled driverless cars are safer than those driven by people. At that point, he said, "We will simply require a living space on wheels."

ONLY PASSENGER

Traveling on a scheduled Air Zimbabwe flight from Johannesburg, South Africa, to Victoria Falls, Zambia, UK professional chess player Nigel Short found he was the only passenger on board a Boeing 737 plane with a capacity of over 130. None of his fellow passengers had turned up, so the flight attendants addressed Short by name for the safety drill and other announcements.

SPY SHIP *Aji Petri*, a Soviet ship that was used to spy on the United States and the UK during the Cold War, has been renamed *La Sultana* and transformed into a luxury yacht available for charter for €225,000 ($246,532, or £173,957) a week. The 213 ft. (65 m) long, six-deck vessel boasts seven stately cabins and has been fitted with marble baths, elegant wood panels, an indoor swimming pool, an outdoor Jacuzzi, and a helipad.

RELUCTANT PASSENGERS Matthew and Pamela Menz, along with their two adult children Justin and Jennifer, were trapped in their minivan as it was dragged 16 miles (26 km) along Interstate 75 in northern Michigan after it had become lodged beneath the rear of a tractor-trailer. Driver Matthew had run into the back of the semi during a snowstorm, but the truck driver was unaware of the collision until police officers stopped him near the town of Grayling.

MOTORBIKE PARADE On February 7, 2015, nearly 20,000 motorcyclists formed a line of bikes that stretched for 12 miles (19 km) along roads through Guatemala. They were riding the 137 miles (222 km) from Guatemala City to Esquipulas for the annual Caravana del Zorro, a parade first held in 1961 when just five people took part.

Aviation Simulation

When poor math skills forced him to give up his dreams of being a pilot, John Davis, 54, from Coventry, England, spent 15 years and £20,000 ($31,075) turning his spare bedroom into a replica Boeing 747-400 cockpit. Each year he flies at least 47,000 miles around the world—without leaving his home—in the exact, life-sized replica he built by hand. He also offers his "flight experience" to other plane enthusiasts, nervous fliers, and even professional airline pilots who want to practice in between flights.

Vapor Velocity

Ripley's —— Believe It or Not!
www.ripleys.com/books
Transport

Photographer Joe Broyles, 61, captured this spectacular image of a jet creating an effect known as flow-induced vaporization at the Oceania Naval Air Station in Virginia Beach, Virginia, on September 21, 2015. The rare shot features an F-18 Super Hornet 2 jet with a vapor cone forming around it. The cone lasts just tenths of a second, and is produced when vapor forms around objects flying at high speeds in the right environmental conditions.

TUNNEL VISION The 35.4 mile (57 km) Gotthard Base Tunnel, which takes trains beneath the Swiss Alps, took 2,600 workers 20 years to build. To bore a total of 94 miles (152 km) of tunnels, shafts, and passages, workers cut through 459 million cu. ft. (13 million cu. m) of rock—the volume of nearly nine Empire State Buildings.

TIGHT SQUEEZE Police officers in Guiyang, China, stopped a slow-moving minibus and found 51 passengers squeezed into a vehicle designed to carry six people.

FLYING COMMUTE In clear conditions and winds below 12 mph (19 km/h), Paul Cox of Gwalchmai, Wales, takes to the skies and makes his 10 mile (16 km) commute to work in a paramotor. When he lands at the end of his half-hour journey, he packs the flying machine into a suitcase.

WEDDING TRAIN In August 2015, Megan Grant and Michael Hayward got married on board a train traveling from Fremantle to Perth, Western Australia. The on-train ceremony was a surprise for the 30 guests as well as the other passengers.

PAPER PLANE Shai Goitein, a former pilot from Haifa, Israel, has developed a gadget that turns an ordinary paper airplane into a remote-controlled machine that can remain airborne for 10 minutes at a time. Attachable to any paper plane, the PowerUp 3.0 is a battery-powered unit with a propeller on one end and a receiver on the other. The plane is then controlled by a smartphone app that allows the user to change its flight path by tilting their phone.

NATURAL JOB Erkan Geldi was born on board a Turkish Airlines flight from Izmir to Frankfurt, Germany, in 1990—and now after completing college he works as a flight attendant for Turkish Airlines. He was born when his mother went into labor during the descent, and he was named after the pilot who was flying the plane that day.

STRAIGHT ROAD Saudi Arabia's Highway 10 from Haradh to the border with the United Arab Emirates runs for 162 miles (260 km) without a single bend.

SERIAL OFFENDER A driver in Kuwait racked up an unbelievable 1,645 traffic violations, leading to fines of nearly $200,000 (£130,068).

>30,000 yak bones!

Dragon Racer

Carving artist Su Zhongyang, along with 19 other carvers, spent three and a half years creating this massive dragon sculpture out of 30,000 yak leg bones and pure gold that decorate a BMW Z4 in Guangzhou, China. The steering wheel, gear stick, and interior panel were also decorated with delicate bone carvings.

RAIL ATLAS Colonel Michael Cobb spent 18 years compiling a 646-page atlas of Britain's railways from 1807 to 1994. He traced every route by hand, and at age 91 the work earned him a PhD from Cambridge University.

DESPERATE PASSENGERS Too late to board their flight after being delayed in traffic on the way to Malta's international airport, Italian couple Matteo Clementi and Enrica Apollonio forced open a security door and ran out onto the tarmac, waving to the pilots in a desperate attempt to stop the jet from leaving without them. They were still not allowed on board, and were arrested and fined over $2,500 (£1,622).

ROAD RAGE Finding a parked car blocking a designated cycle lane in Sao Paulo, Brazil, a cyclist single-handedly lifted the empty vehicle—a Fiat weighing about 1,630 lbs. (740 kg)—out of the way with his bare hands. He then hopped back on his bike and rode off.

WRONG TURN Early morning subway commuters in Dortmund, Germany, were surprised when a Ford Focus automobile pulled into the station instead of their expected train. While driving along a set of above-ground train tracks, a drunk driver accidentally followed a U-Bahn commuter train into an underground tunnel for 1.5 miles (2.4 km) until he reached the Barop Parkhaus station. Regular train service was delayed for several hours while the car was pushed out of the station and off the tracks by hand.

FLYING BIKE Part-tricycle, part-gyrocopter, the $395,000 (£256,276) Dutch-built Pal-V (Personal Air and Land Vehicle) bike can travel at up to 112 mph (180 km/h) on the road and fly in the air for up to 300 miles (480 km) at altitudes as high as 4,000 ft. (1,200 m).

ELECTRIC SPEEDSTER The battery-powered Green Team E0711-6 electric car, developed by engineers and 40 students at the University of Stuttgart in Germany, can go from 0 to 62 mph (100 km/h) in just 1.779 seconds—faster than a Formula 1® race car.

MERCEDES PENS Costas Schuler, a graphic designer from Forestville, California, spent more than five years covering almost every inch of both the interior and exterior of a 1981 300SD Mercedes Benz® automoblie with over 10,000 colored pens. He stuck each pen individually to the car with silicon glue.

MOVIE MACHINES Brothers Marc and Shanon Parker of Port Canaveral, Florida, design and build replicas of famous movie vehicles, including Batman's Tumbler from the *Dark Knight* trilogy, an Optimus Prime truck from *Transformers*, and the Ecto-1 car from *Ghostbusters*. Their street-legal versions have proved so popular that they have been purchased by stars such as 50 Cent, Flo Rida, and Lil' Wayne.

PRINTED CAR Arizona-based company Local Motors has created a 3D-printed car with a top speed of 40 mph (64 km/h). The battery-powered two-seater Strati is built from layers of black plastic reinforced with carbon fiber and can be printed in under two days. It is made from just 49 parts, compared to a typical vehicle's 5,000. The tires, battery, wiring, windshield, and suspension are made using traditional methods, but the body, chassis, dash, center console, and hood are constructed with a printer that can make parts up to 10 ft. (3 m) long.

SHIP FITTINGS Maritime historian Peter Knego loved the old cruise ship *Aureol* so much that when she was broken up, he arranged for an entire shipping container to be filled with its fittings—including a mahogany bar, maple panels, cabinets, chairs, and light fixtures—and transported them from Alang, India, on an eight-week journey to Los Angeles for installation in his home in Moorpark, California. He has since moved to a larger California house to accommodate hundreds of items he has retrieved from more than 30 scrapped vessels.

CAP RETURNED Former petty officer Roger Dewar of Hobart, Tasmania, was reunited with the Australian Navy cap that he had swapped while on shore leave in the Philippines 51 years earlier. In 1964, he met a group of US sailors and agreed to swap caps with electrician's mate Ray Silvia. Half a century later, Robert Musker, Silvia's former brother-in-law, discovered the cap with Dewar's name inside in a Malden, Massachusetts, basement and tracked down its original owner.

EMERGENCY LANDING Just after 10 am on July 12, 2015, a pilot dramatically landed a single-engine airplane on the grass median between the two lanes of the busy Route 72 highway in Stafford Township, New Jersey, after it ran out of power. The pilot navigated the plane, carrying four passengers from a local skydiving school, through power lines and came within a few feet of cars before touching down safely.

UNSTOPPABLE MACHINE Developed in South Africa, the Marauder, a six-cylinder turbo diesel-engined armored military vehicle, has a top speed of 75 mph (120 km/h) and is so tough it can smash through solid walls, survive land mine explosions, and withstand blasts from ballistic missiles.

UNDERWATER CAR US retailer Hammacher Schlemmer offered a $2 million (£1.3 million) car for sale that could be driven underwater—at 75 mph (120 km/h). Inspired by the submarine *Lotus* driven by James Bond in the movie *The Spy Who Loved Me*, the two-seater Submarine Sports Car is powered by an electric motor and uses propellers at the rear and water jets at the front to provide steering and lift. It floats on water but submerges to a depth of up to 33 ft. (10 m) with the pull of a lever. The vehicle features two scuba tanks so that the driver and passenger can remain underwater for an hour.

RAINBOW TUNNEL

China's first "rainbow tunnel" opened in Zhengzhou, the capital of Henan province, in 2015, and may have been inspired by the a race featured in the video game *Mario Kart*®! While the middle section is constructed from ordinary concrete, the 984 ft. (300 m) combined length of the north and south ends are made up of blocks of colors that transition from purple to blue to help drivers get used to the change of light as they enter and exit the tunnel. The 1,312 ft. (400 m) long tunnel cost nearly 100 million yuan ($16 million, or £11 million).

Sol Cinema

Jo Furlong saw more than just a beat-up, 45-year-old trailer lying in an empty lot. He saw the possibility of creating a solar-powered, fully functioning movie theater! With the help of artists Ami and Beth Marsden and filmmaker Paul O'Connor, and using mostly recycled materials, Furlong created the Sol Cinema, the world's smallest mobile movie house! Seating eight adults or 10 young people, the entire cinema—including video projectors, surround sound systems, laptops, hard drives, and lights—is run off the energy generated by two 120W solar panels. Furlong and his team dress in vintage ushers' uniforms to bring the cinema to music festivals, private parties, and corporate engagements throughout the year.

Ripley's Asks

Sol Cinema shared more about their lights, camera, and all the solar action!

Q How long did it take to build the Sol Cinema? How much did it cost?

A It took three months to build after a year of working our way through many different designs. Getting the solar element just right took the longest to work out. It cost around $31,000 (£20,000) to build.

Q What do you do when it rains—or snows?

A We can still gather plenty of energy on cloudy days. In fact, solar panels work better when they are cold. Last year we performed all day at the Birmingham Film Festival during a snowstorm, and our audiences were snug and warm in the Sol Cinema.

Q What's next for Sol Cinema?

A We have plans for building a larger outdoor solar-powered cinema, and we may also build a series of Sol Cinemas to accommodate growing demand.

Solar-Powered Stella

In 2013, Dutch engineers at Eindhoven University of Technology built Stella, the world's first solar "energy positive" car that produces more energy than it uses. Big enough to seat a family of four, Stella uses large solar panels to travel around 250 miles (402 km) without sunshine. When fully charged, it can drive up to 420 miles (676 km), nearly twice as far as a standard electric car! Made with lightweight, high-grade aluminum and carbon fiber, the car weighs a mere 838 lbs. (380 kg), almost 2,500 lbs. (1,120 kg) lighter than the average electrical car.

Ripley's Research

The sunlight that shines on the Earth in one hour could meet world energy demand for one year! A **solar panel** is a large, flat rectangle made up of individual solar energy collectors called solar cells. Each solar cell is a blue-black octagon about the size of an adult's palm. **These cells are designed to capture sunlight and use it to generate electricity**, much like a battery's cells make electricity from chemicals.

Cutting-Edge CLASSIC

Everything old is new again—if you can get it to work. Anthony Dunkin and his colleagues at Quantum Power UK in Oxford, England, created an innovative way to bring the past into the future by installing solar power technology into a classic Ford Model T. The one-of-a-kind vehicle, called MAX, is the world's "oldest" solar-powered car.

CANARY FUNERAL In 1920, 10,000 people lined the streets of Newark, New Jersey, to pay their respects to a local pet canary called Jimmy, who was carried in a coffin by a 500-person funeral procession, complete with a 15-piece band.

TOY CAR After her driver's license was taken away, 20-year-old Texas State University student Tara Monroe bought a small pink battery-powered toy Barbie® Jeep for $60 (£39) on Craigslist and drove that around the San Marcos campus at its top speed of 5 mph (8 km/h).

DÉJÀ VU Police officers clocked a 33-year-old man from West Hartford, Connecticut, driving at 112 mph (180 km/h) on Interstate 89 in Vermont—while he was on his way to court to pay a speeding ticket.

$8 MILLION JANITOR Ronald Read of Brattleboro, Vermont, worked as a janitor, held his coat together with safety pins, and drove an old, second-hand car—but he secretly played the stock market. When he died in 2014 at age 92, he left behind an estate valued at more than $8 million (£5.2 million).

PAW EXCUSE Arrested on suspicion of drunk driving following a high-speed chase in Manatee County, Florida, Reliford Cooper III told police officers that it was not him who was driving the car—but his dog.

BURIED TREASURE Eric Schmitt and his family, from Sanford, Florida, found $1 million (£646,224) worth of buried treasure in water just 15 ft. (4.5 m) deep off Fort Pierce—from a ship that sank 300 years earlier. They retrieved 40 ft. (12.1 m) of ornate gold chain and 51 gold coins, including a single coin, the Royal, that is believed to have been made for King Phillip V of Spain and is worth about $500,000 (£329,783). The ship sank during a hurricane in 1715 while en route from Cuba to Spain, killing the entire crew.

CHANCE REUNIONS Just three weeks after realizing that one defendant was a former classmate, Florida Judge Mindy Glazer discovered that she had crossed paths with another defendant in another case. In the first case, she recognized burglary suspect Arthur Booth as an old classmate from Nautilus Middle School, Miami. In the second, she realized that fraud suspect Alon Glenn had been on the same Caribbean cruise ship as she had over the weekend.

PROLONGED PIT STOP A French family accidentally left behind their three-year-old daughter at a highway rest stop near Loriol and drove another 90 miles (144 km) toward the Riviera without her. They only realized that they had forgotten one of their three children when they heard an alert on the radio.

POTTER PROPOSAL Samuel Goetsch flew his girlfriend Stephanie Dodd, a big Harry Potter fan, 5,000 miles (8,000 km) from Houston, Texas, to England just so that he could propose to her on platform three of the Surbiton train station in Surrey, a key location in *Harry Potter and the Half-Blood Prince*.

SCRAPS AHOY!

Seale, Alabama artist Butch Anthony proved that one man's trash can become another's treasure—or chance to search for it. Joined by Dutch artists Diederick Kraaijeveld, Nick Wagemans, and Gideon Elings, Anthony built the *Llatikcuf*, a pirate ship created from castoff items and trash, and sailed her on a 10-day adventure down the Chattahoochee and Apalachicola rivers to the Gulf of Mexico. They built the boat using an old pontoon boat with a 90-horsepower motor Anthony had found on Craigslist, as well as a pickup truck camper shell, a chandelier crafted from animal skulls, and a disco ball. The artists also used debris they picked up during their trip to create and exhibit artwork along the way.

Steampunk Train

Commissioned by Ripley's in 2015 for our New York City Odditorium, this interactive, steampunk-inspired train is Gladbrook, Iowa artist Patrick Acton's largest matchstick creation ever—built with over one million matchsticks and 35 gallons of wood glue!

Called *Plane Loco*, the train measures over 20 ft. (6 m) long, 9 ft. (3 m) high, and has a wing span of 13 ft. (4 m). It is Acton's own design (based loosely on a 2-6-0 steam locomotive from the early 1900s and Leonardo da Vinci's wing design from the 1500s), and took over 3,000 hours to complete. Guests at our Times Square Odditorium can play with the train's working headlamp, bell, and use a lever to open the firebox doors. Acton has also added a moveable throttle, brake lever, a forward and reverse lever, and many other valves and gauges that will give Ripley's Believe It or Not! visitors a chance to play railroad engineer!

BUBBLE RUN In October 2014, Iranian runner Reza Baluchi was rescued by the US Coast Guard after trying to cross the Atlantic Ocean from Florida to Bermuda—a distance of more than 1,000 miles (1,600 km)—in a giant inflatable ball. He was trying to run inside the plastic floating orb—like a hamster in a wheel—but was picked up after four days at sea still just 70 miles (112 km) off the Florida coast. Officials said he was disoriented and asking for directions to Bermuda.

SUNFLOWER TRIBUTE Grieving farmer Don Jaquish planted a 4.5 mile (7.2 km) long, 60 ft. (18 m) wide strip of more than five million sunflowers along Wisconsin State Road 85 in Eau Claire in memory of his late wife, Babbette.

WRONG DIRECTION Jake Boys of London, England, decided to surprise his girlfriend Emily Canham with tickets to see One Direction—but booked flights to the wrong country. The tickets were for the band's gig in Cardiff, but Boys thought that was the capital of Ireland and not Wales.

PHONE TRACKER Ben Wilson used an app to find his iPhone® that survived a 9,300 ft. (2,835 m) fall from a light aircraft and dropped in a pasture 50 miles (80 km) from his destination of Wichita Falls, Texas.

DIFFERENT GLASGOW Mary and Jack McQueen thought they had found bargain flights online costing a total of $960 (£615) from Glasgow, Scotland, to Las Vegas, Nevada, only to discover that they were booked to fly out from Glasgow, Montana, instead. Happily, the cost of their flights was refunded once the error was spotted.

BRICK MERCEDES Artist Dai Yun from Xi'an, China, built an accurate life-sized sculpture of a German Mercedes-Benz® automobile from red bricks. In addition to the bodywork, the wheels, seats, wing mirrors, steering wheel, license plate, and even the Mercedes logo itself are all made of brick.

SYNCHRONIZED SEESAWS Liu Haibin has built a high-tech seesaw that enables him to play with his son 730 miles (1,168 km) away. He made two identical seesaws equipped with motion sensors—one in his home in Xiamen City, China, the other in Tengzhou City, where his wife and young son live. Through Internet signals and remote sensor data, the two seesaws are synchronized and fitted with monitors so that father and son can see and interact with each other while they play.

CLOSED COFFIN Jenny Buckleff, who used to work as an embalmer at a funeral parlor, arrived for her wedding to Chris Lockett in Llangefni, Wales, in a closed coffin pulled by a motorcycle.

7 Feats

LAVA
Kayakers

Believe it or not, these fearless explorers floated on FIRE! In 2013, Brazil's Pedro Oliva paddled a kayak within feet of the red-hot lava flows pouring down from Kilauea volcano on the Big Island of Hawaii. When he decided to get out and explore the coastline on foot, he accidentally set fire to his paddle! Oliva and his colleagues Chris Korbulic and Ben Stookesberry were exploring some of Hawaii's lesser-known kayaking routes for the TV program *Kaiak*, an adventure series on the Brazilian channel Canal Off. The team explored four islands—Big Island, Maui, Kauai, and Oahu—scouting over 300 waterfalls and rivers.

Rush Hour Rescue

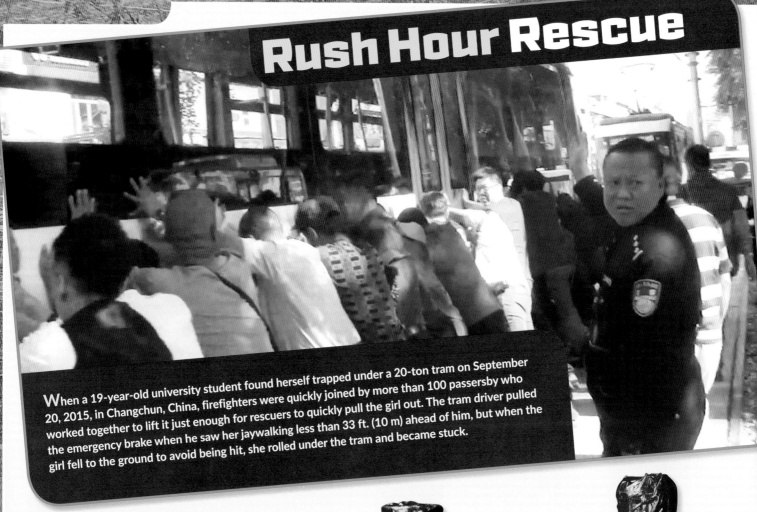

When a 19-year-old university student found herself trapped under a 20-ton tram on September 20, 2015, in Changchun, China, firefighters were quickly joined by more than 100 passersby who worked together to lift it just enough for rescuers to quickly pull the girl out. The tram driver pulled the emergency brake when he saw her jaywalking less than 33 ft. (10 m) ahead of him, but when the girl fell to the ground to avoid being hit, she rolled under the tram and became stuck.

FOOTBALL FATALITIES During the 1905 US college football season, 18 players were killed on the field and 150 were seriously injured.

WONDER SHOT During halftime in the NBA® game between the Detroit Pistons and the New York Knicks in Auburn Hills, Michigan, on February 27, 2015, one of the Pistons's dancers, Kathryn Martin, scored a half-court shot with her back to the basket.

LIGHTNING HANDS Martial arts expert Ian Bishop from Barry, Wales, can throw 13 punches in one second—the time it takes to blink an eye.

CHEW ON THIS

Retired teacher Bruce Wilcox of Tustin, California, has collected 28 years' worth of gum confiscated from his students!

TORONTO BOBBLEHEADS Mark Wlodarski of Mississauga, Ontario, Canada, has a collection of more than 400 bobbleheads, including players from the Toronto Raptors, the Toronto Blue Jays, and the Toronto Maple Leafs. He keeps most of the plastic figurines, some of which are 3 ft. (0.9 m) tall, in 10 glass cabinets at his home.

SPACE PRIZE By becoming the first player to hit a hole-in-one on the par-3 15th hole during the 2014 KLM Open tournament at Zandvoort, the Netherlands, British golfer Andy Sullivan won a trip into space. The $100,000 (£61,483) prize featured a 30-minute flight to an altitude of 330,000 ft. (100.58 km).

DARING JUMPER Swedish stuntman Alassan Issa Gobitaca—also known as Al the Jumper—vaults over cars that are speeding toward him at 80 mph (128 km/h). He jumps at the very last second so that the car passes safely beneath him. He has also cleared two fast-moving motorcycles, one following right behind the other, with a single jump.

DIZZY HEIGHT Romanian extreme sports enthusiast Flaviu Cernescu defied high winds and a sheer 544 ft. (166 m) drop to ride a unicycle along the narrow 6 in. (15 cm) wide ledge that runs along the top of his native country's tallest dam, the Vidraru.

LUCKY COURSE In just two months in 2015, 10 different golfers ranging in age from 11 to 79 scored holes-in-one at the Nashawtuc Country Club in Concord, Massachusetts.

BLIND AMBITION Erik Weihenmayer and Lonnie Bedwell, who are both blind, successfully kayaked the Grand Canyon Rapids on the Colorado River in September 2014—a 277 mile (443 km) journey that took them 21 days. When Bedwell first took on the challenge of the Colorado River in 2013, he hauled a borrowed kayak to the pond on his farm at Dugger, Indiana, and practiced rowing 1,500 times.

SUPER FIT Welsh-born Carlton Williams of Margaret River, Western Australia, completed 2,220 push-ups in one hour on July 25, 2015, averaging just one push-up every 1.6 seconds.

WHIP CRACKER Nathan "Whippy" Griggs, from Mataranka in Australia's Northern Territory, can crack a whip 530 times in one minute—nearly nine cracks per second.

LONG SERMON Pastor Zach Zehnder gave a sermon in Mount Dora, Florida, that lasted more than two days. He began presenting the Bible from Genesis to Revelation at 7 am on November 7, 2014, and finished at 12:21 pm on November 9—53 hours and 18 minutes later.

MUSICAL RUN Harriette Thompson of Charlotte, North Carolina, completed a full 26 mile (42 km) marathon—at age 92. She finished the 2015 San Diego Rock 'n' Roll Race in 7 hours, 24 minutes, and 36 seconds and, as a classically trained pianist, kept her mind focused for the whole distance by mentally playing piano pieces that she had performed in the past. She has been running marathons since she was 76.

ROLLER COASTER RIDE Frenchman Julien Dupont rode around a 50-year-old wooden roller coaster with a maximum height of 100 ft. (33 m)—on a motorcycle. Instead of the usual purpose-built car, he took to his motorbike to tackle the 0.75 mile (1.2 m) long Montaña Rusa ride in Mexico City, which was once the world's tallest roller coaster.

Ripley's —— Revisited
Eccentric Enigma

Covered from his shaven head to his toes with a blue jigsaw puzzle tattoo, circus performer, musician, and actor The Enigma left us guessing after being featured in 2005's *Planet Eccentric*. This former member of the Jim Rose Circus, who also had horns implanted in the skin surrounding his skull, is now a legend in the body modification world. He has numerous television and magazine appearances to his credit, and is a popular performer at music festivals, tattoo conventions, and school anti-bullying lectures. By captivating audiences for over 20 years with his unique combination of circus stunts and offbeat humor, The Enigma has literally changed the face of live entertainment.

TO DIVE FOR

Gary Hunt of Great Britain won the coveted World Championship title.

Diver Todor Spasov of Bulgaria.

Catapulting themselves from a platform over 88.5 ft. (27 m) above an Olympic-sized swimming pool, these graceful divers participated in the 16th FINA World Championships in Kazan, Russia, in the summer of 2015. Against a backdrop of traditional Russian onion-domed buildings, the divers seemingly flew across the blue sky. Gary Hunt of Great Britain was awarded the World Championship title with a total of 629.30 points.

Flying on Water

In September 2015, Shi Liliang, a Shaolin monk, successfully performed the legendary Shaolin Qing Gong "flying on water" stunt across a 410 ft. (125 m) wide river in Quanzhou, China. The 33-year-old monk took small, quick steps across the water's surface using 200 floating plywood planks. Shi, who has been practicing walking on water for the past 10 years, succeeded in breaking his previous record of 387 ft. (118 m), which he set in October 2014.

STRANGE TECHNIQUE Jason Palmer, a professional golfer from Leicester, England, always plays chip shots and bunker shots one-handed. Since adopting his unusual technique out of frustration during a tournament in Spain in 2010, he has enjoyed five tournament wins, and graduated to the prestigious European Tour.

ICE BREAKERS During their careers, an estimated 68 percent of professional hockey players have lost at least one tooth in action.

SPEEDY SOLUTION Marcin Kowalczyk solved a Rubik's® Cube puzzle in 21.17 seconds in Szczecin, Poland, while blindfolded. He did it by first memorizing the cube's pattern. He once solved 41 Rubik's Cubes in under an hour while blindfolded.

CAREER CHANGE Future NBA® Hall-of-Famer Tim Duncan was training to become a member of the 1992 US Men's Olympic swim team until Hurricane Hugo hit his home in St. Croix, the Virgin Islands, in 1989 and destroyed the only pool he could train in. With a morbid fear of sharks, he was too scared to swim in the ocean, so he began playing basketball just to keep in shape.

HOVER FLIGHT Romanian-born Canadian inventor Catalin Alexandru Duru flew 905 ft. (276 m)—the length of two football fields—on a hoverboard at a height of around 16 ft. (5 m) above the surface of Lake Ouareau in Quebec before the batteries ran out. His propeller-based craft took 12 months to design.

UNIFORM DILEMMA The University of Oregon football team—the Ducks—have 512 different uniform combinations to choose from before every game.

SWORD SWALLOWER Entertainer Veronica Hernandez from Dallas, Texas, swallowed a 14 in. (35 cm) long sword when she was nine months' pregnant and just a few days away from giving birth.

SLINKY COLLECTOR Susan Suazo of Los Lunas, New Mexico, has been collecting Slinky® toys for over 40 years and now has more than 1,000. They fill one room of her house, including 200 that hang from the ceiling and several that glow in the dark. She has vintage animal Slinkys, a gold-plated Slinky, and has twisted the colorful coiled spring toys into elaborate floral decorations and built them into ornamental pyramids.

MATH DEGREE Baltimore Ravens offensive lineman John Urschel has a master's degree in mathematics, and in 2015 he published a paper in the *Journal of Computational Mathematics*.

FAST GOALS Senegalese soccer player Sadio Mane scored three goals in just 2 minutes and 56 seconds for Southampton in an English Premier League game against Aston Villa on May 16, 2015. Allowing for the 30 seconds needed to restart the game after each of the first two goals, it means he scored three times in less than two minutes of actual playing time.

SURF SESSION Ben Shaw surfed continuously for 29 hours and 10 minutes off Kure Beach, North Carolina, riding more than 300 waves in that time. He entered the water at 6:30 am on August 20, 2014, and kept catching waves until 11:40 am the following day.

DAM SHOT In June 2015, Brett Stanford, who, with Scott Gaunson, Kyle Nebel, and Derek Herron, is a member of Australian basketball trick-shotters How Ridiculous, landed an incredible basket from a distance of 415 ft. (126.5 m) off the top of the Gordon Dam in Tasmania. Earlier in the year, the group had turned its attention to golf to claim the world's first-ever underwater hole-in-one when Stanford successfully chipped the ball off a tee on the beach and into a bucket on the ocean floor 8.2 ft. (2.5 m) down.

FANTASTIC FLIP Self-taught acrobat Raymond Butler performed a complex double backflip and landed perfectly in a pair of pants. After a year of training, he pulled off the stunt at a sports hall in Westwood, Massachusetts, by running up, spinning in the air, and landing feet first in the waiting pants which were being held by two friends. He had previously launched a single backflip into a pair of pants, in the process jumping a height of nearly 7 ft. (2.1 m).

UTV WHEELIE Driving a utility vehicle with the front wheels raised high off the ground, Canadian stuntman Roger LeBlanc performed a spectacular wheelie for nearly three-quarters of a mile (1.207 km) at Moncton International Airport, New Brunswick.

CAR PUSH Macedonian strongmen Aleksandar Chekorov and Aleksandar Smilkov pushed a Daewoo Matiz car a distance of 60 miles (96 km) in 24 hours around an indoor sports hall in Skopje at an average speed of 2.5 mph (4 km/h).

LATE STARTER Mardelle Peck of Northern California started racing motorcycles at age 65, and within two years had graduated from novice to expert class.

STEADY HANDS Balancing them carefully, waiter Oliver Struempfel carried 27 full glasses of beer—weighing a total of 136 lb. (62 kg)—for a distance of 131 ft. (40 m) at the 2014 Gillemoos Beer Festival in Abensberg, Germany.

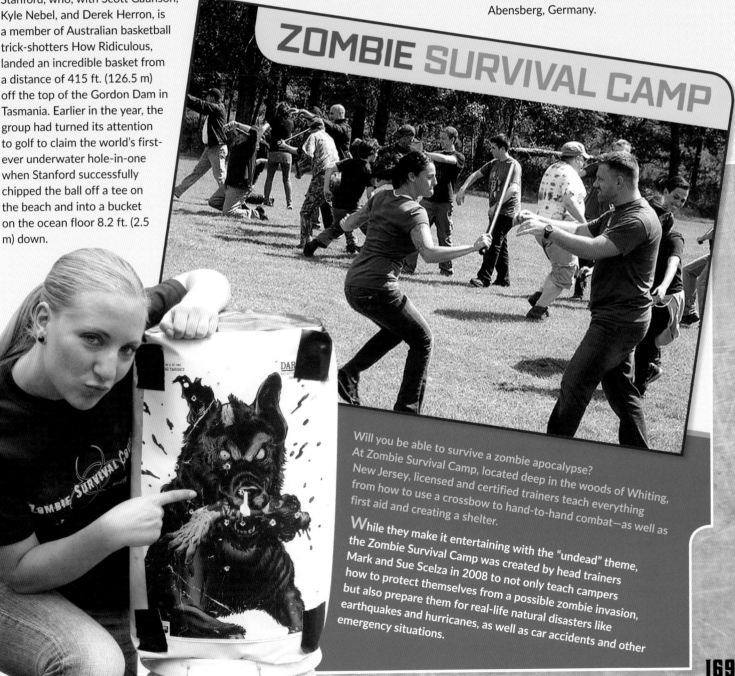

ZOMBIE SURVIVAL CAMP

Will you be able to survive a zombie apocalypse? At Zombie Survival Camp, located deep in the woods of Whiting, New Jersey, licensed and certified trainers teach everything from how to use a crossbow to hand-to-hand combat—as well as first aid and creating a shelter.

While they make it entertaining with the "undead" theme, the Zombie Survival Camp was created by head trainers Mark and Sue Scelza in 2008 to not only teach campers how to protect themselves from a possible zombie invasion, but also prepare them for real-life natural disasters like earthquakes and hurricanes, as well as car accidents and other emergency situations.

In 2015, Australian motorbike stunt rider and celebrated X Games gold medalist Robbie "Maddo" Maddison became the first person in history to successfully "surf" aboard a dirt bike through waves at Teahupo'o and Papara in Tahiti, a French Polynesian island in the Pacific Ocean. Mounting a modified KTM250SX dirt bike on a pair of custom-designed water skis allowed Maddison to hydroplane for long distances without sinking (although inflatable floats were attached to the bike, just in case!)

MULTI-TASKING DAD Watching his team's game against the LA Dodgers at Wrigley Field on June 23, 2015, Chicago Cubs fan Keith Hartley nonchalantly caught a foul ball one-handed while bottle-feeding his seven-month-old son Isaac with the other.

LASTING MARRIAGE With a combined age of 211, Karam and Kartari Chand of Bradford, West Yorkshire, England, celebrated their 90th wedding anniversary in December 2015. They share the same birthday—November 23—Karam having been born in 1905 and his wife in 1912. They first met in Punjab, India, as teens.

SAUNA DASH In the Otepää Sauna Marathon, held every February in Estonia, as many as 1,000 competitors brave freezing conditions to visit more than 20 local saunas in the fastest time. Wearing only swim suits, the participants receive extra points for taking the plunge in ice pools—and are rewarded at the finish with an open-air bath in hot beer.

Wash 'n Scare

Twenty-four-year-old Mohammad Izani Ramli of Malaysia is very close to his king cobras—living with them, training them, and even taking baths with them! Ramli, who began studying snake charming in 2011, captures wild venomous snakes to work with in his home and releases them back to the wild after about two months. He is comfortable living and working in such close proximity to king cobras, copperhead racers, mangrove snakes, and other venomous varieties despite having suffered a bite from a monocle cobra in 2013.

TWO WHEELS
HANG TEN

SINGLE HANDED New York Giants wide receiver Odell Beckham Jr. made 33 one-handed catches in a minute from passes by New Orleans Saints quarterback Drew Brees on the ESPN® Super Bowl XLIX set in Glendale, Arizona. Each pass traveled at least 10 yards (9 m).

TRUCK FLIP On June 13, 2015, at MetLife Stadium, New Jersey, 11-time Monster Jam world champion Tom Meents became the first person ever to land a front flip in a monster truck. Meents, from Paxton, Illinois, had to hit 6,200 RPMs in the 10,500 lb. (4,767 kg), 1,500-horsepower Max D truck on his approach to ensure the vehicle launched properly and achieved the historic 360-degree flip. A week later, he landed an incredible double backflip in the same truck at the Gillette Stadium in Foxborough, Massachusetts, by speeding directly into a huge wall of dirt and bouncing backward through the air for two complete revolutions.

YOUNG GOLFER To raise money for charity, six-year-old Ryan McGuire of Foxborough, Massachusetts, played 100 holes of golf in a single day at a par-3 course in Norton.

ROYAL PATRONAGE Horse racing fan Queen Elizabeth II has missed only two runnings of the Epsom Derby since her coronation in 1953. She missed both the 1984 and 2004 races because she had to attend anniversaries marking the 1944 D-Day landings during World War II.

53 MARATHONS Amy Hughes from Shropshire, England, ran 53 UK marathons in 53 days in 2014. She began in Chester on August 6 and finished—1,388 miles (2,222 km) and five pairs of training shoes later—in Manchester on September 27.

FAMILY JUMP When Marie Kimmey of Hyrum, Utah, went skydiving for the first time at age 91, she was followed out of the airplane at 12,000 ft. (3,658 m) by 11 other family members spanning four generations.

CENTENARIAN SWIM In Matsuyama, Japan, on April 4, 2015, 100-year-old Mieko Nagaoka became the world's first centenarian to complete a 1,500 meter (4,921 ft.) freestyle swim in competition. Nagaoka, who did the backstroke all the way, took up swimming at age 82.

OCEAN SWIM On August 16, 2015, at just 12 years of age, Brooklyn Douthwright, of Riverview, New Brunswick, Canada, swam 9.4 miles (15 km) across the Northumberland Strait from Cape Jourimain, New Brunswick, to Borden-Carleton, Prince Edward Island. The tough ocean swim took her about four hours.

TAX DISCS Jude Currie, a 12-year-old schoolboy from Surrey, England, has collected more than 12,000 UK stickers verifying he's paid his car tax, the oldest dating back to 1926. He has also collected over 600 car hubcaps.

PILLOW FIGHT A total of 4,200 students at the University of California, Irvine, staged a mass pillow fight in 2014.

HIGH HEELS "Slackline Girl" Faith Dickey of Austin, Texas, walked a slackline hundreds of feet above the ground in Ostrov, the Czech Republic, while wearing 3 in. (7.5 cm) high heels. To make her feat even more amazing, the shoes were a few sizes too big, and it was raining.

CONCERNING GURNING

Each September, competitors wearing horse collars test their skill at gurning—or twisting and contorting their faces into ugly expressions—at the World Gurning Championships held at the Egremont Crab Fair in England. The fair was first held in 1267, and one theory has it that the gurning contest got its start from the faces people made when they bit into the sour crab apples grown in the area.

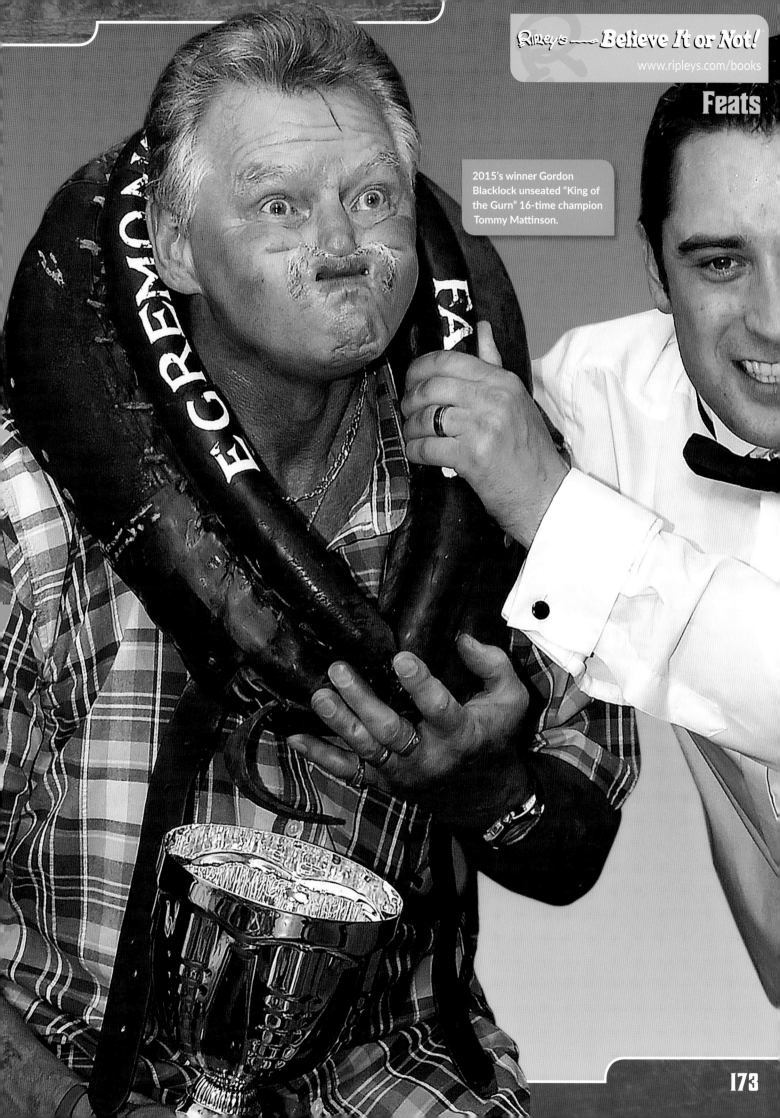

2015's winner Gordon Blacklock unseated "King of the Gurn" 16-time champion Tommy Mattinson.

HIGH FIVE While speeding down the side of a mountain in Chamonix, France, at around 60 mph (96 km/h), Australian wingsuit flyer Nathan Jones kept so close to the rocks and flew with such accuracy that he was able to high-five a cardboard hand held aloft on a stick.

MARATHON MAN Rob Young of London, England, ran 370 marathons in a year between April 13, 2014 and April 13, 2015—despite missing three and a half weeks with a leg injury. His schedule included 29 ultra-marathons, which meant that he clocked up a total of 10,178 miles (16,284 km) with a combined elevation of 473,242 ft. (144,280 m)—that's the equivalent of climbing Mt. Everest more than 16 times. Most weekday mornings he got up at 2:45 am in order to run a marathon before going to work.

TOOTHPASTE LINE Students at John Carroll University, Ohio, carefully arranged 2,178 tubes of toothpaste end-to-end to create an unbroken line that stretched several times up and down the gym floor.

BOUNCING ALONG Jerry Knox of Los Angeles, California, ran the 2015 London Marathon in 4 hours and 10.4 seconds while dribbling two basketballs the entire distance.

DESERT MARATHON Dave Heeley, 57, from the West Midlands, England, completed a six-day, 157 mile (251 km) race across the Sahara Desert even though he is blind. The Marathon des Sables is described as the "toughest footrace on Earth," where competitors carry provisions on their backs and temperatures can reach 122°F (50°C).

FIRE TUNNEL South Africans Enrico Schoeman and Andre de Kock successfully rode motorcycles though a 394 ft. (120 m) long tunnel of fire. The flames roared 400 ft. (120 m) into the air, and the heat in the tunnel hit 900°F (482°C).

CRAZY RIDER On March 28, 2015, French mountain biker Eric Barone—known as "The Red Baron" because of his red speed suit—rode down a steep, 42-degree, snow-covered slope in the Alps at a speed of 138.7 mph (223.3 km/h). Barone did not ride a bicycle at all for eight years following a 2002 crash in Nicaragua, which left him with two torn shoulders, a broken femur, and six broken ribs.

LUCRATIVE CONTRACT In 2014, baseball slugger Giancarlo Stanton signed a 13-year contract with the Miami Marlins worth $325 million (£206 million), which works out to $25 million (£16 million) a season, or $154,321 (£97,860) per game.

SUPER SCOOTER Russell Smith of London, England, rode the length of Britain—975 miles (1,560 km) from Land's End, Cornwall, to John O'Groats, Scotland—on a foot-powered scooter. He completed the journey, which featured a combined ascent of 47,000 ft. (14,329 m), in 21 days, averaging around 45 miles (74 km) a day.

SIX MONARCHS During her 114-year life, Ethel Lang of Barnsley, South Yorkshire, England, lived through the reigns of six British monarchs—Queen Victoria, King Edward VII, King George V, King Edward VIII, King George VI, and Queen Elizabeth II. She died in January 2015 and was the last person living in the UK to have been born during the reign of Queen Victoria.

Scorpion Queen

A Thai woman known officially as the Scorpion Queen wows tourists daily with her bizarre show of bravery at the Tiger Zoo in Pattaya, Thailand—covering her body in the deadly critters! She walks around the park covered in venomous scorpions that crawl all over her, while park visitors—at least those who dare to come close enough—take selfies with her.

Mountain Biking High

Ripley's — Believe It or Not!
www.ripleys.com/books
Feats

Professional cyclist and surfer Tito Tomasi from Nice, France, braved the wind and 27°F (–3°C) temperatures to plunge down the slopes of the Aravis mountains on his mountain bike in December 2015. Tomasi scaled 2,624 ft. (800 m) of the Pointe de Merdassier peak, and then pedaled at breakneck speeds for four hours to descend the mountain.

ROCKET CAR Schoolchildren from Nottinghamshire, England, built a rocket-powered model car that can travel at 858 km/h (533 mph)—double the top speed of a real sports car. The Young Engineers Club at Joseph Whitaker School included four girls and 14 boys aged between 11 and 17, and their achievement was so impressive they received a congratulatory message from NASA.

SUPERSONIC FALL In October 2014, Alan Eustace jumped from a balloon at 135,000 ft. (41,148 m) over New Mexico to complete the highest-ever sky dive, falling at 822 mph (1,322 km/h)—faster than the speed of sound.

VERTICAL RUN Poland's Piotr Lobodzinski took just 10 minutes, 1 second to race up the 82 floors of the tallest building in Beijing—the China World Summit Wing Hotel. He beat 1,000 other runners to win the race, which started from the ground floor lobby and went up 2,041 steps to a height of 1,000 ft. (330 m), finishing on the rooftop.

NOISE BOOST According to a University of Nebraska study, tennis players can hit the ball four percent harder when they grunt.

TRASH COURSE Alfred Evans built a mini golf course in Brooklyn, New York, out of trash. Located between two bus stops along the Brooklyn-Queens Expressway, the urban course includes holes made of a small stroller tire and an empty Pringles® can, and features such hazards as lampshades, traffic cones, and automobile steering wheels. Evans, who is nicknamed "Tiger Hoods," even included a flashlight so that he could play his course at night.

EXTENDED CLUB At the Rolling Hills Country Club in Arlington, Texas, golf professional Michael Furrh used a 20.5 ft. (6.25 m) long driver—more than five times the length of a conventional club—to hit a golf ball a distance of 63 yards (57.6 m).

HISTORIC CLIMB In January 2015, American professional climbers Tommy Caldwell and Kevin Jorgeson achieved the first continuous free climb up El Capitan's notorious Dawn Wall in Yosemite National Park, California—an ascent higher than the world's tallest building, Dubai's Burj Khalifa. It took them 19 days to scale the sleek, 3,000 ft. (914 m) high granite face of the wall, regarded as the toughest of the 100 or more routes to the summit. The pair rested, ate, and even slept on the wall, using a "portaledge" bolted to the face of the rock.

BEE BLANKET Gao Bingguo of Shandong Province, China, who has been a beekeeper for over 35 years, covered himself with an estimated 1.1 million bees weighing a total of 240 lb. (109 kg). He was stung 2,000 times during the challenge.

Mind
OVER
Body

Starting with a Fisher-Price® magic set he received for his fifth birthday and progressing to mind-over-body feats, 38-year-old Dai Andrews has increased his skills beyond tricks and illusions, performing escape artistry, fire eating, and his personal favorite, sword swallowing. His performances include swallowing a saber blade curved 120 degrees, and even a sword heated with a blowtorch! Making these feats even more impressive is that he struggles with essential tremors, a chronic, degenerative nerve condition that causes his hands to shake occasionally. Dai has traveled to over 40 countries around the world—studying yoga and traditional mind-over-body demonstrations with the *sadhus* and *fakirs* of India as well as martial arts in China and Thailand.

> "I have bested my own demons and applied the lessons of masters from around the world to my own life. And, if I'm lucky, I'll pass that lesson on to my audiences as well, showing them that the only limits they have are the ones they set for themselves."

SEVEN Swords!

Ripley's Asks ?

Dai Andrews shared what makes him push the performance envelope.

Q *Did you go anywhere in particular to learn a specific skill?*

A My travels have taken me to almost every island in the Caribbean, across North and South America, China, Japan, India, Cambodia, Thailand, Vietnam, Myanmar, and almost every country in Europe—so many places, just trying to seek out individual masters who have something unique to share.

Q *Who was the most interesting master that you've learned from so far?*

A The most interesting people for me were the sadhus in India. These are men who invented yoga; many say they also invented sword swallowing, fire eating, and other arts.

Q *How much time has passed between your travels? Was it a continuous search or just a few months here and there?*

A I continue to search the world even today looking for new and amazing things to add to my performances. I'm leaving a little more than a week from now to head to Honduras to study free diving to master the ability to control my breathing and add a new depth of underwater performance.

Q *What's the hardest thing to perform? What's the easiest?*

A In many ways, the 100-foot of rope escape that I do is both the most difficult and the easiest trick that I perform. I find it incredibly interesting because it's up to the audience to present me with the challenge. I let them tie me up any way that they want and I escape in less time than it takes them to tie me up. This can be simple or it can be difficult. It's all up to the audience.

Q *Have you had any injuries? If so, what were the injuries?*

A Bruising of the esophagus is something I've encountered more than once, putting me off solid food for several days in a row, but I consider myself very fortunate to have avoided any injury more serious than that.

177

BULKING UP

In 2015, in a grueling three-week-long challenge, 32-year-old powerlifter Andrew Rodichev became the first person ever to climb Russia's Mount Elbrus while carrying a giant 165 lb. (75 kg) barbell across his shoulders. At 18,501 ft. (6 km) high, the peak of Mount Elbrus is a challenge to even the most seasoned of mountaineers due to its harsh conditions, so once Rodichev made it safely to the top, he decided to leave the barbell there as proof of his amazing feat!

DOUBLE ACES Husband-and-wife golfers Tony and Janet Blundy both hit holes-in-one with consecutive shots on the same hole, beating odds of 26 million to 1. Tony aced the par-3, 142 yard (130 m) 16th hole at Ledge Meadows Golf Course in Grand Ledge, Michigan, on May 24, 2015, and then Janet aced hers moments later from the women's tee.

WEATHER WATCH Richard G. Hendrickson, a farmer from Bridgehampton, New York, served as a volunteer observer for the US Weather Bureau for more than 85 years, during which time he filed over 150,000 individual observations. He logged his first observation in 1930, and filed two daily reports until his death at the age of 103 in 2016!

PITCHER'S RITUAL Before a practice session, Washington Nationals pitcher Max Scherzer gets his manager to hum "The Star-Spangled Banner" for him so that he can envision the atmosphere of a real baseball game.

Tough Cookie

Eight-year-old boxing prodigy Evnika Saadvakass packs a real punch—100 punches in less than two minutes, to be exact! Under the watchful eye of her dad and trainer, professional boxer Rustram Saadvakass, she and her brothers and sisters have trained five days a week since she was three—often in the woods outside their home in Voronezh, Russia. She can also throw 47 punches in 30 seconds with one hand.

GOOSE BUMPS As part of the 2015 Grelka Fest ski festival, 1,835 people—wearing just bikinis or swimming trunks in bitterly cold temperatures—skied down snowy slopes in Sheregesh, Russia.

WATERFALL PLUNGE Laso Schaller, from Brazil, jumped 192 ft. (58.8 m) from high on the Cascata del Salto waterfall in Switzerland into a small pool below, his descent taking just four seconds. His jump was higher than leaping from the top of the Leaning Tower of Pisa.

SKI FLYER Towed by a boat, water skier Freddy Krueger from Winter Garden, Florida, hit a ramp at 80 mph (128 km/h) and flew a distance of 312 ft. (95m)—almost the length of a football field—through the air on a lake at Grand Rapids, Michigan, on August 7, 2015.

PORK SPRINT Since 1925, the Tillamook County Fair in Oregon has staged annual Pig-N-Ford races where competitors grab a live, 20 lb. (9 kg) pig from a bin, hand-crank their Model T Fords, and drive the antique automobiles for three laps around the track while carrying the pig under one arm. The drivers have to stop their cars at the end of every lap to pick up a new pig.

BALL BALANCING Juan Marquez Nieto walked for 57 days with a soccer ball balanced on his head. He set off from Mexico's southeast coast on November 23, 2014, and walked 1,240 miles (1,990 km) to Mexico City, averaging about 22 miles (35 km) a day.

GOAT GRAB After scoring a goal for FC Cologne against Eintracht Frankfurt in Germany's Bundesliga in March 2015, soccer player Anthony Ujah apologized to the Cologne mascot, a real goat named Hennes VIII, whose horns he had playfully pulled in celebration.

SIGNED BASEBALLS Since the team's first season in 1998, more than 400 players, managers, and coaches have worn Tampa Bay Rays uniforms—and every one of them has signed a baseball for Jeff McKenney and his family. Jeff's daughter Jennifer once drove 14 hours from Florida to Durham, North Carolina, racing against a hurricane all the way, to acquire the autographs of Jay Buente and Alex Torres.

BARREN STATE Of the 18,500-plus players that have played on Major League Baseball® teams since 1851, only 11 have been born in Alaska.

PAPER BALL At the 2014 Minnesota State Fair, the Minnesota Pollution Control Agency, from St. Paul, displayed a giant ball of paper measuring 9.6 ft. (2.9 m) tall and 32.2 ft. (9.8 m) in circumference and weighing 426 lb. (193 kg). The ball, which was built around a cardboard frame and held together with paper netting, was created to demonstrate how much recyclable paper state residents throw away every 30 seconds. The agency then recycled the ball, turning it into cardboard for cereal boxes.

WORLD RUN Kevin Carr from Devon, England, ran around the world in 621 days. Between July 2013 and April 2015, he ran 16,300 miles (26,080 km), the equivalent of a marathon a day for nearly two years. Carrying all his equipment in a buggy which he pushed as he ran, he traveled through 26 countries, wore out 16 pairs of shoes, and was attacked by bears, hunted by packs of wild dogs, and run over twice.

HOT WORK Appearing on a December 2014 episode of the United States's TV talk show *Jimmy Kimmel Live!*, sidekick Guillermo Rodriguez wore 25 Christmas sweaters at the same time.

BLIND THROWS All four members of a pub darts team from Cornwall, England, are blind. Calling themselves The Optimists, Richard Pryor, Rachael Beresford, Carol Pirret, and Sharon Waters sense where the board is with the help of a piece of string attached to the bull's-eye. They grab the string with their spare hand and throw with the other.

BUNKER HELL The Whistling Straits golf course in Mosel, Wisconsin, has more than 1,000 bunkers, built with 13,000 truckloads of sand.

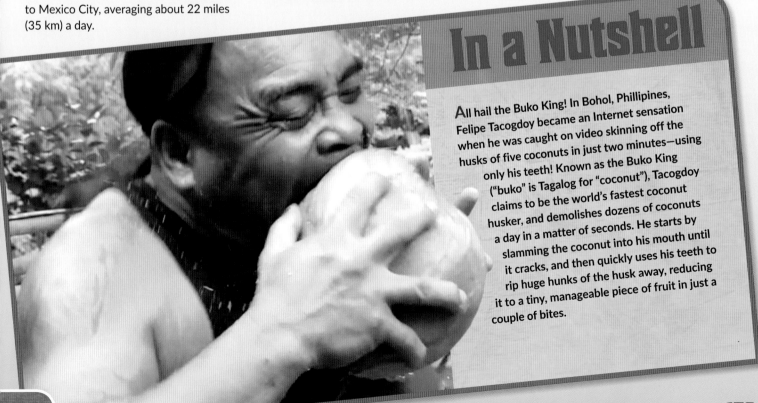

In a Nutshell

All hail the Buko King! In Bohol, Phillipines, Felipe Tacogdoy became an Internet sensation when he was caught on video skinning off the husks of five coconuts in just two minutes—using only his teeth! Known as the Buko King ("buko" is Tagalog for "coconut"), Tacogdoy claims to be the world's fastest coconut husker, and demolishes dozens of coconuts a day in a matter of seconds. He starts by slamming the coconut into his mouth until it cracks, and then quickly uses his teeth to rip huge hunks of the husk away, reducing it to a tiny, manageable piece of fruit in just a couple of bites.

SUMO SURPRISE

In January 2016, 390 lb. (163 kg) sumo wrestler Kotoshogiku won the New Year Grand Sumo Tournament—and became the first Japanese-born wrestler to win a championship in 10 years! Although sumo has been long considered Japan's national sport, it had been dominated by Mongolian athletes during the previous decade, as well as by a Bulgarian and an Estonian winner.

Ripley's Research

In 1891, **Nikola Tesla** developed the Tesla coil, which is in fact two coils—one sitting inside the other. **When an alternating current builds up in the smaller coil, it creates a magnetic field that induces a current in the larger one.** Early radio antennas and telegraphy used the invention, but variations of the coil can also do things that are just plain cool—like shooting lightning bolts.

We all dream of superpowers, but these performers ha[ve] the power of science to do battle with lightning bolts! K[nown] the Lords of Lightning, creator Carlos Van Camp of New [York] and his troupe don chain mail suits and stand atop specia[lly] constructed Tesla coils. The 20,000–25,000 watts of elect[ricity] they generate is conducted through the suits' metal, allowin[g the] performers to "throw" the estimated three million volts of ele[ctric] sparks at each other in an amazing display of wizard-like warfare[.]

LORDS OF LIGHTNING

>Russia's newest sport!

Part wrestling, part mixed martial arts, and part *Game of Thrones*—Russia's latest sport, M-1 Medieval, is as epic as it sounds: two mixed martial artists wearing chain mail and armor duel using gleaming, blunted swords and colorful shields in a full-combat tournament. Unlike the usual Renaissance fair spectacles, each M-1 fight is structured similar to professional boxing, consisting of a trio of three-minute rounds that are judged by five professional judges. M-1 plans to add weight divisions and create titles for eventual champions in 2016, adding an organizational aspect to this knightly sport.

Medieval Mayhem

Dragon Dancing

with SHARKS!

The traditional dragon dance is used to celebrate the Chinese Lunar New Year, but on February 16, 2015, divers at China's Beijing Aquarium performed one with a twist—the dance took place in the shark pool! As they swam by, sharks and rays seemed to join in the dance as divers moved to Korean singer Psy's hit single, "Gangnam Style," captivating the audience with a colorful underwater performance.

LIMBO QUEEN In 2015, Shemika Charles, 22, from Buffalo, New York, became the first person in the world to limbo under a car—a clearance of about 9 in. (22.5 cm). Training for six hours a day, she can limbo while spinning plates in both hands and from her mouth, and can also limbo blindfolded with her hands full. Her mother, Sherrie, was a limbo dancer for 16 years.

CLIFF ROUTE Polish mountain biker Michal Kollbek rode horizontally across a vertical cliff face hundreds of feet above the ground, knowing that one slip would result in almost certain death. The treacherous White Line route in Sedona, Arizona, is a thin line of sandstone extending all along the face of the red cliff with barely space for a wheel. Before tackling the ride, he adjusted the suspension and let the air out of his tires to achieve extra grip.

HIGH SCORE When FC Infonet Tallinn beat Virtsu Jalgpalliklubi 36–0 in a 2015 Estonian Cup match, it was the highest score in a professional soccer competition since Scottish club Arbroath crushed Bon Accord 36–0 in 1885, 130 years earlier.

BABY DRIVER Dutchman Max Verstappen drove in the 2015 Formula 1® season when he was just 17—too young to be allowed to drive unaccompanied on a public road in his homeland.

IMPROVED FITNESS Following two years of training, 34-year-old John Bocek completed 5,801 chin-ups in 24 hours in Arlington, Virginia, on May 30–31, 2015, averaging 240 per hour. Ironically, he admitted that in high school he could barely do one pull-up.

LOST EAR NHL® New York Rangers defenseman Kevin Klein lost part of his ear after taking a high stick from Zach Sill of the Pittsburgh Penguins on December 8, 2014—but he had the chunk reattached with the help of 13 stitches, returning to the ice later in the same game to score the game-winning goal.

BOXING BLING US boxer Floyd Mayweather Jr. put his money where his mouth is by spending $25,000 (£15,853) on a custom-made mouth guard that was embedded with diamond dust, gold flecks, and fragments of real $100 (£63) bills. His name was also stamped on it.

MONSTER CATFISH Using just a rod and reel, Italian fisherman Dino Ferrari caught a monster 280 lb. (127 kg), 8.7 ft. (2.6 m) long wels catfish in the Po delta in 2015. It took him 40 minutes to reel in the fish, which was almost big enough to swallow him, before measuring it and releasing it. Wels catfish sometimes attack humans. When one dragged a Hungarian fisherman underwater by his right leg in 2006, the man barely escaped with his life.

CALENDAR BOY In just 30 seconds, eight-year-old Aryan Parab from Mumbai, India, can calculate the day of the week on which any date falls right up to the year 2068. He can also remember the birthday of every person he has ever met, including classmates and neighbors.

BOWLED OVER Adam Barta of Girard, Ohio, knocked down 2,708 pins in one hour during the National Bowling Association's Reed-Hawthorne Memorial Classic Tournament on February 15, 2015.

BALLOON FLIGHT Erik Roner from Tahoe City, California, tied 90 balloons—inflated by 50 tanks of helium—to a lawn chair and soared 8,000 ft. (2,438 m) into the air. He then used a shotgun to pop the balloons, and as he began to descend, he deployed a parachute and floated safely to the ground.

SPEED SKIER Italian speed skier Simone Origone sped down a steep mountainside in the French Alpine resort of Vars completely unaided at 156.9 mph (252.454 km/h)—nearly double the average speed in an Olympic downhill ski event.

SHARK THREAT Wearing a snorkel mask and battling ocean currents, Kevin Hays of Renton, Washington, solved a Rubik's® Cube in just 15 seconds while submerged in a cage in shark-infested waters off Hawaii.

COWHIDES It takes approximately 3,000 cows to supply the National Football League® with enough leather for a year's supply of footballs.

FIRE JUMP Daredevil Alexander Chernikov from Novoaltaysk, Russia, doused himself in gasoline, set his pants on fire, and jumped off the roof of a 100 ft. (30 m) tall building into a pile of deep snow. Although he was treated for burns, he survived because the snow put out the flames.

GREAT SKATE

For over four years, 70-year-old Wu Xiuying of Jilin, China, has been regularly roller skating by the Songhua River—and balancing pumpkins and fishbowls on her head at the same time! The playful, petite skater stands 4 ft. 11 in. (1.49 m) tall and can easily balance up to five gourds or glass bowls on her head as she glides.

Even without the use of his legs, Michael Mills of Covington, Georgia, is an incredible athlete. In his latest feat of strength, the wheelchair-bound Mills successfully pulled a 4,000 lb. (1,814 kg) SUV 330 ft. (100 m), hand-over-hand, on April 18, 2015.

At the age of 16, Mills was pronounced dead for 28 minutes after being hit head-on by a drunk driver. A final attempt to revive him miraculously worked, but he was told he would never walk again. Overcoming this disheartening news, Mills now takes on able-bodied sports, becoming the first paralyzed person to complete a Spartan Race in 2013. He is the only paralyzed person to climb Georgia's 825 ft. (251 m) tall Stone Mountain, and he has even reached the top of Philadelphia's famous Rocky steps!

WHEELCHAIR PULL

Ripley's Asks ?

Michael gave us the inside track on his incredible feat.

Q How did you prepare for this incredible stunt?

A I started training for my pull the day after Christmas—December 26, 2014. I started out with a much smaller automobile and a much shorter rope. I moved up in weight on a weekly basis by adding an extra person or two in the automobile. Then, as the weight progressed, I added the distance. I also did a lot of strength training in the gym three days a week.

Q Was a special wheelchair used?

A No special chair was needed! The chair I am using today is the chair I used to earn this record.

Q What inspired you to take on this challenge?

A I was told it was not possible. I love a challenge, and I love it when someone does not believe that I can do something. I love showing people that anything is possible. That is all I need to get me motivated.

DANGER HOLE Every year, 125,000 golf balls are hit into the water on the infamous 17th hole of the Stadium Course at Sawgrass, Ponte Vedra Beach, Florida.

HOCKEY VETERAN Dutch-born defenseman Jan Loos played in a competitive hockey game at age 85 when he joined his team in the Huff N Puff League in London, Ontario, Canada, on December 19, 2014. He still played three 80-minute games a week in a league where Peter Schussler retired from refereeing at age 90.

COCONUT SMASH Balashankar Budati from Chirala Mandal, India, can use a machete to smash a coconut balanced on the throat of his wife Bhramharamba without hurting her.

CHOP CHOP At a 2015 contest in Florence, Italy, Australian lumberjack Brad Delosa chopped four tree trunks in half in just 58 seconds using a combination of ax and saw techniques in four disciplines— hot saw, single buck saw, standing block chop, and underhand chop.

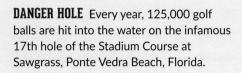

Flipping out There

Toby Segar, 21, from Surrey, England, performed a backflip on the edge of Trolltunga, a cliff hanging 2,297 ft. (700 m) over a mountain on the north side of Lake Ringedalsvatnet in Norway. Not content with merely doing a backflip on the rock—whose name translates as "Troll's Tongue"—Toby actually stood right on the edge of the precipice to perform the stunt.

IN A SPIN On January 19, 2015, 11-year-old ice figure skater Olivia Rybicka Oliver of Halifax, Nova Scotia, Canada, spun a dizzying 342 rotations in one minute at Poland's National Stadium in Warsaw—nearly six spins per second.

EUROPEAN SPRINT Gunnar Garfors, Tay-young Pak, and Øystein Djupvik—three friends from Norway—visited 19 countries in 24 hours in 2014. They set off from Greece at midnight on September 22 and, traveling by rental car and commercial flights, passed through Bulgaria, Macedonia, Kosovo, Serbia, Croatia, Bosnia, Slovenia, Austria, Hungary, Slovakia, the Czech Republic, Germany, the Netherlands, Belgium, Luxembourg, France, Switzerland, and finally Liechtenstein.

BACKWARD BASKET In Phoenix, Arizona, on November 12, 2014, Harlem Globetrotters star Corey "Thunder" Law shot a basket from a distance of 82.1 ft. (25 m)—standing with his back to the basket and throwing the ball over his head.

SENIOR PROFESSOR Professor Joseph Crea was still teaching at New York's Brooklyn Law School when he was 99. He first attended the school as a student in 1944, and went on to teach through eight decades, from 1948 to 2014.

5,000TH RIDE On May 24, 2015, 82-year-old Vic Kleman of Pittsburgh, Pennsylvania, celebrated his 5,000th ride on the Jack Rabbit roller coaster at Kennywood Amusement Park, sitting for more than eight hours straight and logging 95 spins around the historic wooden ride. He has been regularly riding the roller coaster—which opened in 1920 and is the fifth oldest in the world—since 1959.

LIVING DICTIONARY University lecturer Li Yanzhi from Shaanxi Province, China, can recite every single word in the *English-Chinese Dictionary* from cover to cover—all 220,000 entries. She has been reading the dictionary, which contains 2,458 pages, regularly since August 2013 for six hours a day beginning at 3 am. It took her just 19 days to memorize it the first time, and she has repeated the feat on 28 further occasions with the help of 465 English language magazines borrowed from the university library.

1,000 GAMES Carl Marston, a UK soccer reporter with the *East Anglian Daily Times* newspaper, has watched more than 1,000 matches while writing about Colchester United. The first Colchester game he covered, on November 21, 1992, was against Rochdale—and the 1,000th, on March 7, 2015, was also against Rochdale.

HEROIC CRAWL Kenyan athlete Hyvon Ngetich was leading the women's race in the 2015 Austin Marathon in Texas with just over 400 meters (1,312 ft.) to go when she collapsed—but instead of quitting, she crawled on her hands and knees to the finish line and still placed third.

ICE WALL In January 2015, Canadian climber Will Gadd became the first person to scale Niagara Falls while it was frozen. He climbed the 147 ft. (45 m) wall of ice just feet away from the Horseshoe Falls, where 150,000 tons (136,000 tonnes) of water thundered past him every minute at speeds of up to 70 mph (112 km/h).

BALANCING ACT Naib Subedar Azad Singh, a soldier from Goa, India, walked 28.5 miles (45.6 km) in eight hours while balancing a soccer ball on his head. He has also cycled 64 miles (103 km) with a water bottle balanced on his head.

BUSY MAILMAN Eight-year-old Josh Johns of Manchester, England, has received more than 4,000 postcards sent by complete strangers from as far away as Japan and Antarctica.

8 Art

Rose Petal
Portraits

Mexican artist Ricardo Amezcua creates remarkable likenesses of famous ladies—and what makes them even more remarkable is that they are hand-painted on canvases covered in rose petals. After the petals are meticulously applied in an even layer, the artist delicately paints each portrait on top of them, creating a découpage effect. The Miley Cyrus painting shown here is 20 in. x 20 in. (51 cm x 51 cm), the Rihanna canvas is 20 in. x 16 in. (51 cm x 41 cm), and the Amy Winehouse is 18 in. x 14 in. (46 cm x 36 cm). They are part of a series of 16 of Amezcua's portraits in Ripley's collection, which also includes likenesses of Marilyn Monroe, Jennifer Aniston, and Mother Theresa.

TIME to RIDE

You wouldn't lose track of time riding this bike! This intricate model of a motorcycle is made from no less than 112 watches and 14 wristbands and its head lamp is made from a working alarm clock that tells the time. This addition to Ripley's collection was created by Orlando, Florida, artists Luz Marina Escobar and Luis Alfonso Blanco. Being a motorcyle-racing champion in his home country of Colombia helped Blanco get all the details exact.

SCREW PORTRAITS Using thousands of ordinary gray screws, Marlboro, New Jersey artist Marc Schneider creates incredibly detailed portraits that look exactly like black-and-white photographs. After modifying the pixels in a photo of his subject into a grayscale template, he painstakingly arranges the hand-sprayed screws to replicate the picture on a block of plywood, paying particular attention to the eyes and mouth. For his portrait of Jimi Hendrix, he used 4,270 screws.

CLASSIC TOUCH The Prado Museum in Madrid, Spain, has created 3D replicas of classic paintings by artists including Leonardo da Vinci, Francisco Goya, and Diego Velázquez so that blind visitors can "see" the artworks by touching them. Fully sighted guests can also savor the experience by putting on a pair of special blackout eyeglasses.

RIB NECKLACE Known for performances designed to test his pain threshold— usually without using anesthetic—Chinese extreme performance artist He Yunchang had one of his ribs surgically removed so that he could wear it as a necklace. He has also painted the fingernails and toenails of 10 mannequins with his own blood, burned his clothes while wearing them, and encased himself in a cube of quick-setting concrete for 24 hours.

PET PROJECT Russian artist Svetlana Petrova includes her big ginger cat Zarathustra in every painting she does. She has added her pet to classic works by Sandro Botticelli, Salvador Dali, and Francisco de Goya—and also incorporated it into her version of Leonardo da Vinci's *Mona Lisa*, whose enigmatic smile is explained by the presence of the cat on her lap.

HELI ARTIST Heiner Börger of Frankfurt, Germany, has produced over 120 huge abstract paintings with a helicopter instead of a brush. He creates his unique artworks by hovering his helicopter perilously close to the ground above canvases that have recently been doused with paint. He disperses the colors with the downward draft of the helicopter's rotor blades, and uses the landing skids to form impressions in the paint.

SNOW TURTLE Every winter, brothers Austin, Trevor, and Connor Bartz, of New Brighton, Minnesota, shovel snow from their neighbors' gardens to build giant sculptures of sea creatures. In 2015, they spent 300 hours making an impressive snow turtle that measured 37 ft. (11.3 m) long, 31 ft. (9.5 m) wide, and 12 ft. (3.6 m) tall. In previous years, they handcrafted a puffer fish, a walrus, and a 16 ft. (5 m) long shark—all from snow.

BARGAIN BUY Jesse Ronnebaum of Batesville, Indiana, haggled with a yard sale seller to buy a painting of seven men playing pool for just 50 cents instead of the $1 sticker price. Ten years later in 2015, he discovered that the painting is a 1910 work by Chicago's Palette and Chisel Academy of Fine Arts and is now worth $10,000 (£6,498).

STRAW PEACOCK

Quebec City artist Nathanael Cantin used over 15,000 neon drinking straws to create this one-of-a-kind peacock statue. This brightly colored bird stands 67 in. (170 cm) high and 52 in. (132 cm) long—and glows in the dark!

BATTLEFIELD MODEL In 1975 when he was 16, Willy Smout began making a scale model of the Battle of Waterloo, where Napoleon Bonaparte was defeated by the British Army in 1815. He finally completed it 40 years later—over three times longer than the duration of the real Napoleonic Wars. The miniature battle scene covers 430 sq. ft. (40 sq. m) of the basement of his home in Schaffen, Belgium, features 3,000 hand-painted soldiers, and cost him $170,000 (£111,560) in model-making and research.

TIRE LANDMARKS Singaporean designer Thomas Yang paints pictures of world landmarks with bicycle tire tracks. He coats the rubber tire treads with black pigment and rolls them repeatedly over the canvas to form lifelike images of such famous sites as the Empire State Building, the Tower of London, and the Eiffel Tower.

EMOJI PORTRAITS California rapper and artist Yung Jake has constructed accurate portraits of Kim Kardashian, Miley Cyrus, and Wiz Khalifa out of emoji images. Using a computer mouse and a blank screen, he is able to shape detailed facial features of his celebrity subjects with hundreds of text-message pictograms.

MINIATURE PETS As mementos for their owners, Lucy Francis Maloney of Welch, Minnesota, makes realistic miniature models of deceased pet dogs using chicken wire and real animal hair. Working from photos of people's beloved pets, she re-creates the dogs in precise detail, giving them glass eyes and using fur from goats, dogs, camels, or alpacas.

INCENSE STICKS Korean artist Jihyun Park uses incense sticks to burn thousands of tiny holes into sheets of rice paper to create intricate landscapes of clouds, trees, and mountains.

MODEL WIFE As a tribute to his late wife Tajamulli, to whom he was married for 53 years, 80-year-old Faizul Hasan Quadri has spent over three years and $175,000 (£115,282) building a huge 27 ft. (8.2 m) high model of the Taj Mahal on his land in the village of Kaser Kalan, Uttar Pradesh, India.

OPTICAL ILLUSION Natalie Fletcher of Bend, Oregon, paints human bodies in bold, swirling patterns to make it appear that parts of their torso are twisted or even contain gaping holes. She paints her human canvases in bright base colors before adding black contour lines to create the optical illusions.

CRIME PAYS Former armed robber Nigel Milsom won Australia's prestigious $100,000 Archibald Prize in 2015 for his black-and-white portrait of Charles Waterstreet, the flamboyant barrister who represented him in court. Milsom was jailed for two years and four months for the robbery, but struck up a friendship with Waterstreet, the inspiration behind the hit Australian TV legal drama *Rake*.

HOLEY HANDS Using just an eyebrow pencil and eye shadow, Italian makeup artist Luca Luce creates amazingly realistic 3D optical illusions of holes in his hand. One artwork makes it appear that a jigsaw puzzle piece is missing from his palm, while another shows a paintbrush seemingly poking through a hole in the middle of his hand.

MINI CERAMICS Ceramic artist Jon Almeda of Tacoma, Washington, makes tiny pieces of pottery—tea kettles, vases, cups, and bowls—that are only about 1 in. (2.5 cm) long, so tiny they can sit on a coin or the head of a toothbrush. He uses a specially designed, small-scale pottery wheel to create his perfectly detailed mini masterpieces by hand, which, although they appear fragile, are solid and able to endure normal glazing and high-temperature firing.

SPARK YOUR CITY

On August 27, 2015, London commuters, tourists, and residents were greeted by a giant interactive "urban jungle" kaleidoscope, complete with swirling images, shapes, and colors. The trippy tunnel was installed overnight by the Kipling® luggage company as a one-day event that was part of Spark Your City, a global movement dedicated to sparking joy in everyday city life.

Pursuit of PERFECTION

To perfect his skills, Chinese artist Qin Kun, who has been practicing the art of origami since 2003, spent a year at an animal husbandry school in Nanning to study the bone, muscle, and hair of the animals he fashions. All of his spellbinding works are intricately folded from just one piece of square paper, without using glue or scissors. His most expensive work is the origami mantis pictured top right, priced at $33,069 (£23,580).

Dismaland

From August 22 to September 27, 2015, visitors from around the world took part in underground artist Banksy's *Dismaland*, an art exhibition/dystopian amusement park in the seaside town of Weston-super-Mare in Somerset, England. The project had been kept secret until its unveiling, with locals being told that a Hollywood film crew was shooting a movie at the site. At the conclusion of the exhibition, the structures and material from the park were recycled for use in a refugee camp in France.

EGG ETCH

To celebrate the 70th anniversary of the end of World War II, 63-year-old farmer Li Aimin hand-carved the portraits of 254 former Chinese leaders, as well as Soviet Union leader Joseph Stalin, US President Franklin D. Roosevelt, UK Prime Minister Winston Churchill, and images of the anniversary celebration itself on eggshells. The painstaking process took eight months—and over 300 eggs—in total.

STICKY STATUE Canadian artist Douglas Coupland invited people to stick thousands of pieces of used colored chewing gum onto a 7 ft. (2.1 m) fiberglass statue of his own head in Vancouver, British Columbia. Called *Gumhead*, the sticky statue soon started to melt in the summer heat and attracted clouds of bees and wasps.

SCORCH MARKS Using a process called pyrography, artist Jordan Mang-osan decorates slabs of wood with scorch marks from the sun. He sketches a design onto a block of wood, and then uses a magnifying glass to focus the sun's rays on particular areas, using the heat to etch permanent dark lines into the wood. Each intricate artwork can take the Filipino artist several months to complete.

STAMP IMAGE More than 3,000 volunteers in Malaga, Spain, took 22 hours to create a huge mosaic from 230,000 postage stamps. The mosaic depicts the uppercase letter Ñ—a letter that is unique to the Spanish-language alphabet and considered to be a symbol of Spain and its former colonies. They stuck the stamps to a piece of paper that covered an area of 2,371 sq. ft. (220.3 sq. m).

CEREAL MUSICIANS New York City–based illustrator and photographer Sarah Rosado uses corn flakes to create portraits of famous musicians, including Michael Jackson, Bob Marley, Alicia Keys, John Lennon, and Guns N' Roses guitarist Slash. Rosado first sketches the picture, then crushes cereal over the drawing, using a pin to maneuver each individual corn flake fragment into position.

INVISIBLE MURALS Artist Peregrine Church of Seattle, Washington, creates street artworks that are invisible until they come into contact with water. Using stencils and a waterproof superhydrophobic coating, he has spray-painted more than 20 "rainworks" on walls and sidewalks across the city. The part of the concrete he sprays stays dry and light-colored in the rain, but everything else gets darker as it becomes wet. The contrast creates the image. When he wants his hidden pictures to appear, he simply throws a bucket of water over them. His pieces can last up to 12 months, depending on how much the sidewalk location is used. He does it to give people something to look forward to on the average 155 days it rains each year in Seattle.

ANIMATED COUPLE For Valentine's Day 2015, New York City's Brian Flynn commissioned US artist Dylan Bonner to draw Flynn and his girlfriend, Manini Gupta, as various Disney® couples, including the Little Mermaid and Prince Eric, Aladdin and Princess Jasmine, and Mulan and Shang.

PENCIL TIPS In his spare time, jeweler Tom Lynall from Birmingham, England, carves tiny detailed sculptures into the tips of pencils. He uses a scalpel blade for cutting into the graphite, as well as several pins with modified ends for special tasks. Each piece takes him up to 25 hours to complete.

BIG BRONZE BOOTS

These one-ton shoes were created by shoe lover Zheng Changgan from Shanghaixixin Village in Fuzhou, southeast China. He has spent almost 180,000 RMB ($29,000, or £18,475) creating a giant pair of his ideal shoes in bronze. Each shoe measures 7.5 ft. (2.3 m) long, over 2.5 ft. (0.8 m) wide, and over 4 ft. (1.23 m) high. Zheng Changgan fell in love with bronze shoes in 1986 when he made more than 30 pairs to give as gifts.

Auto Art

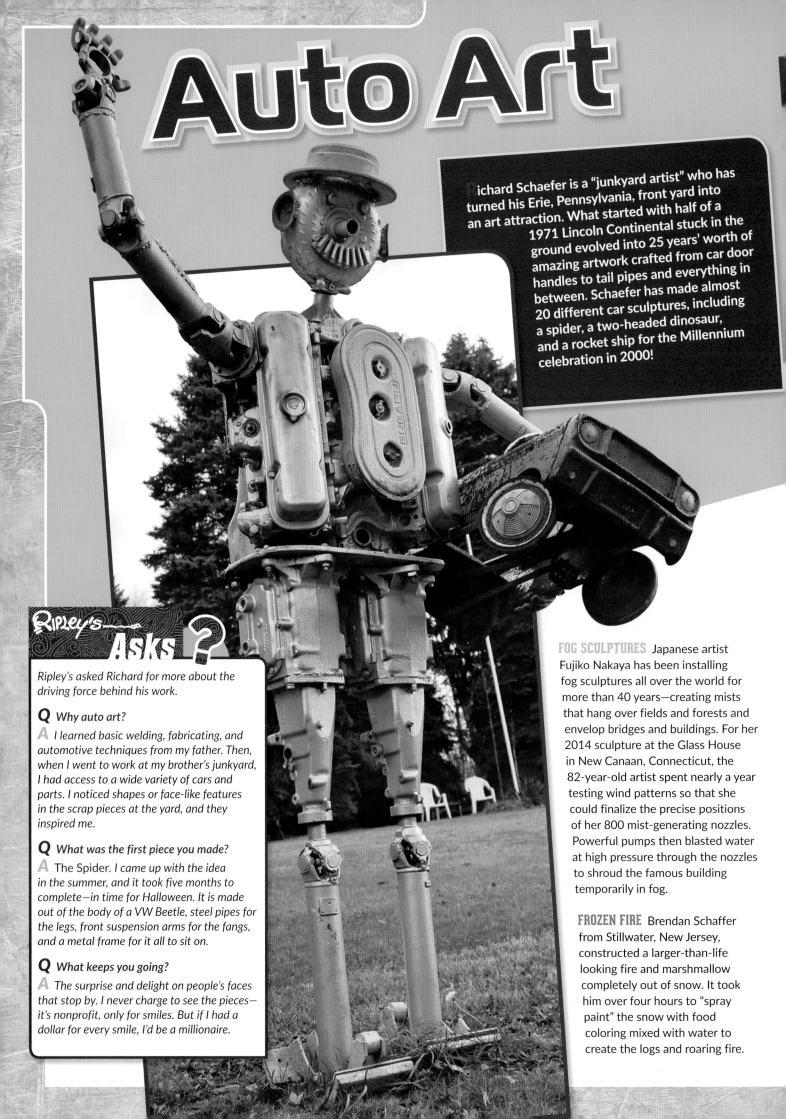

Richard Schaefer is a "junkyard artist" who has turned his Erie, Pennsylvania, front yard into an art attraction. What started with half of a 1971 Lincoln Continental stuck in the ground evolved into 25 years' worth of amazing artwork crafted from car door handles to tail pipes and everything in between. Schaefer has made almost 20 different car sculptures, including a spider, a two-headed dinosaur, and a rocket ship for the Millennium celebration in 2000!

Ripley's Asks

Ripley's asked Richard for more about the driving force behind his work.

Q *Why auto art?*

A *I learned basic welding, fabricating, and automotive techniques from my father. Then, when I went to work at my brother's junkyard, I had access to a wide variety of cars and parts. I noticed shapes or face-like features in the scrap pieces at the yard, and they inspired me.*

Q *What was the first piece you made?*

A The Spider. *I came up with the idea in the summer, and it took five months to complete—in time for Halloween. It is made out of the body of a VW Beetle, steel pipes for the legs, front suspension arms for the fangs, and a metal frame for it all to sit on.*

Q *What keeps you going?*

A *The surprise and delight on people's faces that stop by. I never charge to see the pieces— it's nonprofit, only for smiles. But if I had a dollar for every smile, I'd be a millionaire.*

FOG SCULPTURES Japanese artist Fujiko Nakaya has been installing fog sculptures all over the world for more than 40 years—creating mists that hang over fields and forests and envelop bridges and buildings. For her 2014 sculpture at the Glass House in New Canaan, Connecticut, the 82-year-old artist spent nearly a year testing wind patterns so that she could finalize the precise positions of her 800 mist-generating nozzles. Powerful pumps then blasted water at high pressure through the nozzles to shroud the famous building temporarily in fog.

FROZEN FIRE Brendan Schaffer from Stillwater, New Jersey, constructed a larger-than-life looking fire and marshmallow completely out of snow. It took him over four hours to "spray paint" the snow with food coloring mixed with water to create the logs and roaring fire.

Ripley's — Believe It or Not!
www.ripleys.com/books
Art

BODY SHOCKERS Los Angeles, California artist Jonathan Payne makes grotesque sculptures of mixed-up body parts from polymer clay, acrylics, and hair. His "Fleshlettes" series fuses realistic-looking human eyeballs, fingers, toes, teeth, tongues, warts, and more into horrific mutations, and includes a gross tongue with teeth in place of taste buds.

HONEY COATED For his "Preservation" series, Los Angeles-based photographer Blake Little took pictures of models—including a baby, an 85-year-old woman, and a dog—covered from head to toe in honey. The models posed for around an hour in the sticky honey, which was shipped to Little in 5 lb. (2.3 kg) containers. Every week, he used 1,000 lbs. (454 kg) of honey, which was collected for re-use as it dripped off the subjects. As the models automatically kept their eyes closed, the pictures show their different physical reactions to being drenched in honey. One said she found the substance heavy and weird but admitted that it made her feel "protected in a way."

SCARY PUMPKINS Hollywood artist Jon Neill creates scary Halloween images by carving wrinkly faces and mouths full of crooked teeth into large pumpkins—some weighing as much as 1,700 lbs. (772 kg). He is always on the lookout for pumpkins with character and says, "If I can see a hint of an expression or an attitude in a pumpkin, I look to get that one to carve."

CANDY MOSAIC More than 200 people joined forces to create a 1,577 sq. ft. (146 sq. m) mosaic of candy manufacturer Arcor's logo from over 300,000 pieces of candy in Buenos Aires, Argentina.

CHILD PRODIGY Five-year-old Iris Grace Halmshaw from Leicestershire, England, has autism and struggles to conduct a conversation—but creates colorful paintings that sell for over £1,600 ($2,500).

> ▶▶ ARTISTS FROM MORE THAN 45 COUNTRIES COME TO THE ANNUAL WORLD BODYPAINTING FESTIVAL IN AUSTRIA TO COMPETE IN FIVE DIFFERENT CATEGORIES, INCLUDING BRUSH, SPONGE, AND AIRBRUSH.

MINIATURE HOUSE Leonard Martin of Dorset, England, spent $9,000 (£6,323) and 26 years—over a third of his life—building Langdon Hall, an incredible 6 ft. (1.8 m) long, 3.5 ft. (1.1 m) tall Georgian dollhouse, complete with six rooms, marble and wood floors, plastered ceilings (gilded with 24-karat gold leaf), and chandeliers containing $150 (£105) worth of Swarovski® crystals. He individually cut out 5,000 cardboard bricks for the front of the house, made all the furniture, and illuminated each room with electric lights.

SELFIE VIDEO Homer, Alaska artist JK Keller took a shot of himself every day from age 22 to 39, to create a time-lapse video showing the aging process.

PAPER SETS Bruna Salvador Conforto from Louveira, Brazil, builds intricate models of *Harry Potter* movie sets from paper. She cuts, folds, and paints all of the paper pieces, then carefully positions them on the set with tweezers. She has also re-created Monica's apartment from the TV hit *Friends* with paper, a challenge that took her two years.

SKATER GIRL Tian Haisu, a student at the California College of Art, paints with roller skates. She attaches a pot of black paint to the wheels of a modified pair of skates and then rides in patterns over a large white canvas to create designs resembling Chinese calligraphy. She calls her art form "landskating," and some of her paintings are as big as 40 ft. x 20 ft. (12 m x 6 m).

HAPPY FACES Japanese artist Asano Makoto uses a tiny plastic spoon to carve smiling faces into tubs of ice cream. Each face is carved out of a different flavor of ice cream, with sauces and toppings forming features such as hair and beards.

CERAMIC ICES Ceramics artist Anna Barlow of London, England, makes realistic sculptures of ice cream desserts, complete with porcelain cherries and glazed wafers. When the ceramics are firing in the kiln, the glaze acts like molten sugar, helping to create the illusion of melting ice cream.

TOP INCH For his artwork *The Intruder*, Ecuadorian artist Oscar Santillan took the topmost rock from the summit of England's highest mountain—the 3,209 ft. (978 m) Scafell Pike—thereby reducing its height by 1 in. (2.5 cm).

BLIND ARTIST John Bramblitt from Denton, Texas, creates vivid paintings that have been exhibited in over 30 countries, even though he has been blind since 2001. While Braille writing on his tubes of paint helps him identify the colors, he uses a special type of fabric paint with raised edges so that he can feel what he is painting.

SCHOOL MURALS Ninety-year-old janitor Valery Khramov, a former art teacher, has spent 25 years painting the drab walls of his school in Yekaterinburg, Russia, with beautiful scenes depicting fairy tales and the changing seasons.

When book historian Erik Kwakkel studies 800-year-old books and manuscripts at Leiden University in the Netherlands, he's more interested in the doodles in the margins! Known as pen trials, most of these small sketches, doodles, and practice strokes were made by medieval scribes testing the ink flow of a pen or quill. However, Kwakkel's research revealed that some of the funny faces, letter strokes, random lines, or geometric shapes were also the result of many of our own doodles—boredom.

MEDIEVAL Doodles

Erik Kwakkel gave us the big picture on these little doodles.

Q Is there a common theme that pervades many of the doodles?
A In my experience, the theme or appearance of doodles is not related to a specific time period or type of book. That said, it is striking how many law books have faces doodled in the margins, for reasons unknown to me.

Q How do you feel when you come across these doodles in ancient books?
A What happens to me when I encounter a doodle is best described as a "historical sensation"—a sense of personal connection to medieval times... the doodle (and also the fingerprint) produces a sense of closeness to the past.

Q What was the most unexpected doodle you've discovered during your research?
A I recall seeing a "wobbly" doodle with the name of the child written underneath it and it was easy to see a young boy or girl leaning over the book with a pen in utter boredom, wishing his homework was done—I see my own 10-year-old son do the same thing. That sense of connection and familiarity over a span of five or ten centuries is what makes these doodles most attractive.

Buddha Blowout

On August 27, 2015, the largest number of Buddha statues in the world—a total of 9,900—were displayed in an exhibition center in Zhengzhou, China. The statues were painstakingly hand-carved from jujube wood in various sizes.

TEABAG PORTRAIT "Red" Hong Yi, an artist based in Shanghai, China, created a portrait of a tea-maker from 20,000 teabags. She soaked the bags individually in hot water, and by changing the temperature and amount of water, she was able to achieve 10 different shades of brown. The bags were arranged in position and stapled to wire mesh to complete the picture, which took her a total of two months to complete. Previously, Yi made a portrait of Chinese movie director Yimou Zhang using 750 pairs of white, black, and gray socks.

NATURE COLLAGES Seattle artist Bridget Beth Collins creates colorful collages of birds, marine creatures, and human faces from flower petals, leaves, berries, and twigs.

PLASTIC BAGS South African artist Mbongeni Buthelezi produces amazing works of art from discarded plastic bags. He tears the colorful bags into strips and melts them with a heat gun before applying them onto a black plastic background to form lifelike portraits and landscapes.

TYPE FACES Álvaro Franca of Rio de Janeiro, Brazil, draws detailed portraits of his favorite authors, including J.D. Salinger and Jack Kerouac, using just a typewriter. By changing the number of strikes and the letters he uses, he is able to vary the shading, as an "m" makes a darker spot than an "i" because of its density.

SNOW TANK Alexander Zhuikov, a student from Novosibirsk, Russia, sculpted a life-sized tank from 20 tons of snow. Using spades, knives, and trowels, it took him a month to create a 20 ft. (6 m) long, 6.5 ft. (2 m) high solid replica of a Soviet-era SU-122-54 tank. Each and every part was made of snow except for the cardboard gun barrel.

BEATLE STATUE Leonard Brown created a life-sized statue of an old lady inspired by the title character in the Beatles's 1966 song "Eleanor Rigby," made from £1 million ($1.5 million) in old bank bills. The thousands of used £5, £10, and £20 bills that make up the sculpture were supplied by the Bank of England in the form of shredded pellets. Some of these filled the figure's chest cavity, while others were mashed and molded over the statue's steel frame. It took the artist, who was born in the Beatles's home city of Liverpool, six months to complete.

YARN BOMB GRANNY

At 104 years old, great-grandmother Grace Brett just might be the oldest street artist in the world! She yarn-bombed her town of Selkirk, Scotland, with the help of the Souter Stormers, a group of "guerrilla knitters" who also yarn-bombed 46 landmarks in the Scottish county of Borders in 2015. Brett and her fellow Stormers spent nearly a year secretly planning the project. "I thought it was a really good idea to decorate the town and enjoyed having my crochet included," Brett said. "I liked seeing my work showing with everyone else's, and thought the town looked lovely."

HAZMAT
Surfing

When Bellingham, Washington, photographer Michael Dyrland traveled to Los Angeles in August 2015, he planned on trying his hand at surfing at Venice Beach, but friends warned him of runoff contamination. "I was shocked. Because it rains so infrequently in L.A., all the sewage, garbage, oil, and [fecal matter] runs right down the streets into the sand and the ocean," Dyrland said. Teaming up with the Surfrider Foundation, a non-profit organization devoted to protecting beaches and oceans, Dyrland created the photo series "HAZMAT Surfing," which envisions what surfing might look like 25 years from now if ocean health continues to worsen.

Christina in RED

Believe it or not, these amazingly vivid photographs are from 1913, over 100 years ago—making them some of the very first color photos ever taken! Mervyn O'Gorman took these pictures of his daughter, Christina, at Lulworth Cove in Dorset, England, using Autochrome, one of the first color photo technologies available. Autochrome used glass plates coated in potato starches to filter pictures with dye, making the color very deep and rich. He asked his daughter to wear red clothing because that color worked very well with the early technology.

MONSTER BRUSH Sujit Das from Assam, India, paints with a brush that is 28 ft. (8.5 m) long and weighs 48 lb. (22 kg). He crafted the brush from pieces of bamboo and wooden logs. The bristles are made of horse-tail hair. He needs an extra-large canvas, measuring 6 ft. x 4 ft. (1.8 m x 1.2 m), so that he can use the brush to paint portraits of famous Indian people such as Mahatma Gandhi.

SPOCK MOSAIC William Shatner honored fellow former *Star Trek* actor Leonard Nimoy by making a portrait of Mr. Spock from thousands of individual fan selfies. Shatner asked fans of the series to tweet him pictures of themselves performing Spock's famous Vulcan salute, and then turned the photos into a mosaic.

MISSING MASTERPIECE A $15 million (£10.5 million) Pablo Picasso painting, *The Coiffeuse*, which had been missing since it was stolen from a storage room in Paris, France, in 2001, turned up in December 2014 in Newark, New Jersey—after being smuggled into the US from Belgium as a Christmas present declared to be worth just $37 (£26).

COMPUTER AQUARIUMS Jake Harms of Hildreth, Nebraska, has converted more than 1,000 old Apple iMac® computers into beautiful aquariums, lamps, and clocks, which he sells to customers all over the world.

STADIUM REPLICA Ninety-two-year-old Joe Duncan spent a year building an exact replica of Progressive Field, home of the Cleveland Indians MLB® baseball team, in the attic of his house in Sharon Center, Ohio, using wood, chicken wire, art supplies, and baseball figurines.

TRASH ICONS Nadia Luongo from Naples, Italy, has created portraits of pop culture icons such as Marilyn Monroe, Freddie Mercury, and David Bowie using household trash and food items—including bottle caps, buttons, recording tapes, beans, and tomato ketchup.

CORKNEY COX For the premiere of the fifth season of the TV show *Cougar Town*, artist Scott Gundersen of Grand Rapids, Michigan, made a mural of star Courteney Cox from 60,000 recycled wine corks. He did a pencil drawing of her and then pinned each cork to the canvas, using different hues of red wine on the corks to create light and shade. It took him 200 hours of preparation followed by 10 days of pinning the corks.

Ripley's —⌐ **Believe It or Not!**
www.ripleys.com/books
Art

Over 100 years old!

These beautiful antique photos were made with potato starch!

GUITAR PICKS Manchester, England's Ed Chapman made a portrait of Jimi Hendrix using 5,000 Fender® guitar picks. The picture was later sold at an auction for $37,200 (£24,382).

ICE REPLICA In February 2015, five men used chainsaws and ice cutters to build a frozen replica of the ancient English monument Stonehenge 3,900 miles (6,240 km) away in Rock Lake, Wisconsin. Each of the 6 ft. (1.8 m) tall ice pillars weighed 300 lb. (136 kg), while the blocks placed horizontally on top of them weighed an additional 200 lb. (91 kg). It took Drew McHenry, Kevin Lehner, Quinn Williams, Alec Seamars, and Patrick Shields two weeks to create their "Icehenge," but as temperatures rose it soon melted.

PAPER DRESSES Asya Kozina, an artist from St. Petersburg, Russia, created a range of elaborate wedding dresses made entirely from sheets of plain white paper. She based her designs on traditional Mongolian costumes worn hundreds of years ago.

COW ART Rancher Derek Klingenberg of Peabody, Kansas, patiently used his feed truck to move cows around a field until they formed the shape of a smiley face, which he then filmed from above with a camera drone. It took several minutes for the cows to get in line, and he had to double back at one point when the cows forming one of the eyes finished their food and started to move away.

>50 pages on microfilm!

LUNAR BIBLE

During his historic *Apollo 14* Moon walk in 1971, astronaut Edgar Mitchell carried 100 of the 300 one sq. in. (6.5 sq. cm) microfilm King James Bibles that he'd brought aboard. In 2000, that microfilm was divided and placed for posterity inside custom-made Fabergé eggs. Ripley's proudly owns three of these ultra-rare Lunar Bibles!

APOLLO 14 Lunar Surface Bible Text Fragment - 50 Pages -

Renovation Revelation

MOUTH STICK Paralyzed from the shoulders down after a diving accident at age 17, Henry Fraser from Hertfordshire, England, uses his mouth to draw pictures of sports stars such as Formula 1® racing driver Lewis Hamilton and former French soccer star Thierry Henry. He uses a drawing app and a mouth stick, which has a stylus on the end that acts like a pen.

PHOTOGRAPHIC MEMORY Dutch artist Stefan Bleekrode can draw amazingly detailed ink sketches of cities he has visited—just from memory. He has drawn accurate aerial views of cities such as London, New York, and Paris, featuring buildings, bridges, and even streetlights. Each of his large-scale drawings takes him nearly six months to complete, and sells for up to $6,000 (£3,933).

GIANT NEEDLES Laura Birek of Los Angeles, California, knits huge blankets using 5 ft. (1.5 m) long needles, which she made from 1.5 in. (3.75 cm) diameter PVC pipes with duct tape added to the ends to form tips. She had previously tried using broomsticks as needles but found them too small. The yarn she uses for her "Giganto-Blankets" comes in balls that are bigger than her cats.

MUNCHABLE MILLINERY Phil Ferguson from Melbourne, Australia, crochets colorful headwear in the shape of food—including pizza and burger hats—and then posts pictures of himself wearing the creations to his more than 130,000 followers on Instagram.

ANIMAL LOLLIPOPS Using a 500-year-old Japanese art form called *amezaiku*, Shinri Tezuka crafts pieces of syrupy, glass-like candy into lollipops in the shape of goldfish, frogs, tadpoles, and other creatures. After heating the syrup candy base, he has just three minutes to mold it into shape using a special pair of scissors before it cools and hardens. He then paints it with organic coloring.

REPLACEMENT MODEL When US artist Grant Wood (1891–1942) planned his famous *American Gothic* painting, he originally wanted his mother Hattie as the female model, but he then decided that standing for so many hours would prove too tiring for her. Instead, he dressed his 32-year-old sister Nan as his mother to pose in her place.

FEATHER PAINTINGS Jamie Homeister of New Albany, Indiana, paints images of parrots and other birds on the very feathers they have recently shed.

FUNGAL PHOTOGRAPHY South Korean artist Seung-Hwan Oh deliberately distorts photographs with mold, even though each fungal picture can take him years to complete. He allows mold to grow on the negatives by storing the film in a warm, wet environment where fungus can thrive. He sometimes also takes mold that grows on bread and rice and pastes that into the prints to add further distortion. However, he is only able to use one out of about every 500 original frames because the mold does not always grow in the way he wants.

HONEYCOMB MAP Chinese artist Ren Ri created an amazing map of the world with beeswax. He placed a world map inside a hive and, by controlling the movement of the queen bee, he was able to manipulate the other bees into building at the desired locations on the map. Using the same technique, he has also made accurate beeswax maps of individual countries, including the United States, France, and Japan.

COLOR CHIPS Peter Combe, a Canadian artist based in San Francisco, creates 3D pixelated portraits that look as realistic as photographs but are actually made using color chart paint swatches hand-punched into small disks. He has paint swatches in more than 1,100 colors, and he carefully fits them into specially cut grooves on his canvas material with the help of a vintage operating room lamp. Sometimes he places the chips so that the colored side faces away, making the color not directly visible but reflected off the back.

GHOST SHIP A ghostly ship was projected onto a canal in Amsterdam, the Netherlands, using water, lights, and wind. The brainchild of Romanian art collective VisualSKIN, it was created by mounting four water pumps onto a pontoon and floating them into the canal. Two were placed facing each other 79 ft. (24 m) apart and the other two were positioned opposite each other at a distance of 20 ft. (6 m) across the center of the first two. When the pumps were activated, they formed two 30 ft. (9 m) high screens of water that intersected through the middle of each other at right angles. This enabled a 3D image to be created by using gobos and spotlights to project the lengthways and sideways images of a 17th-century ship onto the screens. When the wind blew, the hologram swayed eerily against the night sky.

Dawn of Chimes

In 2014, Grand Rapids, Michigan artist Stanley Skopek created *Dawn of Chimes*, a dinosaur formed from numerous brass musical instruments. As a lifelong fan of Ripley's, Skopek's dream is to have one of his incredible musical instrument 3D sculptures in every Odditorium in the world! You'll be able to see this 6 ft. (2 m) high and 12 ft. (4 m) long rhapsodic raptor at the new Ripley's Believe It or Not! Odditorium in Amsterdam.

TEA MOSAIC A mosaic covering an area of 931 sq. ft. (86.5 sq. m) was created in a park in Jinan, China, using 5,280 bowls of black tea and milk tea.

JOINT EFFORT Ruth Oosterman of Toronto, Ontario, Canada, converts the scribbles of her two-year-old daughter Eve into beautiful paintings. She studies the random black ink lines that Eve has drawn and looks for shapes that could form the basis of an image, such as a woman's face or a bird's beak, before applying watercolor paints and turning it into an adult artwork.

BALLOON SCULPTURES In his spare time, Japanese chemical engineer Masayoshi Matsumoto makes incredible animal sculptures from multiple layers of balloons. Each sculpture can take him up to six hours to make—and even the creatures' beady eyes are made of balloons.

STEEL SKULL Subodh Gupta from New Delhi, India, made a sculpture of a human skull from hundreds of reused stainless steel kitchen utensils. When completed, his statue weighed nearly a ton and stood 7.9 ft. (2.4 m) tall.

PAPER BRIDGE A temporary bridge over a river in England's Lake District was made entirely out of paper. Created by artist Steve Messam, the 16 ft. (5 m) long bridge was built out of 22,000 sheets of red paper and had no glue, bolts, or bindings—but was strong enough to take the weight of walkers and cyclists.

CLASSIC COMBINATION Los Angeles–based digital artist Vartan Garnikyan blends classic paintings with modern pop art to create works like *Starry Knight*, which combines Heath Ledger as the Joker in the Batman movie *The Dark Knight* with Vincent van Gogh's *Starry Night*. He has also transformed Leonardo da Vinci's *Mona Lisa* into the Joker.

ROCK TAPESTRY Left paralyzed from the chest down by a motorcycle accident, Colin Booth of Newport, Wales, spent almost 20 years creating an 8 ft. (2.4 m) tall tapestry tribute to UK rock band Status Quo by sewing with a needle between his teeth.

PILL PICTURE To mark European Antibiotics Awareness Day, Welsh artist Nathan Wyburn created a portrait of Alexander Fleming, the discoverer of penicillin, from 25,800 empty pill capsules and powder. He has also made a portrait of actor Rowan Atkinson (Mr. Bean) from baked beans, and one of Barack Obama using pizza toppings.

ROYAL EGGS Dutch artist Tiety Entjes-Weij paints portraits of members of the British and Dutch royal families—including the Duchess of Cambridge and Queen Maxima of the Netherlands—on hard-boiled eggs. She has been painting on eggs since 1975, and each picture takes her about six weeks. She uses goose and swan eggs because they provide both a bigger and sturdier canvas—smaller eggs have more fragile shells.

BATTLEFIELD SCENE To mark the 100th anniversary of World War I, Vipula Athukorale, a Sri Lankan–born chef from Leicester, England, spent three weeks making a 1.5 ft. (45 cm) tall sculpture of a battlefield scene out of 53 lb. (24 kg) of pastry margarine. He has also used margarine to craft a 1 ft. (30 cm) long Rolls-Royce automobile containing four passengers.

MERRY KEG-MAS!

In 2014, the Genesee Brewing Company of Rochester, New York, built a 23 ft. (7 m) tall Christmas tree out of 300 empty stainless steel beer kegs. The 10-story tree—trimmed with 600 ft. (183 m) of green lights—greeted guests to the brewery's Visitor Center during the holiday season.

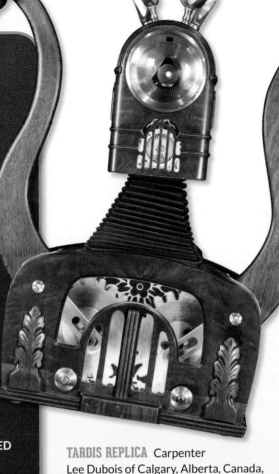

Ripley's — Believe It or Not!
www.ripleys.com/books
Art

Nemo Gould

alifornia artist Nemo Gould used found materials to create *Parlorgeist*, a moving "kinetic sculpture" that reflects Gould's love of science fiction, mechanical design, and the generally bizarre. The 29 in. (74 cm) tall steampunk-inspired sculpture is made from an old radio, a clock, an ashtray, a mirror stand, door stops, fondue fork handles, wallpaper, an angle grinder, gears, motors, brass, wood, candlesticks, and meat grinder handles. Its robot-like arms and head sway rhythmically—and the red LED eye in the center of its head blinks!

TARDIS REPLICA Carpenter Lee Dubois of Calgary, Alberta, Canada, spent four months building a full-size wooden replica of the TARDIS, the time machine from the long-running UK science fiction TV program *Doctor Who*.

PENCIL SHAVINGS South African schoolteacher Meghan Maconochie makes amazing portraits of iconic figures including Bugs Bunny, Kurt Cobain, Harry Potter, and Nelson Mandela—not with conventional pencils, but with pencil shavings. After making a sketch of her subject on white paper, she sharpens her pencils and applies a thin layer of the shavings to the outer edges of the drawing. She then adds further layers of shavings to give the piece a sculptural look. She sometimes goes through an entire box of pencils to create a single sketch.

MATCHSTICK MODELS Airplane enthusiast Norman Dawson of Berkshire, England, spent more than two years building scale models of a Concorde jet and a Boeing 747 from over 5,000 matchsticks.

BROTHERLY LOVE Spanish surrealist painter Salvador Dali (1904–1989) believed he was the reincarnation of his older brother, also named Salvador, who died of gastroenteritis nine months before the artist was born.

Go Ahead, Make My Mosaic

If you were going to make an image of a famous actor out of bullets, would there be a better choice than Clint Eastwood? This portrait of the award-winning actor, director, and gun enthusiast was created by mosaic artist Doug Powell. The 54-year-old made it from 6,615 12-gauge shotgun shells that were collected from the Volusia County Trap and Skeet Club in New Smyrna Beach, Florida. Powell is an activist as well as an artist, so the color of some of the shells have a powerful meaning as well. He incorporated pink shells to represent breast cancer awareness, while the white shells are for the US veterans' service charity Wounded Warrior Project.

9 Food

Molten 'Mallow

A normal campfire just won't do for daredevil Simon Turner, who toasted his marshmallows over the edge of an active lava lake! Using a tent pole, Turner dangled the treat over Marcum Crater on the island of Ambrym in Vanuatu. Turner and his cameraman, Bradley Ambrose, had to rappel more than 1,300 feet (396 m) toward the molten lava, which can reach 2,000°F (1,093°C)!

ROAST CAMEL As part of a tourist festival in Xinjiang, China, hundreds of people gathered to feast on a whole roast camel. To cook the 990 lb. (450 kg) animal, chef Momin Hopur and his team spent five days building a 13 ft. (4 m) tall kiln with more than 10,000 bricks. The camel, coated in a bright yellow marinade, was then hoisted into the kiln by crane.

MONSTER TURNIP Mr. Li, a gardener from Yunnan Province, China, grew a monster turnip that was 4 ft. (1.2 m) long and weighed 33 lb. (15 kg). The giant vegetable, which was grown naturally without the help of any fertilizers, weighed more than the average three-year-old child.

BUGS GALORE Camren Brantley-Rios, a student at Auburn University in Alabama, ate insects for breakfast, lunch, and dinner for a whole month. His meals included scrambled eggs with waxworms, bug-burgers with cheese and Creole crickets, sautéed cockroaches, and chocolate-covered crickets.

SUPER SPUD

Mr. Chen, a farmer in China's Sichuan province, harvested an extraordinarily large root vegetable, measuring almost 28 in. (70 cm) long and weighing 32 lbs. (14.6 kg)! Chen noticed a seedling growing in his backyard in the spring of 2014, but he was shocked to find this monstrous hand-shaped veggie growing the following year, as he never fertilized or tended to it. He decided to use it to make soup—noting it tasted like a yam!

SAND LOVER Ninety-two-year-old Sudama Devi from Kajri Noorpur, India, eats 2.2 lbs. (1 kg) of sand every day—and has never needed to visit a doctor. She first ate sand when she was 10 and now consumes four plates of it a day, sometimes mixing it with water to make a revitalizing drink.

CHOCOLATE TOWER Andrew Farrugia from Malta created a 44.2 ft. (13.4 m) tall model of Dubai's Burj Khalifa skyscraper using 9,240 lbs. (4,200 kg) of Belgian chocolate. It took Farrugia and his team 1,050 hours—over 43 days—to complete.

FRUITY EGGS By feeding chickens large amounts of the peel of yuzu, a Japanese citrus fruit, farmers in Kochi Prefecture have created eggs called "yuzu tama" that smell and taste like the fruit.

CHEESE PHOBIA Anna Bondesson from Bara, Sweden, has an extreme phobia of cheese. She is so terrified of cheese that she bursts into tears just looking at it. All types of cheese send her into a panic, and even hearing someone talking about cheese is enough to scare her.

EDIBLE ART

Shockingly beautiful, these curious cakes are created by Annabel de Vetten, the force behind Conjurer's Kitchen in Birmingham, England. Her bizarre baking caters to the offbeat, unusual, and sometimes macabre. Ranging from artistic to anatomical, these confections are detailed to death—intricacies that can be attributed to de Vetten's experience as a taxidermist, sculptor, and fine art painter. She does warn, "Some of the edibles aren't to everyone's taste!"

STRANGE Slices

Bernard Jordan of Butlers Pizza in Cape Town, South Africa, once hand delivered a pizza to Corne Krige, the captain of the Fedsure Stormers rugby team in Sydney, Australia, a **DISTANCE OF 6,861 MILES** [11,042 km].

The **FIRST BITCOIN** transaction was for a pizza.

Americans eat approximately **100 ACRES OF PIZZA** a day.

Neighborhood Pizza in Florida offers the "Everglades Pizza" with **PYTHON MEAT, ALLIGATOR SAUSAGE,** and **FROGS' LEGS!**

Pricey Slice of Pie ➔

New York City's Nino's Bellissima Pizzeria offers a **$1,000 PIZZA** topped with six varieties of caviar, chives, fresh lobster, and crème fraiche.

On June 20, 2015, pizza-makers at Expo Milano created the **WORLD'S LONGEST PIZZA,** measuring nearly a mile long. The record-setting pie featured 1.5 tons of mozzarella and 2 tons of tomato sauce, and weighed about 5 tons in all!

In 2001, Pizza Hut® delivered a pizza to the **INTERNATIONAL SPACE STATION.**

In 2006, Cristian Dumitru of Romania ate **200 POUNDS** of pizza in one week!

Rest in Pizza

When a loved one bites the crust, may they rest in pizza. In the Light Urns, from Three Rivers, California, provides one of the most creative urns on the market—a pizza box!

NEW FOR EASTER

RABBIT PIZZA
MADE FROM REAL RABBIT. LIKE THIS BILLBOARD.

Bunny Billboard

Rabbits are considered damaging pests in New Zealand, so if you can't beat them, eat them! For Easter 2014, Hell Pizza debuted a pie topped with smoked wild New Zealand rabbit, toasted pine nuts, beetroot and horopito relish, cream cheese, rosemary, and fresh spring onions. To advertise this adventurous pizza, the chain erected a billboard covered with hundreds of real rabbit skins! The pelts were ethically sourced from a professional animal tanning company, who obtained them from a local meat processing company where the skins are a regular byproduct.

Loaves of Fun

Lou Lou P's Delights of Leeds, England, has a Kenwood Chef mixer, a couple of baking trays, and an unerring compulsion to create ridiculous and delicious food art. From sloth brioche to Donald Trump piñata cookies, and even doughnuts inspired by the horror film *The Ring*, Lou Lou P is no stranger to offbeat bakes.

The Pugloaf and the Unicorn burger bun were born from the same batch. First came the Pugloaf, whose furrowed brow was quite challenging to craft. Lou Lou P baked the canine carb slowly in order to retain its light beige fur color. Once cooled, edible dusts were painted on to create the pug's puppy dog eyes, ears, and snout. With the leftover dough, Lou Lou P whipped up a Unicorn burger bun!

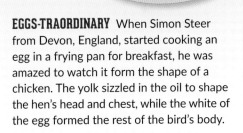

EDIBLE CUP Fast-food restaurant KFC® has created an edible coffee cup. Called the "Scoff-ee Cup," it is made from a cookie-like, wafer-thin biscuit wrapped in sugar paper and lined with heat-resistant white chocolate, which allows it to keep the coffee hot while the cup stays crispy.

GENEROUS TIP A man so enjoyed the gumbo he shared with a friend at Washington, DC's Blue 44 restaurant in May 2015 that he left a $2,000 (£1,271) tip on a $93 (£59) bill.

CHEESE BAN Before the 2015 NFL® playoff game between the Seattle Seahawks and the Green Bay Packers, Bainbridge Island City Manager and Seahawks fan Douglas Schulze banned the possession and consumption of cheese inside City Hall in a friendly jab at Packers fans, who are popularly known as "cheeseheads."

HISTORIC CAKE Baker Christine Jensen from Cornwall, England, spent 94 hours creating a full-size replica of the Magna Carta—the historic document signed by King John in 1215—made entirely of cake. She painstakingly copied out the 4,000 Latin words of the original medieval script by writing them in food dye on fondant.

CURRY TATTOO Glasgow, Scotland's Beth Faulds got the logo of the city's Shish Mahal curry house inked on her hip in exchange for her curry-loving father Norman being able to enjoy free meals there for a year. Norman has been a regular at the Shish Mahal for nearly 50 years.

JUMPING MAGGOTS The tiny, 0.3 in. (8 mm) long maggots that infest Sardinia's casu marzu cheese can jump 6 in. (150 mm) when disturbed—the equivalent of Russia's 2012 Olympic high jump champion Ivan Ukhov leaping 126 ft. (38.4 m) into the air.

HIGH ENERGY Sarah Weatherill from Coventry, England, drank as many as 24 cans of Red Bull® energy drink every day for nearly six years. She had to undergo hypnosis to break her expensive $8,000 (£5,084)-a-year devotion to the caffeine-filled fluid.

EGGS-TRAORDINARY When Simon Steer from Devon, England, started cooking an egg in a frying pan for breakfast, he was amazed to watch it form the shape of a chicken. The yolk sizzled in the oil to shape the hen's head and chest, while the white of the egg formed the rest of the bird's body.

TALL ORDER Sugardale Foods of Ohio created a sandwich with an incredible 40 layers. It stood 26 in. (66 cm) tall, weighed 9 lbs. (4.1 kg), and contained 160 slices of bacon, 42 slices of bread, 5 lbs. (2.3 kg) of peanut butter, and 3 lbs. (1.4 kg) of Marshmallow Fluff®.

PEANUT POOL The Candy Factory in North Hollywood, California, made a 444 lb. (201 kg) peanut butter cup. The ingredients were so heavy that workers were unable to find a bowl large enough to use as a mold, so they instead poured the melted chocolate and peanut butter into a children's wading pool.

The Royal Carriage

Created by chef Ash Elsayed, this 300 lb. (136 kg) handcrafted confection is made entirely of a mixture of salt, corn starch, and water! Measuring 8 ft. (2.5 m) long and 2 ft. (0.6 m) high, it took more than 200 hours of planning, construction, and hand sculpting to complete. The masterpiece was awarded the gold medal by Société Culinaire Philanthropique at the 1994 Salon of Culinary Arts Competition in New York City, and is now part of the Ripley's Believe It or Not! collection.

CHEESED OFF English Stilton cheese is licensed to be produced in Derbyshire, Leicestershire, and Nottinghamshire in the UK, but not in the Cambridgeshire village of Stilton with which it shares its name.

FAST FOOD Runners in the Half and Half 13 mile (21 km) race in Washington, DC, must eat a chili dog and potato chips halfway through the course before they are allowed to finish.

AGED MARTINI Celebrated Las Vegas bartender Salvatore Calabrese created a martini containing spirits with a combined age of more than 350 years. The gin and orange bitters were both from 1900, and the vermouth from 1890.

Cookie Canvas

We've all heard the saying, "Don't play with your food!" But Tisha Cherry Saravitaya of Brooklyn, New York, breaks this rule by using a unique canvas for her work—OREOS®. Using the crème filling, Saravitaya paints pop-culture-inspired masterpieces—from Warhols to emojis—on the cookies!

FIERY BURGER Loren Gingrich, owner of the Xtreme Smokehouse and Grill in Washington, Iowa, has created the "Hellfire Burger," a burger with a rating of more than one million on the Scoville heat scale—200 times hotter than a single jalapeño pepper. The burger, which is topped with cayenne pepper, pure chili extract, and a hot pepper relish, is so fiery that customers have to sign a waiver and wear gloves and goggles before they can take a bite.

TESTICLE BEER Iceland's Stedji Brewery launched a new limited-edition beer flavored with smoked whales' testicles. The Hvalur 2 beer was made by curing the testicles of fin whales and then salting and smoking them.

KFC EXPEDITION Brian Lutfy and Neil Janna drove their four sons 1,000 miles (1.609 km) from Montreal, Quebec, Canada, to Corbin, Kentucky, just for a taste of KFC® chicken. The trip to the original home of KFC and back took them 34 hours through two Canadian provinces and five US states.

MR. BEAN Gary Watkinson from Huddersfield, England, eats beans on toast for every meal. Apart from eating French fries when traveling (and that is only when he cannot find any beans), the 25-year-old has never eaten anything other than beans on toast since he was a young boy.

BONE IDOL A restaurant in Guadalajara, Mexico, is decorated with 10,000 animal bones—some real, and others cast aluminum replicas. Called "Hueso" (Spanish for "bone"), it was designed by architect Ignacio Cadena, and almost every vertical inch of its interior is adorned with whitewashed skulls, mandibles, and vertebrae.

HEAVY DESSERT Thirty pastry chefs in Gemona, Italy, helped make a giant tiramisù weighing 6,647 lb. (3,015 kg)—similar to the weight of a Hummer. The coffee-flavored dessert was so heavy it had to be weighed by crane.

BACON BLITZ Matt "Megatoad" Stonie from San José, California, ate 182 slices of bacon in five minutes at the 2015 Daytona 500 in Florida.

LADY IN LICORICE

Believe it or not, this luscious dress is made out of licorice! Created from Twizzlers® by Wilmer Lam of Orlando, Florida, there are more than one million miles (1.6 million km) of the tasty candy produced each year. That's enough Twizzlers to stretch from the Earth to the Moon and back again—five times!

ANCIENT PRETZELS Two 250-year-old pretzels were discovered by archaeologists during an excavation in Regensburg, Germany. Unearthed beneath the floor of a former bakery, the charred remains of the burnt pretzels had survived since the 18th century.

CEREAL FAN Cheshire, England's Natalie Swindells lives on four bowls of Rice Krispies® a day and claims she is healthier than most people. She rarely eats anything else except bread, and has not tasted a vegetable for nearly 20 years.

ANT GIN Distiller Will Lowe has created a gin made from the essence of 62 ants in his laboratory in Cambridge, England. His "Anty Gin," which costs over $200 (£285) per bottle and is the world's first gin to be made from insects, gets its typical citrus flavor not from lemon or lime peel, but from red wood ants. He began by soaking 6,000 ants in high-strength ethanol and then distilled the liquid to make an ant concentrate, which he mixed with juniper, stinging nettles, and other woodland plants.

CHIP DIET Debbie Taylor from Essex, England, has eaten only corn chips for over a decade. Although she cooks proper meals for her partner and children, she eats two family-sized bags of corn chips a day and nothing else.

MAGIC INGREDIENT Ninety percent of ancient Roman dishes included garum, a liquid made from the guts of a fish that had been left to ferment in the sun for three months. Garum was also used to treat dog bites and remove unwanted body hair and freckles.

SPACE COFFEE In 2015, Italian astronaut Samantha Cristoforetti became the world's first orbiting barista when she fired up an espresso coffee machine on the International Space Station 250 miles (400 km) above Earth.

SUPER SUNDAE Nearly 200 volunteers in Nashville, Michigan, helped create an ice cream sundae that stretched 1,800 ft. (549 m) down the M-66 Highway and into the middle of town. The super sundae was made from 7,200 scoops of ice cream, 3,600 cherries, 72 cans of whipped cream, 28 gallons (106 liters) of chocolate syrup, and 56 gallons (212 liters) of strawberries. It occupied more than 270 tables and was served with the help of 8,300 spoons.

POETIC PAYMENT In 19th-century Hungary, impoverished poets in Budapest coffeehouses would scribble sonnets on a napkin in lieu of paying for their drinks.

KRISPIE COLOSSUS Students at the University of Wisconsin-Madison made a Rice Krispies® cereal treat weighing 11,327 lb. (5,138 kg). The colossus, made by combining the crispy cereal, marshmallows, and butter, measured 10 ft. x 10 ft. (3 m x 3 m), and stood 6.5 ft. (2 m) tall.

SHEEP CAFÉ As 2015 was the Year of the Sheep in South Korea, Seoul restaurant owner Lee Kwang-ho kept two live sheep in his Nature Café to entertain customers. Visitors flocked to the café from as far away as New Zealand and Saudi Arabia.

FLESH BURGER By studying the journals of famous cannibals, London, England, food creatives "Miss Cakehead" and James Thomlinson devised a burger that tastes like human flesh. The burger, which was launched to celebrate season five of the TV horror drama *The Walking Dead*, was made from a mix of pork, veal, chicken livers, and bone marrow to replicate the taste and texture described by cannibal author William Seabrook, who said human flesh tasted like "good, fully developed veal, not young, but not yet beef."

LUXURY CAVIAR Strottarga Bianco, a white caviar created by Austrian fish farmer Walter Gruell and his son Patrick, can cost as much as $40,000 (£25,420) per teaspoon. It comes from the roe of the rare albino sturgeon and is laced with 22-karat gold.

NEON ICE CREAM For a nighttime festival in Melbourne, Australia, chef Steve Felice created fluorescent ice cream. He used UV-reactive food dye, which causes the liquid nitrogen ice cream to glow in the dark. He launched his neon range with flavors that include pine-lime, mango passion fruit, and raspberry.

PRISON FOOD In 2015, a restaurant staffed entirely by prisoners was voted the best diner in Cardiff, Wales, on the website TripAdvisor. The Clink Restaurant at Cardiff Prison was ranked number one out of 946 eateries in the Welsh capital.

STEAK DINNERS Although she weighs only 120 lb. (54 kg), competitive eater Molly Schuyler from Sacramento, California, devoured three 72-ounce steak dinners—three steaks, three baked potatoes, three shrimp cocktails, three salads, and three rolls—in just 20 minutes during a food challenge in Amarillo, Texas.

FRIED TADPOLES The Thai dish *huak tod* is made from fried tadpoles. A seasonal delicacy that is only available in the rainy months, it is often served with the tadpoles wrapped in a banana leaf.

ANT SUPPERS When bad weather and flooding left him stranded on a mountain in Turkey in January 2015, student David Mackie of Nottinghamshire, England, survived for eight nights in the wild by eating ants.

CHOCOBATCH

Who wouldn't want enough Belgian chocolate to make a life-sized statue of one of the world's most famous actors? This replica of British actor Benedict Cumberbatch was sculpted from about 500 bars of melted chocolate, and took a team of eight chocolatiers 250 hours to create it. When the "Chocobatch" was displayed at a London shopping center on April 3, 2015, fans even severed its fingers for a snack.

MONKEY BAR
Open since 1519, In't Aepjen, one of the oldest bars in Amsterdam, the Netherlands, used to accept sailors' monkeys as payment for drinks. The monkeys were brought back from Indonesia, which was then a Dutch colony, but there were soon so many running around the bar that customers complained of fleas. The animals were eventually re-housed in what became the forerunner of the city's Artis Royal Zoo.

PICKLED EGGS
Terry Nugent from Kent, England, can eat three pickled hen's eggs in just 22 seconds. In a single day, he often eats 15 of the pungent snacks—hard-boiled eggs that have been cured in vinegar or brine.

Breakfast IN BED
Breakfast in bed is the ultimate way to eat your eggs and bacon, and 418 people took this morning meal to the next level on August 16, 2015. Setting the record for the most people eating breakfast in bed, participants started their day by comfortably lounging in the garden of the Sheraton Langfang Chaobai River Hotel in Hebei, China. Although they were already breaking one of Mom's rules ("No eating in bed!"), participants had to keep their backs against the headboard at all times and wait to dig in—72 over-eager eaters were disqualified!

NEVERENDING NOODLE

In China, it is customary to eat noodles on hot summer days, especially on the summer solstice. The saying goes, "After eating noodles on the summer solstice day, daylight gets shorter day by day." On July 23, 2015, to help with the summertime sadness, students at Yangzhou University created a 984 ft. (300 meter) long noodle!

EYE WATERING
The Crocodile Inferno curry, served at Tony Uddin's restaurant in Staffordshire, England, is twice as potent as tear gas and is so hot that kitchen staff have to wear gas masks to protect their faces from the chili fumes.

GIANT CONE
Norwegian ice cream company Hennig Olsen made an ice cream cone that stood 10 ft. (3 m) high and weighed almost a ton. In addition to containing 13 gallons (60 liters) of chocolate and 242 lbs. (110 kg) of waffle biscuit, the giant cone was able to hold 238 gallons (1,080 liters) of ice cream—enough for nearly 11,000 people to have two scoops each.

NOODLE LOVER
In the past two decades, Japanese noodle fan Toshio Yamamoto has tasted more than 5,600 varieties of instant ramen noodles from 40 countries.

DONUT LINE More than 100 volunteers in Hamburg Township, Michigan, laid out 24,000 donuts to create a line that stretched for over two miles (3.2 km).

CURRY TAKEOUT When Whitney and Adam Gardner moved from Sussex, England, to Brittany, France, they missed their favorite Indian takeout restaurant so much that they arranged for family members to collect curries and drive the food on a 500 mile (800 km), six-hour journey through the Channel Tunnel to their new home.

CHIPOTLE LIFE Andrew Hawryluk of Los Angeles, California, ate at Chipotle® restaurants for 186 days straight—more than half a year. Every day he ate the same meal at the Mexican restaurant chain: white rice, chicken, guacamole, and lettuce topped with Tabasco® chipotle sauce, spending a total of over $1,800 (£1,190). The idea started as a joke when he told his brother he was going to eat at Chipotle every day for Lent, but at the end of the 40 days he just kept going.

FOUR YOLKS Spotting a gigantic egg—three times the size of a normal egg—in the shop in Gloucester, England, where she works, Jan Long, at odds of 11 billion to one, cracked it open to find four yolks inside.

BEATLE DIET When the Beatles visited India in 1968, drummer Ringo Starr packed two suitcases—one full of clothes and the other full of cans of baked beans because his stomach could not cope with spicy food.

MICE WINE Baby mice wine, a traditional health tonic in China and Korea, is made by placing up to 15 live baby mice, so young their eyes are still closed and their fur has not yet grown, into a bottle of rice wine and leaving them to drown and ferment for at least a year. By the end of the process, the corpses will have sunk to the bottom of the bottle, allowing the liquid to be drunk without swallowing the mice.

SWEET SAUSAGE Keen to create a mix of sweet and savory, Liam Bennett of Carmarthenshire, Wales, has invented the "dausage," a cross between two of his favorite foods—a donut and a sausage. It looks just like an ordinary sausage except that it is filled with either jam or custard.

The gourd was lowered into the water with a crane.

Aboard a Gourd

Cinderella feared her carriage would turn into a pumpkin, but Todd Sandstrum prefers it! On September 5, 2015, Sandstrum broke the record for the longest distance traveled in water by a pumpkin. He hollowed out the 817 lb. (371 kg) gourd, lowered it into Massachusetts's Taunton River by crane, and propelled the pumpkin 3.5 miles (5.6 km), surpassing the previous 3 mile (4.8 km) record.

BIG BERRY In 2015, Koji Nakao from Fukuoka, Japan, grew a giant strawberry that was 3.2 in. (8 cm) high, 4.7 in. (12 cm) long, and weighed 8.8 oz. (250 g), making it the heaviest strawberry grown anywhere in the world for over 30 years.

TASTY TREAT Dubai's Scoopi Café sells an ice cream that costs a whopping $817 (£519). The confection, called the "Black Diamond," contains Madagascar vanilla ice cream, Iranian saffron, Italian black truffles, and 23-karat edible gold.

FAMILY BUSINESS Allan Ganz of Peabody, Massachusetts, has been selling sweet treats from an ice cream truck for nearly 70 years. He started at age 10 in 1947 with his father Louis, who went on to sell ice cream until he was 86. Allan's season runs from April to October, during which he only takes one day off—his birthday in July. He drives around 70 miles (112 km) a day, and his truck has covered more than 150,000 miles (240,000 km).

TORPEDO JUICE US Navy servicemen in the Pacific Theater in World War II drank "Torpedo Juice," made from fruit juice and the 180-proof grain alcohol that fueled torpedoes.

FAVORITE PUB In 2015, Des Pirkhoffer drove 800 miles (1,287 km) from his home in Austria to Southampton, England, just to attend the reopening of his favorite pub. He drove for 15 hours before spending the night in a tent outside the Frog and Frigate, where he had worked for five years in the 1980s.

GIANT EGG Seventy chefs in Bariloche, Argentina, created a handmade Easter egg which stood 28 ft. (8.5 m) high, had a diameter of 19.7 ft. (6 m), and contained 17,637 lb. (8,000 kg) of chocolate. The egg was so big that the town's mayor had to crack it open with a pick-axe.

EXPENSIVE CHOCOLATE A single bar of To'ak chocolate costs over $250 (£159). Only fine grade cacao grown by 14 farmers on the coast of Ecuador is used to make the luxury chocolate. It takes 36 separate steps to create a bar, which is eaten using wooden tongs so that the chocolate's aroma can be fully appreciated.

FREE HUGS Tim Harris, owner of Tim's Place, a former restaurant in Albuquerque, New Mexico, gave free hugs to every customer—and gave out over 70,000 hugs from 2010 to 2015.

FROG BURGER In 2015, the Orbi Yokohama Museum Café in Japan sold deep-fried frog burgers made with lettuce, chili sauce, and an entire frog, whose legs protruded from the side of the bun.

SURGICAL SUSHI

A standard written exam simply will not do to secure a prestigious surgical internship at Japan's Kurashiki Central Hospital. Instead, students must complete three tasks requiring very steady hands and incredible focus—fold miniature cranes using 1.5 cm (0.59 in.) origami paper, reassemble an insect, and create tiny sushi! Using just one grain of rice, students must assemble the sushi with only a surgical knife and a pair of tweezers!

HUNGRY HIPPOS Former president Theodore Roosevelt supported a 1910 bill to import African hippos to the Louisiana bayou to satisfy the United States's demand for meat. The American Hippo Bill nearly passed, but fell one vote short.

RAT'S HEAD When Buckinghamshire, England's Terri Powis opened a bag of supermarket frozen spinach, she found a thumb-sized severed rat's head, perfectly preserved.

CREME CRAZY Emma Dalton from Worcestershire, England, can eat 20 Cadbury Creme Eggs® in 10 minutes—a total of 3,000 calories, which is more than her recommended intake for a whole day. She trains by eating 4.4 lb. (2 kg) of chocolate every day.

LOYAL CUSTOMER Jack King of Salt Lake City, Utah, ate in Benihana® restaurants 579 times in 2014 at a total cost of around $6,900 (£4,385). He visited his local branch at least once almost every day, and if he was out of town for the day he took the opportunity to eat at other branches.

$100 DONUT A $100 (£64) donut on sale at the Dolicious Donuts bakery in Kelowna, British Columbia, Canada, in 2015 was made of 24-karat edible gold flakes, edible sugar diamonds, aged chocolate balsamic vinegar, and infused with ice wine.

OLD FRIES A portion of McDonald's® fries survived for six years without going moldy—and looked so appetizing on the bar of a hotel in Reykjavik, Iceland, that a customer ate them. The fries were purchased by Hjörtur Smárason when all three Icelandic branches of McDonald's closed in 2009. They were then exhibited in a museum for three years before being displayed on the bar of his local hotel.

Sky Dining

Lifted by crane and strapped in, these diners are enjoying their meal nearly 100 ft. (30 m) above the Dianchi International Exhibition and Convention Center in Kunming, China. Taking the culinary experience to new heights is Belgian-based restaurant service "Dinner In The Sky." The company has suspended its 3-ton dinner tables in over 43 cities worldwide!

HOT ICE The Ice Cream Store in Rehoboth Beach, Delaware, sells Ghost Pepper ice cream, which is so fiery customers need to sign a waiver before eating it. The sauce from Ghost Pepper chilies is so potent that villagers in areas of India smear it onto fence posts to keep elephants away.

FUN FOOD Every morning since 2012, Anna Widya from Hong Kong, has used fried eggs, fruit, sausages, and vegetables to make artistic breakfasts and ensure her three oldest children get a healthy start to the day. She makes her colorful designs, which include smiling pigs, ice cream sundaes, and a portrait of Lady Gaga, using a cookie cutter and sushi wrap.

VINTAGE BURGER Casey Dean and Edward Nitz of Adelaide, Australia, have a McDonald's® burger that is more than 20 years old. They bought the Quarter Pounder with Cheese for a friend in 1995, but when he failed to show they decided to keep it—and it remains perfectly preserved in its original wrapping.

WURST CHALLENGE Competitors at the 2015 Wurst Challenge in Ypsilanti, Michigan, had to attempt to eat their way through 200 ft. (60 m) of sausage. While each of the 10 finalists was faced with a 20 ft. (6 m) long coiled bratwurst, the winner, William Henderson, managed to devour 3.26 lb. (1.5 kg) of meat.

TUMMY TRANSLATOR Domino's® Pizza has launched a "Tummy Translator" app, which employs technology that can apparently interpret your stomach gurgles to find out what type of pizza you want to order. Users select whether they are "peckish," "nibbly," "hungry," or "famished" before placing the cell phone against their stomach so that the app can translate their rumblings and suggest the ideal pizza for their state of hunger.

PIE CHART Martin Tarbuck from Wigan, Lancashire, England, spent two years traveling all over the UK and tasting 400 pies in his quest to find Britain's best pie. Sampling such baked delicacies as steak pie, chicken and mushroom pie, and Cornish pasties, he rated each one according to taste, texture, presentation, and price in his book, *Life of Pies*.

BIG CHEESE When Britain's Queen Victoria married in 1840, she was presented with a half-ton wheel of cheddar cheese. At more than 9 ft. (2.7 m) tall, a slice of the cheese was almost twice the height of the 4.9 ft. (1.5 m) tall monarch.

MASSIVE MUSHROOM

This 200-year-old giant wild Lingzhi mushroom was discovered in China and placed in the Museum of Ancient Carved Stone in January 2015. At its widest point, the Lingzhi measures over 3 ft. (107 cm) and weighs an unbelievable 16.4 lbs. (7.44 kg). Also known as "immortality mushrooms," Lingzhis have been used in traditional Chinese medicine for over 2,000 years!

hat better way to make vegetables interesting to kids than plant them in a toilet! In Heze City, China, an anonymous man grows vegetables in his rooftop garden in crop-yielding commodes—yes, he grows his greens in toilets. Taking his toilet theme even further, the gardener uses nutrient-rich human excrement, or nightsoil, as fertilizer—a method used in China for thousands of years.

TOILET TO TABLE

MOOSE CHEESE In Sweden, moose cheese costs $450 (£297) a pound—because it is so rare. Christer and Ulla Johansson are among the few farmers that produce it, and although they have 14 animals, only three can be milked, and then only from May to September. It takes up to two hours to milk a moose.

CHOCOLATE MAZE As a homage to the movie *Maze Runner*, food artist Prudence Staite from Gloucestershire, England, and YouTube vlogger Doug Armstrong from London, built an edible maze from 4,640 chocolate sticks. The maze, which used 22 lbs. (10 kg) of Belgian chocolate, took 56 hours to complete. It measured 4 ft. x 4 ft. (1.2 m x 1.2 m) and contained a whopping 143,840 calories—nearly two months' worth of normal calorie intake for a man.

GORILLA POOP In 2015, the café at Japan's Kyoto University sold a limited-edition cheesecake made with gorilla poop. Bacteria extracted from gorilla feces was cultivated in a laboratory and turned into yogurt for use in the cheesecake.

KETCHUP QUEEN Samantha Archer from London, England, goes through 1,217 fluid ounces (36 liters) of ketchup a year—more than 100 bottles. She has been crazy about ketchup for more than 25 years and consumes an average of two bottles per week, spending $300 (£191) a year to feed her habit. As well as having ketchup on every meal—even curry, salad, and cheese—she eats ketchup sandwiches and has spoonfuls straight from the bottle as snacks.

SPREADABLE BEER Italian chocolatier Pietro Napoleone and brewery Alta Quota collaborated to create Birra Spalmabile, a breakfast spread made of 40 percent beer.

PUMPKIN MONSTERS For Halloween, farmer Tony Dighera from Fillmore, California, grew 5,500 pumpkins in the shape of Frankenstein's monster. He made the molds himself for his Pumpkinsteins, which sell for over $75 (£50) apiece, and it took him four years to perfect the ghoulish gourds.

ZOMBIE DANCE A dish of recently killed cuttlefish can be temporarily brought back to life by pouring ordinary soy sauce over it. Although the animal is dead, the high levels of salt in the sauce trigger the cuttlefish's still-active muscle cells, causing them to spasm in such a way that the fish performs an eerie zombie dance. It is served in Japanese restaurants as the "dancing squid rice bowl."

VINTAGE ALE A 140-year-old bottle of Allsopp's Arctic Ale, brewed in Staffordshire, England, for an 1875 Arctic expedition led by Sir George Nares, sold in 2015 for $5,000 (£3,305).

UNDERWATER BAR The Clear Lounge® Bar on the Mexican island of Cozumel is located underwater in a 13,000 gallon (49,210 liter) aquarium tank. Guests wearing clear diving helmets that release mint- or citrus-scented oxygen can move around the tank playing board games, shooting bubble guns, or having their pictures taken in an underwater photo booth.

Cheese Bank

Ripley's ——— *Believe It or Not!*
www.ripleys.com/books
Food

Since 1953, Credito Emiliano, a bank in Reggio Emilia, Italy, has offered small business loans in return for a curious collateral—Parmigiano-Reggiano cheese. Credito Emiliano does not simply collect the pungent Parmesan as insurance—the financial institution goes as far as storing and aging the giant wheels themselves! The cheese is stored in climate-controlled vaults for the duration of the loan, saving farmers many operating costs and enhancing the cheese's value. The more Parmigiano-Reggiano ages, the more valuable it becomes, almost like it is accruing interest in the bank's vault. Credito Emiliano's cheese vault can store 440,000 of the 80 lb. (36 kg) wheels of cheese!

LAVA GRILL Geologists at Syracuse University in Syracuse, New York, teamed up with British chef Sam Bompas to cook 10 oz. (283 g) steaks over specially created artificial volcanic lava that reached a temperature of 2,700°F (1,480°C).

COOKBOOK LIBRARY Linda Deon of San Bernardino, California, has a collection of more than 4,400 cookbooks containing recipes from all around the world. She has been collecting them for over 25 years, and the oldest ones she has date back to the 1800s.

PANCAKE CARTOONS Brek Nebel of Marysville, Washington, makes cartoon pancakes for his young son. He forms the outlines on a cold griddle with a chopstick and chocolate batter, and then adds in different colored batters to illustrate the characters. Among the characters and animals he has whipped up are Super Mario®, a T-Rex, a shark, a bear, and Olaf from the movie *Frozen*.

DEAD LIZARD While Muhammad Hussain and his pregnant wife, Sanam, were cooking lunch at their home in Birmingham, England, they opened a can of tomatoes they'd recently bought from a supermarket—and found a dead baby lizard inside.

Bountiful Bun

This substantial steamed bun, measuring 8.4 ft. (2.6 m) wide and weighing 3,014 lbs. (1,367 kg), stole the show at a food festival in Qinhuangdao, China, on July 24, 2015—setting a world record! It took a team of 25 cooks 13 hours to make this monster, requiring 1,102 lbs. (500 kg) of stuffing and 1,911 lbs. (867 kg) of flour! The bun was filled with 7,000 smaller steamed buns that could easily be shared with festivalgoers.

FOOT SHAPE Japanese farmer Yukihiro Ikeuchi harvested a 3.3 lb. (1.5 kg) foot-shaped radish the size of a US men's size 14 shoe.

100-YEAR EGGS Robert Kerr of Biggar, Scotland, has a pair of real Easter eggs that are over a century old. They were made in 1912 by his mother, Margaret McMeekan, and her twin sister Henrietta, and have been passed down through the family for generations. Chocolate eggs were a rarity in those days, so poorer children used to hard-boil a hen's egg and stain it with tea for the same effect. The girls' names and the date are still visible on the unbroken shells.

GIANT TOMATO Dan MacCoy of Ely, Minnesota, grew an 8.4 lb. (3.8 kg) tomato in 2014—the heaviest grown anywhere in the world for nearly 30 years—even though its northerly location gave it a shorter growing season than most places.

FIZZY APPLE Swiss fruit nursery Lubera spent 10 years creating Paradis Sparkling, an apple that feels like a fizzy drink in your mouth.

LOBSTER BEER The Oxbow Brewing Company in Newcastle, Maine, has created a new beer flavored with lobsters and sea salt. The lobsters were placed in a mesh bag and suspended in a kettle of boiling wort, the liquid extracted during the brewing process. After being used in the beer, the lobsters were eaten.

JAVA JOKE

Located in Insadong, Seoul, South Korea, the Poop Café serves poop-shaped pastries and hot coffee in toilet-shaped mugs. The tasteful décor features stool-themed wall murals, squat toilets turned into mini gardens, and even plush coils of "poop."

FROG JUICE At her food stand in Lima, Peru, Maria Elena Cruz serves the juice of freshly killed water frogs as a supposed cure for asthma, bronchitis, and fatigue. After killing the frogs, she peels off their skin and drops them into a blender with carrots, Peruvian maca root, and honey.

GREAT JOB The Down Café in Istanbul, Turkey, employs only workers with Down syndrome. The café was founded by Saruhan Singen, who has a daughter with the condition and wanted to find a way of giving young people with Down syndrome self-confidence and independence.

DUAL PURPOSE Using careful grafting, UK horticultural firm Thompson & Morgan has created a TomTato, which produces tomatoes and potatoes on the same plant. It produces tomatoes above the ground and potatoes below, and is able to do so because tomatoes are members of the potato family.

PANTONE SMOOTHIES Hedvig A. Kushner, a Swedish art director living in New York, has mixed a series of smoothies to match the different shades of Pantone® swatches. She tweaks the ingredients of her smoothies so that they correspond exactly to the individual colors.

EDIBLE PLATES Belgian designers Hélène Hoyois and Thibaut Gilquin created a range of edible bowls and plates to save washing dishes after meals. The containers are made from a mix of potato starch, water, and oil.

HOT DIET Li Yongzhi eats 5.5 lbs. (2.5 kg) of chili peppers every day. He grows eight different varieties in the backyard of his home in Zhengzhou, China.

Bacon!

About 500 years ago the term "BACON" referred to all pork.

Texas "Top Shot" Dustin Ellermann COOKS BACON slices by wrapping them around the barrel of his assault rifle and FIRING 90 QUICK ROUNDS!

SHAKESPEARE'S *Henry IV, Part 1* and *The Merry Wives Of Windsor* both mention bacon!

Cured, Cooked, and Curated →

Actor Kevin Bacon has been the muse for many BACON INSPIRED works of art, from a life-size bust made of bacon bits by sculptor Mike LaHue to a portrait by Jason Mecier made of... bacon!

Some historians believe bacon made from YOUNG HOGS was a FAVORITE of the early Romans and Greeks.

When he landed in Britain in 55 BC, JULIUS CAESAR brought his own bacon with him!

The FRIED BACON FROG of North America is named for its croak, which sounds like it is saying "Fried Bacon!"

The state of New Hampshire offers SCRATCH-N-SNIFF lottery tickets that smell like bacon!

DONKEY DELICACY Pule cheese, the world's most expensive cheese—costing $1,000 (£661) a pound—does not come from cows or goats, but from endangered Balkan donkeys. All the milk comes from a single herd of 100 animals on a nature reserve in Serbia, and it takes 3.5 gallons (16 liters) of donkey milk to make a pound of cheese. Consequently, only 200 lbs. (90 kg) of Pule cheese are produced each year.

MILE-LONG PIZZA In Milan, Italy, 60 pizza-makers worked together for 18 hours to create a pizza that was almost 1 mile (1.6 km) long. It was made with 1.5 tons of mozzarella and 2 tons of tomato sauce, and weighed a total of nearly 5 tons.

ANT DISHES Voted the world's best restaurant in 2014, Noma, in Copenhagen, Denmark, has a waiting list of 60,000 people—even though one of chef René Redzepi's signature dishes is steak tartare covered in dead ants. On a two-month pop-up residency in Japan, Noma's menu also featured shrimp seasoned with live black ants.

POOP CURRY The Curry Shop Shimizu restaurant in Tokyo, Japan, serves a curry created to taste like poop. The brainchild of movie star/restaurant owner Ken Shimizu, the dish gets its bitter flavor by combining green tea with goya (bitter gourd), and its dung-like color from cocoa powder and water. For added effect, it is served in a toilet-shaped bowl.

WEIGHT LOSS Science teacher John Cisna of Colo-Nesco High School in Colo, Iowa, ate McDonald's® food for every meal for six months—a total of 540 meals—and lost a reported 60 lbs. (27 kg) in weight.

BACON SEAWEED Scientists at Oregon State University have developed a strain of seaweed that tastes like bacon. Using dulse, an edible seaweed that grows wild along the Pacific coast, they created a new form that looks like translucent red lettuce but has a savory flavor when fried.

LATE RETURN A glass was returned to a pub in Plymouth, Devon, England, 74 years after it was taken out. Cyril Smeeth had popped into the West Hoe in April 1941 to get his wife a shot of port before he went out on Home Guard duty, but that night the pub was flattened by German World War II bombers, meaning that he was unable to return the glass the next day as intended. Finally in 2015, his daughter, 77-year-old Inez Jordan, took the engraved glass back to the rebuilt inn.

TITANIC CRACKER

This Spillers and Bakers "Pilot" biscuit managed to survive the doomed 1912 voyage of the Titanic, in which over 1,500 people perished after the "unsinkable" ship struck an iceberg. This surviving snack was part of a ration kit stored on the ocean liner's lifeboats. James Fenwick, a passenger on board the SS Carpathia, which came to the Titanic's rescue, kept the cracker, saving it for years in a labeled photographic envelope. It was purchased at an auction at Henry Aldridge & Son, in Devizes, Wiltshire, for $22,968 (£16,081)—earning the title "most valuable biscuit in the world."

SPILLERS & BAKERS
PILOT

Zoo Feast

MENU

DECEMBER 25, 1870
99th DAY OF THE SIEGE

Appetizers:
Butter, Radishes, Stuffed Donkey Head, Sardines

Soups:
*Puréed Red Beans with Croutons
Elephant Stock*

Main Course:
*Fried Gudgeon—Roasted Camel, English Style
Kangaroo Stew
Bear Chops Roasted with Pepper Sauce*

Roasts:
*Haunch of Wolf, Venison Sauce
Cat Flanked with Rats
Watercress Salad
Antelope Terrine with Truffles
Porcini Mushrooms Bordeaux Style
Buttered Green Peas*

Sweet Course:
Rice Pudding with Preserves

Dessert:
Gruyère Cheese

WINES

1st Service
*Xeres
Latour Blanche 1861
Ch. Palmér 1864*

2nd Service
*Mouton Rothschild 1846
Romanée Conti 1858
Bellenger Chilled
Grand Porto 1827*

Coffee & Liquors

MENU

25 DÉCEMBRE 1870
99ᴹᴱ JOUR DU SIÈGE

Hors-d'Œuvre :
Beurre, Radis, Tête d'Âne Farcie, Sardines

Potages :
*Purée de Haricots rouges aux Croûtons
Consommé d'Éléphant*

Entrées :
*Goujons frits. - Le Chameau rôti à l'anglaise
Le Civet de Kangourou
Côtes d'Ours rôties sauce Poivrade*

Rôts :
*Cuissot de Loup, sauce Chevreuil
Le Chat flanqué de Rats
Salade de Cresson
La Terrine d'Antilope aux truffes
Cèpes à la Bordelaise
Petits-Pois au Beurre*

Entremets :
Gâteau de riz aux Confitures

Dessert :
Fromage de Gruyère

VINS

1ᵉʳ Service
*Xérès
Latour Blanche 1861
Ch. Palmer 1864*

2ᵐᵉ Service
*Mouton Rothschild 1846
Romanée Conti 1858
Bellenger frappé
Grand Porto 1827*

CAFÉ & LIQUEURS

In 1870, during the Franco Prussian War, Paris was entirely surrounded by ene forces. Their goal: to starve the French into submission Parisians eventually resorte to eating cats, dogs, rodent and, before the war was over, about 70,000 horses. In desperation, a zoo in northern Paris called the Jardin d'Acclimatation came to a disconcerting decision- its animals were sold to the kitchen of Chef Alexandre Etienne Choron's restauran Voisin. Choron, the celebrit chef of his time, then treate his patrons to a wild six-course Christmas dinner!

Mystery Machine

In Seattle, Washington's Capitol Hill neighborhood, at the corner of East John Street and 10th Avenue East sits a secret—a vintage soda machine with all six buttons labeled "mystery." The surprise sugary pop is always stocked, but for decades, no one has been able to figure out who is behind this cola conspiracy!

TASTY SOAP While she was pregnant, Jess Gayford from Bristol, England, developed a craving for eating soap. She began by licking a bar of soap, but enjoyed the taste so much she started regularly snacking on bottles of liquid soap.

BEER PALACE The Raleigh Beer Garden in Raleigh, North Carolina, has 366 individual beers on tap—one for every day of the year, even in a leap year.

TEA TASTER Sebastian Michaelis, a master tea blender for the British company Tetley®, has had his taste buds insured for $1.4 million (£1 million). Tetley's team of master blenders taste 40,000 cups of tea every week.

SHARK EYEBALL Keku'l'apoiwa II, the mother of Hawaii's 18th-century King Kamehameha, ate the eyeball of a tiger shark during her pregnancy to ensure that her son grew up to be a powerful leader.

EXPLODING HERRING *Surströmming*— fermented Baltic herring—is a delicacy in northern Sweden, but smells so foul that it is banned from apartment blocks in Stockholm and on many airlines. They also sometimes explode, and if that happens in a supermarket, the entire store usually has to be evacuated. In 2014, a fire at a Swedish warehouse containing 1,000 cans of surströmming caused explosions that lasted for six hours, launching cans all over the surrounding area.

TACO LINE Chefs in Guadalajara, Mexico, created a line of tacos that measured 1.9 miles (3 km) from end to end. More than 130 people spent six hours building the taco line, which used 2,600 lbs. (1,180 kg) of pork and 2,400 lbs. (1,090 kg) of tortillas.

FORTUNE COOKIE Daria Artem of Los Angeles, California, made a fortune cookie that was larger than a person's head. The giant cookie was 11 in. (27.5 cm) wide, 7 in. (17.5 cm) high, 10 in. (25 cm) deep and weighed nearly 2 lbs. (0.9 kg).

UNDERGROUND FARM An underground farm, fitted with lighting and irrigation systems, grows a wide range of vegetables in an abandoned World War II bunker hundreds of feet below the streets of London, England.

Carved Cuisine

Dig into this feast and you'll end up with a few chipped teeth! These dishes are hand carved out of jade by Zhang Shuzhang and his wife Zhang Yuchun, who spent four and a half years making 120 courses, from *dim sum* dumplings to a pig's head! On display in Hangzhou, China, on September 27, 2015, the stones used to set this table are estimated to be worth over $3 million (£2.1 million)!

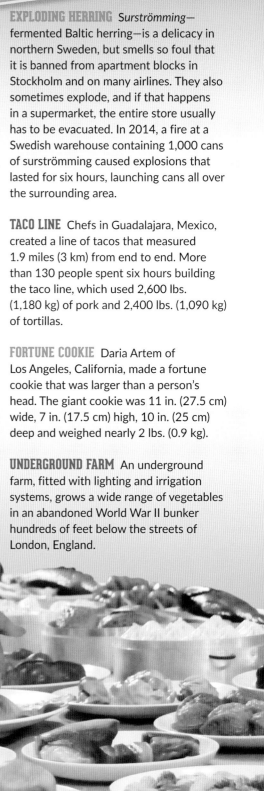

10 Beyond Belief

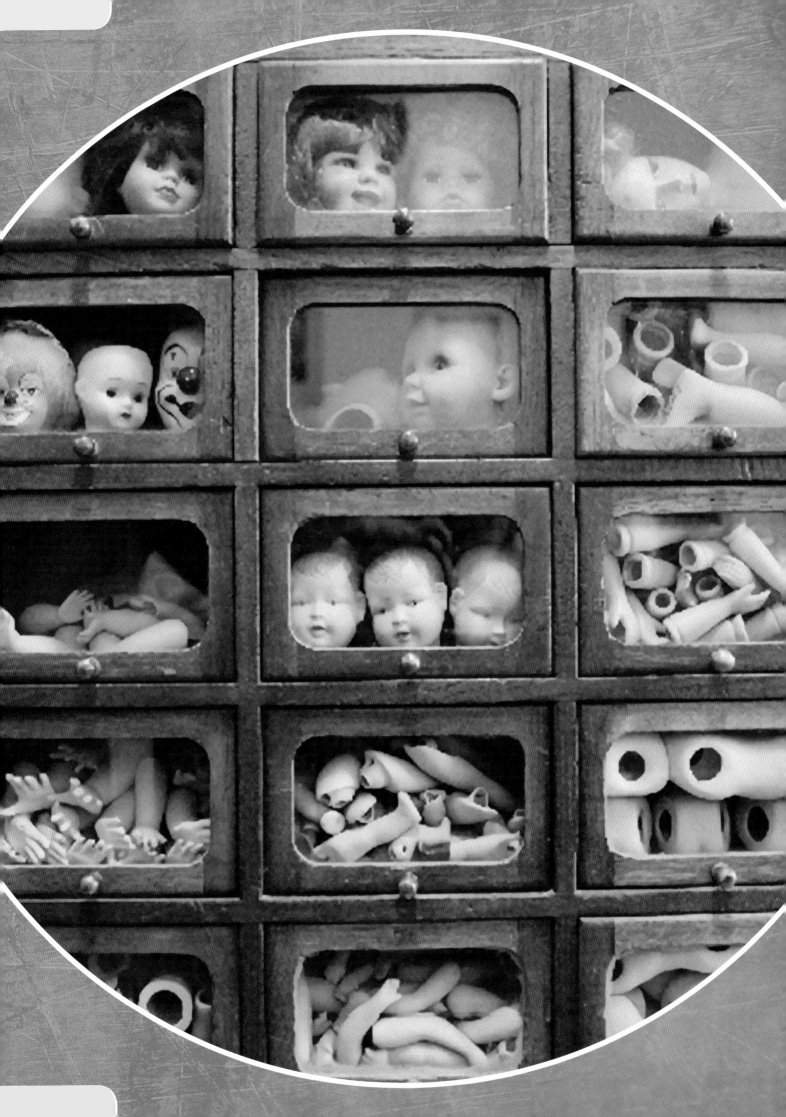

HOT SWEAT James McElvar, a 19-year-old singer with the Scottish band Rewind, was so determined to avoid paying an excess baggage fee on a flight from London to Glasgow that he put on 11 extra layers of clothing and ended up fainting at 37,000 ft. (11,278 m) because his body had overheated. Even though it was the height of summer, he boarded the plane wearing six T-shirts, four sweaters, and two jackets.

BREAK-UP SERVICE For people who hate the uncomfortable task of ending a relationship, Kristy Mazins from Melbourne, Australia, will do it for them. She runs a service called "Sorry It's Over" where, for a small fee, she will send an apologetic message via text, email, letter, or phone call.

Chicken Church

It's not a chicken, and it's not a church. In 1989, Daniel Alamsjah of Jakarta, Indonesia, had a vision of a dove-shaped, nondenominational house of prayer on a hill. Soon, Alamsjah and 30 locals began construction on this unique piece of architecture in the dense forests of Central Java. Although the red-beaked building was never completed—the building has been abandoned since 2000—it still ruffles the tail feathers of fascinated tourists!

On the 15th day of the Chinese New Year, Singkawang, Indonesia, celebrates Cap Go Meh—and the city comes alive! What makes this Chinese New Year celebration so special is the parade of the Tatung, a traditional ritual of rejecting evil spirits to prevent misfortune for the rest of the year. During the Tatung, participants enter a trancelike state and perform such shocking stunts as slicing their tongues, stepping on swords, and piercing wire through their cheeks.

CAP GO MEH

WORK SHY Shri A. K. Verma, an executive engineer at India's Central Public Works Department, was finally fired from his job in 2014 despite not having shown up for work since 1990. India's labor laws make it difficult to dismiss workers for any reason other than criminal misconduct.

MISTAKEN IDENTITY A drunk Frenchman tried to give the kiss of life to an inflatable dinghy he had mistaken for a drowning person. He summoned the emergency services to the waterfront in Vannes, Brittany, but when they arrived they found him performing CPR on a boat.

ROBOT FUNERALS Super-intelligent Aibo robotic dogs are so loved in Japan that owners bury them and hold funeral services for them when they finally break down. About 150,000 Aibos—made by Sony® and selling at $2,000 (£1,282) apiece—were sold in Japan between 1999 and 2006, but it is now difficult to get spare parts.

GROOM DUMPED When Jugal Kishore suffered an epileptic seizure on the morning of his wedding day and was rushed to a hospital, his prospective bride, Indira, decided that rather than miss out on the Hindu ceremony in Rampur, India, she would marry her sister's brother-in-law, Harpal Singh. The switch sparked a brawl and several guests were arrested.

SKELETON PARTY A man snorkeling in the Colorado River in Cienega Springs, Arizona, found two fake skeletons wearing sunglasses and sitting in lawn chairs about 40 ft. (12 m) underwater. The chairs had been tied to large rocks to keep them in place.

DOZY BURGLAR After breaking into a house in Pontypool, South Wales, Matthew Waters ate a whole tub of ice cream from the freezer and then fell asleep in the bedroom, allowing the returning homeowner to provide police with a detailed description.

SELF-SERVICE SHIPPING After competing in Britain in the late summer of 1964, javelin thrower Reg Spiers was unable to afford plane fare back to his native Australia—so he shipped himself home in a wooden crate. With the help of UK javelin thrower John McSorley, Spiers built a box measuring 5 ft. x 3 ft. x 2.5 ft. (1.5 m x 0.9 m x 0.75 m), climbed inside with a couple of cans of peaches and some fruit juice for the 13,000 mile (20,900 km) flight, and was nailed in. McSorley drove him to Heathrow Airport, wrote "Cash on Delivery" on the outside of the box, and loaded it onto a plane bound for Perth via India. Three days later, Spiers landed in Australia, cut himself free under cover of darkness, and hitchhiked home to Adelaide, having traveled halfway around the world for free.

SHOT COMPUTER Lucas Hinch of Colorado Springs, Colorado, became so frustrated with his computer that he took it outside into an alley and shot it eight times—and was then given a citation for discharging a weapon within city limits.

CAMP CASSADAGA

The Cassadaga Spiritualist Camp stems from very mysterious beginnings. In the late 1800s, 27-year-old medium George P. Colby was instructed by his spirit guide, a Native American named Seneca, to bring Spiritualism to Florida. Seneca instructed Colby to search for an area with "rolling hills and linked lakes," which he did in what is now known as Cassadaga.

Est. 1894

Stepping into the quiet town of Cassadaga, Florida, feels both peaceful and alarming. Amidst the unusual architecture and ominous Spanish moss dangling from the treetops, the residents of Cassadaga communicate with the dearly departed.

Camp Cassadaga, as it was once known, is populated by mediums. They claim to use different senses or "clairs" to communicate with spirits. The mediums use hearing (clairaudience), seeing (clairvoyance), knowing (claircognizance), and feeling (clairsentience) to channel messages from spirits—bridging the spiritual and physical world.

THE CASSADAGA SPIRITUALIST PSYCHIC THERAPY CENTER

WALK-INS ARE WELCOME

WELCOME TO CASSADAGA CERTIFIED PSYCHIC MEDIUMS ON DUTY

We Offer Spiritual, Psychic, Tarot Card, Crystal Ball & Palm Readings

OFFICE

WE NOW DO ASTROLOGY CHARTS

KATHY IS HERE

Greetings from CAMP CASSADAGA FLORIDA

© CURT TEICH & CO., INC.

Devil's Chair

Just up the road from Cassadaga is George Colby's final resting place in Lake Helen Cemetery, but Colby isn't the main attraction. According to the legend of the Devil's Chair, shown here, if you sit on this brick throne at midnight, the Devil himself will talk to you. However, medium and long-time Cassadaga resident, Rev. Louis Gates, set the record straight: "We made that story up as kids," he said. In reality, the chair was built by a grieving man who had unexpectedly lost his wife. He would walk from Cassadaga to visit her grave each day and simply wanted a place to sit.

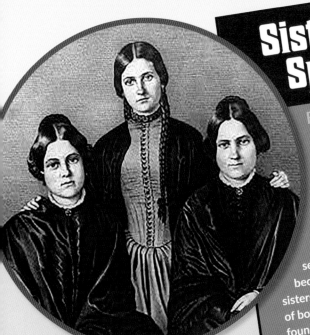

Sisters of Spiritualism

Believe it or not, the science, philosophy, and religion of Spiritualism can be accredited to three young girls—Leah, Maggie, and Kate Fox. In 1848, in the bedroom of their Hydesville, New York, home, these sisters allegedly communicated with spirits through sequences of raps and taps. Quickly becoming a national sensation, the Fox sisters went on tour, drawing large crowds of both believers and skeptics who never found any evidence of trickery.

In the 1920s, magicians, including Harry Houdini, began to prove they could replicate what mediums were doing. Despite his disbelief, after the death of his mother, Houdini sought the help of a medium.

ENCOUNTER THE SPIRIT
GUIDED Walking TOURS
Week Days & Saturdays

FEEL the ENERGY of
CASSADAGA!

SATURDAY NIGHT TOUR
with ORB PHOTOGRAPHY

Ticket Sales in Book Store

Andrew Jackson Davis Building
Certified

MEDIUMS
& HEALERS

BOOKS·GIFTS

Information
REST ROOMS

Do Spirits Return?

HOUDINI
SAYS NO - AND PROVES IT
3 SHOWS IN ONE
MAGIC-ILLUSIONS-ESCAPES = FRAUD MEDIUMS EXPOSED
LYCEUM THEATRE
PATERSON
THURS · FRI · SAT · SEPT 2
MATINEE

Summoning Spirit

Are humans merely susceptible to suggestion, or can we truly communicate with the dead? Skeptics have tried to debunk séances by binding mediums with ropes, gagging them, and even sealing them in "spirit cabinets" to see if phenomena would occur even if they were restrained. Many believe these events can be explained by manipulation, but in Cassadaga they are a truly spiritual experience. Rev. Louis Gates has experienced many forms of phenomena during his séances at the Colby Memorial Temple, including "apports"—objects appearing to materialize and fall from the ceiling!

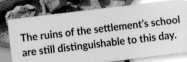
The ruins of the settlement's school are still distinguishable to this day.

Drowned Town Emerges

The largest man-made reservoir in the United States recently lost more than half of its water, revealing some of the Wild West's best-kept secrets. Nevada's Lake Mead has a high water line at 1,229 ft. (375 m) above sea level, but drought conditions in 2015 drained much of the lake, and an eerie 19th-century ghost town emerged.

Founded in 1865, the Mormon settlement of St. Thomas was situated in what would later become Lake Mead. When construction of the Hoover Dam was completed in 1936, the area around the town began to fill with water, gradually displacing the residents. In June 1938, St. Thomas's last resident rowed away from his home. The once thriving town was sunken and soon forgotten. Now, with Lake Mead at its lowest point in over 40 years, St. Thomas is emerging from its watery grave. The ghost town is expected to remain exposed for at least the next two years—but Lake Mead could eventually refill, submerging St. Thomas once again.

Now surrounded by clamshells, this was once St. Thomas's ice cream parlor!

MANGO MISSILE Marleny Olivo was rewarded with a new home after hitting Venezuelan president Nicolas Maduro on the head with a mango. Desperate for a house, she threw the fruit at him with the message, "If you can, call me," along with her name and phone number. In response, he promised to find her an apartment and eat the mango.

FREAK ACCIDENT Larry McElroy of Lee County, Georgia, accidentally shot his mother-in-law, Carol Johnson, after his bullet bounced off an armadillo. The 9 mm ammo killed the armadillo, then hit a fence, traveled 300 ft. (90 m) to fly through the back door of Mrs. Johnson's mobile home and passed through the reclining chair she was lying in, hitting her in the back. Johnson was not badly injured.

SNAKE OBSESSION Sandeep Patel, 27, tried to marry a cobra at Badwapur, India, in 2015 because he was convinced that the venomous reptile had been a beautiful woman in a previous life. Patel, who has apparently exhibited snake-like behavior since childhood, flickers his tongue like a snake and claims that he can even turn into a snake at night by going into a deep trance.

IMPERSONATED GIRLFRIEND Twenty-year-old Ayan Zhademov put on a long black wig, makeup, and his girlfriend's clothes and tried to take an important exam on her behalf in Zhetisai, Kazakhstan. However, he was caught by the examiners when he attempted to speak in a high voice.

LOOK-ALIKE WANTED Renato Tronco Gomez, a politician in Veracruz, Mexico, launched a Facebook competition to find a body double who can attend official events in his place when he is busy. As well as a $2,700 (£1,730) prize, Gomez promised to give the successful applicant training in how to speak and act like him.

GRAVEYARD SHIFT Fire chiefs in Pingliang City, China, decided to toughen up 20 of their firefighters by making them spend the night in a local cemetery.

POOP ROLL In an attempt to avoid being arrested for public drunkenness by police officers in Wilkes-Barre, Pennsylvania, a 45-year-old man fell to the ground and deliberately rolled around in dog poop. His plan failed, and he was taken into custody anyway.

SHARK ATTACK In the United Kingdom, soccer fan Kenneth Meech was fined $140 (£100) in compensation in 2015 for assaulting a steward at an English Conference game at Barnet with an inflatable shark.

WANTED ACTOR In July 2015, US agents arrested a fugitive they had been seeking for several months after they spotted his picture in a newspaper story about a low-budget horror movie in which he was appearing. Bank robber-turned-actor Jason Strange was picked up in Olympia, Washington, after marshals tracked him from the filming location of *Marla Mae*. He had been sentenced to 117 months in prison in 2006, and a warrant for his arrest was issued in 2014 after he walked away from a halfway house near Spokane.

PAPER CRAVING Jade Sylvester of Lincolnshire, England, eats an entire roll of toilet paper every day. Her odd craving started when she was pregnant with her youngest son Jaxon in 2013, causing her to keep two rolls in the toilet at all times—one for normal use and one for eating. She says she likes the texture of the paper rather than the taste.

Doll Hospital

Nestled in Lisbon's Praça da Figueira is the world's oldest doll hospital, the Hospital de Bonecas, founded in 1830. Here, seamstresses and craftsmen turn into nurses and surgeons, repairing childhood treasures from teddy bears to priceless porcelain dolls. Shelves are lined with spare arms, legs, torsos, heads, and blinking eyes—ready for any incoming patient.

GIGANTIC FOOT

Suffering from a condition known as local gigantism, Liu Huichang, a 21-year-old man from China, recently underwent surgery to reduce the size of his massive right foot—which measured an astonishing 17 in. (43 cm) long and 5 in. (14 cm) thick—the equivalent of a US size 31 shoe (UK size 29). Liu decided to undergo surgery not only for himself but also for his grandmother—who had been stitching his shoes by hand for the past 16 years.

DIRTY BEARDS A study by microbiologists in New Mexico showed that because facial hair can collect such large amounts of rancid bacteria, some beards contain more poop than a toilet.

MEMORY LOSS After being involved in a car crash in 2010, 36-year-old Candace Emptage from County Durham, England, lay in a coma for six weeks—and when she awoke, she was convinced she was still 22 and that it was 1996. When she opened her eyes, she mistook an iPhone® for a space-age gadget, thought Michael Jackson was still alive, and had forgotten giving birth to her daughter Maddie.

GUM MAGGOTS When 10-year-old Ana Cardoso complained of a tingling sensation in her gums and of things "moving around," she was taken to a clinic in Brasilia, Brazil, where the dentist discovered 15 maggots living inside her mouth. The fly larvae had wormed their way into her mouth and had probably fed on her ingested food—a condition called oral myiasis.

FOUND GOLD After a 63-year-old businessman was taken to a hospital in Delhi, India, complaining of vomiting and constipation, surgeons found 12 small gold bars—weighing a total of 14 oz. (400 g)—in his stomach.

PAW SCENT Japanese beauty product company Felissimo has designed a beauty cream that leaves users' hands smelling like cats' paws, an odor that is considered soothing to pet owners.

HUGE TUMOR Kapleshwar Lal Das, 66, from Delhi, India, had a five-hour operation to remove an 11 lb. (5 kg) tumor on his kidney. The growth was the size of a watermelon and weighed more than five bags of sugar.

HOPELESS ROBBER In 2015, would-be robber Rory Seager fled empty-handed from an off-track betting shop in Essex, England, after failing to convince the cashier that the can of sardines in tomato sauce that he was carrying was really a bomb.

Belly Button Challenge

A Chinese website where people—including celebrities—post selfies of their attempts at touching their belly buttons by reaching around their backs received more than 130 million hits on Weibo, a Chinese social media site, within 24 hours. If a person successfully completes the "belly button challenge," it is believed that he or she has a good figure. Experts, however, say that the challenge does not necessarily point to a super-fit body, but just shows some people have long arms or are very flexible.

VICTORIAN THROWBACK

Sarah Chrisman and her husband Gabriel reside in Port Townsend, Washington, in a home built in 1888—where it feels as if time has stood still. The couple are commited to living as if they were in the Victorian era. It all began by collecting clothing from the period, but they have now taken it further than simply dressing the part. While they admit that ignoring modern conveniences is difficult, the Chrismans try to limit themselves to 19th-century technologies. They pedal around town on high-wheel bicycles, bathe with Castile soap created by a company started in 1839, and brush their teeth with toothbrushes made of boar bristles. When a modern appliance such as their refrigerator breaks down, they replace it with something more typical of the time, like an icebox. Sarah and Gabriel are living history.

Ripley's—— Asks ?

Ripley's asked these time-travellers to tell us more.

Q *Gabriel, where did your commitment to the Victorian era come from?*

A *Sarah has loved the aesthetic of the Victorian era for as long as she can remember. I studied history and library science in college, and became fascinated by the technology and everyday details of the late 19th century. We both wondered what errors there were in the "modern" view of the Victorians, and began acquiring everyday items from the time, which we could use and learn from.*

Q *How do you approach the Internet? It's unavoidable!*

A *Our rule of thumb is that when something Victorian still exists and we can use it, we do. Sometimes, though, a whole infrastructure is gone. For example, if we were doing this interview in the 1890s, we might be using the telegraph. We must now use the closest modern equivalent, and that's the Internet.*

Q *What is your diet like?*

A *Sarah bakes all of our bread, using a sourdough starter that we keep constantly bubbling in one corner of our kitchen. To keep the starter going we have to feed it every day—it's almost like a pet! Because homemade bread goes stale quickly, a good portion of our diet involves what we think of as "the life-cycle of Victorian foods." We use it in recipes from antique cookbooks to create dishes like Welsh rarebit, which is stale bread baked in cheese sauce. We also eat a lot of seasonal foods, scavenging for wild berries in the summer and nettles in the spring.*

Q *What are your pastimes, Sarah?*

A *We explore the natural world in many of the same ways the Victorians did. For example, we enjoy hiking, fossil hunting, and visiting public arboretums and botanical gardens. We also love riding together. Gabriel has three high-wheel bicycles, and I have a high-wheel tricycle—it's a copy of a Lady's Rudge Rotary Roadster tricycle from around 1885 that weighs about 75 lbs. (34 kg)!*

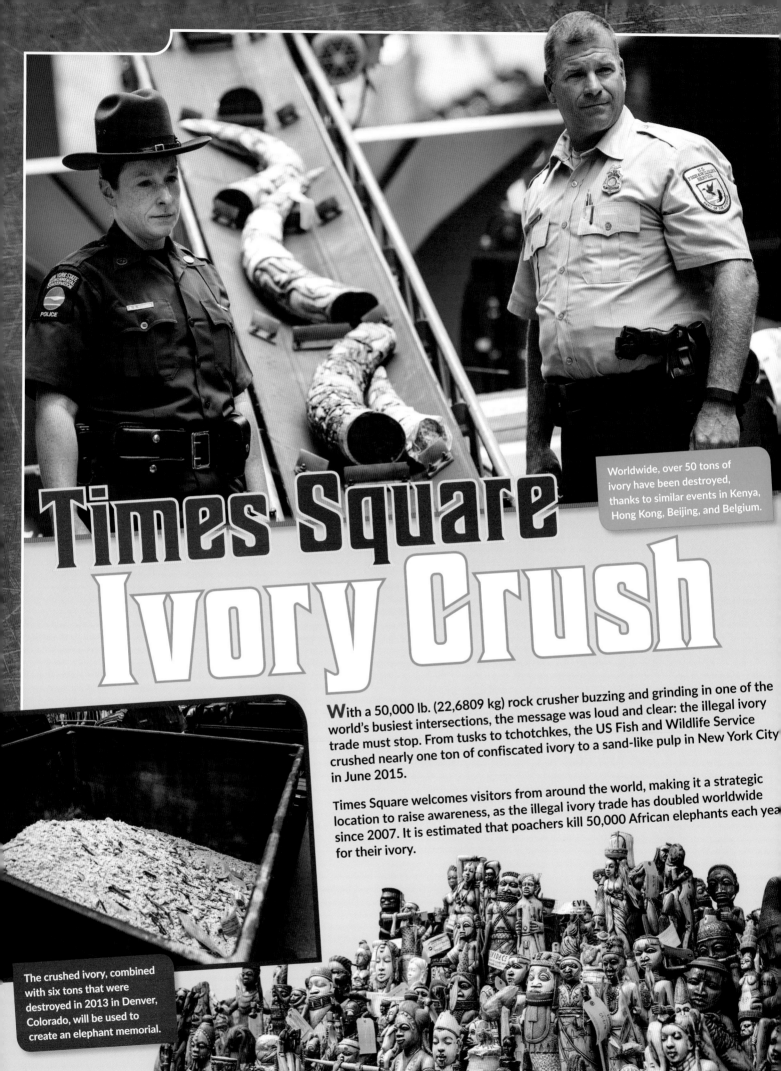

Times Square Ivory Crush

Worldwide, over 50 tons of ivory have been destroyed, thanks to similar events in Kenya, Hong Kong, Beijing, and Belgium.

With a 50,000 lb. (22,6809 kg) rock crusher buzzing and grinding in one of the world's busiest intersections, the message was loud and clear: the illegal ivory trade must stop. From tusks to tchotchkes, the US Fish and Wildlife Service crushed nearly one ton of confiscated ivory to a sand-like pulp in New York City in June 2015.

Times Square welcomes visitors from around the world, making it a strategic location to raise awareness, as the illegal ivory trade has doubled worldwide since 2007. It is estimated that poachers kill 50,000 African elephants each yea for their ivory.

The crushed ivory, combined with six tons that were destroyed in 2013 in Denver, Colorado, will be used to create an elephant memorial.

Beyond Belief

GREAT SURVIVOR 101-year-old Funchu Tamang was pulled out alive from the rubble of his house after surviving for seven days following the devastating earthquake that hit Nepal in April 2015. He had just minor injuries to his hand and ankle.

MISSING RING More than 70 years after RAF Flight Sgt. John Thompson of Derbyshire, England, went missing in action on a secret mission during World War II, his wedding ring was returned to his 92-year-old sister, Dorothy Webster. The pilot's inscribed ring had been discovered in Albania by a local man whose family eventually managed to trace it to the rightful owner.

LUCKY TEETH Hoping to bring good luck to his favorite English soccer team, Walsall FC, Jason Bailey takes his late father's false teeth to every home match. He keeps them in his pocket wrapped in an old handkerchief, and before important games he even kisses the teeth for extra good fortune.

SLEEP EATER Kate Archibald, a student at the University of Aberdeen in Scotland, once ate an entire wheel of Cheddar cheese in her sleep. She wondered why she kept putting on weight until she was diagnosed with Nocturnal Eating Disorder, a condition where her body craves food in the middle of the night. She kept getting out of bed and sleepwalking into the kitchen to raid the fridge.

JAIL BAIT Lamont Cathey, a prisoner at Cook County Jail in Illinois, was taken to the hospital 24 times in 16 months for eating parts of his cell. He swallowed screws, pins, and leather straps from sections of his bed, a prison camera, and medical equipment, racking up more than $1 million (£1,560,440) in medical bills.

FRENCH VACATION Li Jinyuan, the billionaire CEO of the Chinese conglomerate Tiens, celebrated the company's 20th birthday by giving 6,400 of his best salespeople a vacation in France. Some 4,700 hotel rooms and 146 buses were booked for the lucky workers, with the trip costing around $20 million (£13 million).

FAKE TIGER An alarmed passerby called 911 to report seeing a Bengal tiger on top of a vehicle at Lacamas Lake, Washington, but when police officers investigated they found it was nothing more dangerous than a stuffed toy. Connor Zuvich had found the tiger among trash bags at the lake and had decided to strap it to the roof of his SUV.

BIRTHDAY TRADITION Arizona brothers Ron and Jeff Methier have sent each other the same Peanuts™ birthday card back and forth every year since 1973. Each year, they just write their name on the card—except in 1982 and 2010, when Ron sent the card but forgot to sign it.

SOLO SURFER Dodging ferries, whirlpools, and dangerous rocks, Jono Dunnett from Essex, England, windsurfed solo 2,200 miles (3,520 km) around the entire coast of Great Britain on a three-month voyage in 2015.

CARING FRIENDS Ever since her teenage son Zhang Kai died of leukemia in 2004, Sheng Ru-zhi of Hefei, China, has been looked after by seven of his former high school classmates. Each one treats her as if she were his mother, regularly visiting, helping her with shopping and chores, and even coming to her aid during a 2008 earthquake—even though some are now married with families of their own.

MALE DISGUISE Since losing her husband when she was 21 and pregnant, Sisa Abu Daooh of Luxor, Egypt, has spent over 40 years disguised as a man so that she could earn enough money to support her daughter and grandchildren. She worked as a laborer for years, and now works as a shoe polisher—all the time dressed as a man, because her local culture does not welcome women in the workplace.

CHOCOLATE COSTUMES Twelve friends went on a Christmas pub crawl in Dublin, Ireland, dressed as chocolate bars from a Cadbury® assortment box. Two members of the group had traveled all the way from Australia, and one had flown in from Canada. All of the handmade costumes were the idea of Aaron Johnston, who runs a fitness company and was dressed as a Crunchie bar.

MISHEARD ORDER When a baker in Gangi, Sicily, misheard an order, a nine-year-old girl was given a birthday cake, which instead of featuring a bright pink pony with a blue mane, was adorned with a dark-haired 1960s male singer in a sparkly white jacket. The girl's parents had ordered a My Little Pony® cake, but the pastry shop thought they wanted it decorated with Little Tony, an Italian performer who modeled himself after Elvis Presley.

Paracas Skulls

This unusually shaped skull was one of more than 300 found in a mass grave discovered in 1928 by archaeologist Julio Tello in Paracas, Peru—some of the largest elongated skulls ever found. Scientists have long believed that this irregularity was a result of cranial deformation, a practice of binding the head for an extended period of time to form the unusual shape. However, a privately funded DNA analysis of a 3,000-year-old skull found in the region allegedly suggests it may have been genetically deformed instead.

BACON CHURCH Founded in Las Vegas, Nevada, by retired pilot John Whiteside, the United Church of Bacon has over 10,000 members around the world and offers legal weddings, baptisms, and funerals. Anyone wishing to join the church must love the smell of bacon.

WRONG HEARSE Mourners at the funeral of Mair Howard in Pembrokeshire, Wales, delayed her burial by following the wrong hearse for 9 miles (14 km). After leaving the church service, three cars containing Mrs. Howard's nephews and pallbearers were separated from the rest of the convoy and ended up following another hearse to a different cemetery. They only realized their mistake when other family members waiting at the graveside in the rain called to ask where they were.

TRANSPLANT TRAGEDY In 1996, Sonny Graham received a new heart from a donor, Terry Cottle, who had died of a self-inflicted gunshot wound to the head. Graham suddenly developed a craving for beer and hot dogs (Cottle's favorite foods) and even went on to marry Cottle's widow before in 2008 he, too, fatally shot himself in the head at his home in Vidalia, Georgia.

MANNEQUIN BRIDES Kate Holder of Devon, England, posed in a wedding dress in a bridal shop window in Cornwall for 58.5 hours—nearly two and a half days—to win $7,133 (£5,000) toward the cost of her wedding. She and a rival bride, Tara Attis, were allowed to take toilet breaks every four hours but had to sleep in the window.

NO VOTES Farmer Randy Richardson of McIntire, Iowa, was elected to his local school board in 2015 despite failing to earn any votes, not even his own. No votes were cast in the election and McIntire, who was running unopposed, was so busy at work he did not find time to vote for himself.

MOVIE EDUCATION For 14 years, the seven siblings in the Angulo family were hardly ever allowed to leave their 16th-floor apartment on Manhattan's Lower East Side and instead learned about the world by watching and memorizing over 2,000 movies from their father Oscar's collection. Brothers Bhagavan, Govinda, Narayana, Mukunda, Krisna, and Jagadesh, and their sister, Visnu, were unable to venture outside because Oscar kept the only key to the front door, which was always locked because he was afraid that the city would "contaminate" his children.

SURF BREAK A prisoner escaped from a Norwegian island jail on a surfboard. He fled the Bastoy low-security prison by using a plastic shovel to paddle the surfboard 1.8 miles (3 km) to the mainland.

LORD SHIVA

Locals and visitors alike have traveled far and wide to Kolathur village in Tamil Nadu, India, seeking good luck and the chance to worship the Hindu god Shiva face to face, or at least an incarnation of Shiva and his most famous attribute—the third eye. This extra-eyed calf has been hailed as a blessing by Hindus who believe animals, especially cows, are sacred and symbolize the vehicle of gods.

Ripley's — **Believe It or Not!**
www.ripleys.com/books
Beyond Belief

Panjat Pinang is a unique celebration of Indonesia's Independence Day and one of the oldest traditions in the country. Every August 17th, men in teams of four must scale greased betel nut trees, standing on and climbing over their teammates in order to stay balanced. Atop the slippery trees are prizes including bicycles, buckets, food, and clothing. Panjat Pinang was introduced to the country by Dutch colonists as a form of entertainment.

Pole Party

FEARS JUSTIFIED Bradley and Penny Mason bought an unoccupied neighboring house in Meyersdale, Pennsylvania, with the intention of demolishing it because they feared it was a fire hazard—and while they were at the county courthouse signing the deed, the house caught fire.

SHORT REIGN Louis XIX was King of France for just 20 minutes. He succeeded his father, Charles X, on August 2, 1830, but quickly abdicated in favor of his nephew, Henri V, who himself only ruled for seven days.

LIFE SENTENCE After Josten Bundy of Tyler, Texas, pleaded guilty to assaulting his girlfriend Elizabeth Jaynes' ex-boyfriend, Judge Randall Rogers spared him a jail sentence—on condition that he married Jaynes within 30 days.

TANDEM BRIDE Cyclists Anna Reffell and Lee Atkinson of Devon, England, got married in the middle of a 1,400 mile (2,240 km) ride from Scotland to Cornwall. The bride wore a white wedding gown and the groom a suit as they rode 11 miles (18 km) to the ceremony on a tandem bicycle.

FLYING METAL On April 13, 2015, an underground electrical fire caused an explosion that sent a manhole cover flying nearly 300 ft. (90 m) into the air above a street in Buffalo, New York.

FATEFUL SNACK Shane Lindsey was arrested 20 minutes after robbing a bank in New Kensington, Pennsylvania, when he stopped to eat chicken and biscuits at a restaurant just two blocks away.

ROYAL PORTRAITS Since her reign began in 1952, Queen Elizabeth II has had 237 streets named after her and has posed for 129 official portraits.

COMPUTER WITCH To safeguard their computers from mysterious viruses and hackers, some Silicon Valley tech companies employ the services of Californian Wiccan witch Rev. Joey Talley. She has become the go-to person for computer programmers, software designers, and engineers facing problems that they feel might somehow be supernatural. She tackles many of the glitches with lucky charms, but in extreme cases she casts a protection spell over the entire company.

INDECENT PROPOSAL Galveston, Texas, police officer Gregory Parris arranged for a patrol car to turn on the sirens and pull over a vehicle driven by his girlfriend, Sara Wolff, for made-up misdemeanors— just so that he could propose to her.

Rainbow Opal

Millions of years ago when this opal formed, dinosaurs roamed the Earth—and now it is worth a million dollars! The "Virgin Rainbow" is regarded as one of the finest opals of its kind, weighs 72 carats, is about the size of a thumb, and refracts a rich palette of colors. Discovered by Australian opal miner John Dunstan in a mineshaft in Coober Pedy, a town responsible for 90 percent of the world's opal supply, the "Virgin Rainbow" is now displayed at the South Australian Museum.

CASE CRACKED After a security guard named Gu was caught smuggling two suitcases of goods out of a food factory in Pinghu City, China, where he worked, police officers raided his home and found more than 1,000 eggs in his fridge, each carefully labeled with a use-by date. Admitting to the theft, Gu explained that he "really liked eggs."

FREE WIFE When Wina Lia, a 40-year-old widow and beauty salon owner, put her two-bedroom house in Yogyakarta, Indonesia, on sale for $76,500 (£49,104), as part of the deal she offered to marry the buyer.

NEW SHORTS Curt Almond, a restaurant manager from Bristol, England, spent more than $3,000 (£2,000) a year on underwear after becoming addicted to wearing a brand-new pair of boxer shorts every day. He would spend $60 (£40) a week on new Calvin Kleins, which he then threw out after just one day's wear.

LOVE TEST After Wu Hsia broke up with long-term girlfriend Jun Tang to be with Rong Tsao, the two love-struck women argued so much that both ended up jumping into a river in Ningbo, China, to see which one he would save. Wu jumped in and saved Rong, calling his brother to rescue Jun.

GOLD TOOTH Among donations dropped into a Salvation Army collection kettle in Kansas City, Missouri, in December 2014 was a gold tooth, which is worth up to $100 (£64).

JINXED COUPLE Donna and Tim Hillyer of London, England, had two homes destroyed by freak accidents in the span of three months. In November 2014, they were forced to move out of the family home after a car crashed into their living room causing $90,000 (£57,637) worth of damage—and in February 2015 a huge gas explosion destroyed the temporary accommodation in which they were staying while waiting for the first house to be repaired.

Corpse Plant

While many of the flowers in the Rollins College greenhouse in Winter Park, Florida, give off a sweet perfume, there was one hefty 3 ft. (1 m) blossom that, on April 19, 2015, actually produced a horrible odor that had been 11 years in the making.

The Amorphophallus titanum plant, more colorfully known as the "corpse plant," blooms only once in 10 to 12 years—and lasts for only 36 hours before it begins to fade away. In fact, the stench from the 67 in. (170 cm) tall, 30 in. (76 cm) wide plant was so intense that Rollins's greenhouse manager Alan Chryst and biology professor Paul Stephenson had to step out a few times for a breath of fresh air.

Beyond Belief

RARE CRIME In 2015, the remote Scottish island of Canna (population 20) was rocked by its first crime in 50 years after thieves raided its only shop. The last reported crime on the Inner Hebridean Island had been the theft of a wooden plate from a church in the 1960s.

NO RELATION A New York City jury awarded $95,000 (£60,985) compensation to a Manhattan real estate broker named James Ferrari after his Ferrari sports car was seized and auctioned off by the police.

PARALLEL LIVES Monika Tano of Birmingham, England, has given birth to two children on the same days as the Duchess of Cambridge. Her first daughter, Liliana, was born on July 22, 2013—the same day as Prince George—and her second, Aurelia, was born on May 2, 2015—the same day as Princess Charlotte, beating odds of two million to one.

PUNISHING CLIMB After Joseph McElwee was found guilty of being abusive toward a police officer from County Mayo, Judge Seamus Hughes ordered him to climb to the top of Ireland's holiest mountain, the 2,507 ft. (764 m) high Croagh Patrick, as punishment.

DEPUTY MARSHAL In 2015, Sam Harris, a community radio DJ from Middlesbrough, England, was appointed a Deputy Marshal of Dodge City, Kansas—4,484 miles (7,216 km) away.

AROMATIC CLOCK An alarm clock called SensorWake, invented by French teen Guillaume Rolland, uses distinctive smells to get people out of bed. The clock contains special odor capsules, which emit the scent of money, strawberry candy, cut grass, or coffee and fresh croissants to encourage sleepers to wake up.

BOUQUET CATCH Jamie Jackson of Salt Lake City, Utah, has caught 46 bridal bouquets at weddings since 1996—but is still single.

RING RETURNED Nearly half a century after losing his Amesbury High School class ring on a Massachusetts beach in 1966, Dan Toomey of Anchorage, Alaska, was reunited with it. The ring was found by a tourist with a metal detector on the same beach, buried under 8 in. (20 cm) of mud, who then tracked down its owner.

LATE GRADUATION At the age of 94, Anthony Brutto finally graduated from West Virginia University in 2015—76 years after starting. He first enrolled in 1939 and was close to graduating when he was drafted during World War II. He reenrolled in 1946, but was unable to finish because he had to care for his sick wife. It was only after he retired from his job as a machinist 69 years later that he resumed his studies.

SAME BIRTHDAY Over three consecutive years, Virginia mother Shalonda Dominique gave birth to three boys, all on March 13. Her son Tre was born on March 13, 2013, followed by Santana on March 13, 2014, and Harlem on the same date in 2015.

CHATTER BOX

This late 19th-century traveling salesman's kit from the midwestern United States offered dentists—as well as blacksmiths, wigmakers, chemists, and others who "practiced" dentistry at the time—a selection of ready-made false enamel teeth in various shades and sizes for their patients whose own teeth were rotting. Each of the six drawers contains tooth samples carefully secured to small cards with steel pins, which prevented the samples from rattling around or getting lost.

FARE SENTENCE Judge Michael A. Cicconetti ordered Victoria Bascom of Lake County, Ohio, to walk 30 miles (48 km) as punishment for leaving a taxi without paying her $100 fare. The walk equaled the length of her cab journey.

Ripley's —— **Asks** ?

Dying to learn more? Greenhouse manager Alan Chryst tells us about the Rollins College corpse plant!

Q *Corpse plants are very rare. How long did it take Rollins College to grow this particular plant?*

A *We acquired the seeds in 2004 as part of a trade for some of our cocoa seeds, and we'd been cultivating it for 11 years—all in the hopes that it would flower.*

Q *How does the plant prepare itself to bloom?*

A *Each year, it goes through the same cycle. It dies; it comes back. But each time it comes back, it's bigger and bigger and bigger. What it's doing is storing enough energy to produce this massive flower, which only lasts 36 hours.*

Q *When was the corpse plant at its most odorous?*

A *This plant bloomed on Sunday afternoon, and was pollinated Sunday between midnight and 4 am, when the "rotting flesh" smell was the strongest—and the plant actually gave off steam as the night air cooled and the bloom heated up.*

Volcanic View

What looks like a giant trudging through the clouds is actually the aftermath of Chile's Calbuco volcano, which sent a massive plume of ash and smoke 12 miles (19 km) into the sky! Hariet Grunewald of the nearby town of Puerto Montt captured the eerie figure on camera. Some superstitious residents believe this was a sign from the gods, as Calbuco had not erupted in over forty years.

FANCY FLU$H

>Can actually flush!

This fancy toilet is encrusted with 72,000 Swarovski® crystals and valued at $128,000 (£82,920)! Unfortunately, no one will be sitting on this "throne," as it is only used to attract customers in Tokyo's Ginza shopping district.

GRADUATION GUEST When Dawnielle Davison graduated from high school, the guest of honor at the ceremony was Mike Hughes, the firefighter who had dramatically rescued her from a 1998 house blaze in Wenatchee, Washington, when she was nine months old. Hughes later messaged her via Facebook when she was in seventh grade and they remained in contact.

ILLEGAL FISH Boater Muoi V. Huynh of Brockton, Massachusetts, was arrested on suspicion of illegally catching large quantities of sea bass while he was drunk. He was apprehended in Buzzards Bay with a haul of 122 black sea bass when the legal limit is only eight.

DEADLY MACHINES Each year, vending machines account for four times as many deaths in the United States as sharks. There is approximately one fatal US shark attack every two years, but over a 17-year period, 37 people were killed trying to obtain a snack from a vending machine—usually by tilting a faulty one—an average of 2.18 deaths per year.

MASS WEDDING Indian diamond trader Mahesh Savani paid for 111 fatherless brides from humble backgrounds to get married in the city of Surat in November 2014.

GRENADE SCARE A grenade-shaped perfume bottle found in a woman's suitcase on June 30, 2015, caused the Hamilton County courthouse in Cincinnati, Ohio, to be evacuated.

KEEN RECYCLER New Yorker Lauren Singer has produced just one jar's worth of trash in two years. She no longer buys packaged products, buys only secondhand clothes, recycles her waste, and even makes her own toothpaste, deodorant, and laundry detergent.

PERFECT TIME A strontium lattice clock developed by scientists from the National Institute of Standards and Technology and the University of Colorado in Boulder is so accurate it will not gain or lose a second in 15 billion years—approximately the age of the universe.

WEIRD ODORS The Demester Fragrance Library of Great Neck, New York, sells perfume in odors such as dirt, frozen pond, curry, lobster, earthworm, and funeral home.

WALLET RETURNED Thirty-five years after his wallet was stolen while he was on vacation in Devon, John Steel of Wiltshire, England, was reunited with it when it was found in the wall cavity of a house that was being renovated. The wallet contained a picture of him as a boy and a £1 note.

ATE FINGERTIPS Kenzo Roberts, a suspect at Lee County Sheriff's office in Florida, chewed the skin off his fingertips and swallowed the flesh, apparently in an attempt to avoid being identified by his fingerprints.

LEMONADE STALL Five-year-old Na'ama Uzan from Toronto, Ontario, Canada, raised over $25,000 (£16,010) for her disabled brother Nadav by selling lemonade at roadside stalls.

INDEX

Page numbers in *italic* refer to the images

ACKNOWLEDGMENTS

Cover © Markus Gann - Shutterstock.com, © Davydenko Yuliia - Shutterstock.com, © leolintang - Shutterstock.com; 4 (tr) ANA, (cl) Courtesy of Theo Fennell Ltd., (bl) Alek Kurniawan; 5 (tl) In the Light Urns, (bl) David Hedges SWNS.com, (br) Jeff Cremer / @JCremerPhoto; 12–13 John McVitty Photography; 16 John McVitty Photography; 17 ADAM GERBER / CATERS NEWS; 18 BRUNO GRACIANO / CATERS NEWS; 19 (tl) Diovane Moraes Fotografia, (cl) Henry Miller News Picture Service/FPG/Getty Images, (cr) Keystone/Getty Images; 20 (t) Idaho Department of Fish and Game (IDFG), (c, br) THE AMERICAN SOCIETY FOR MICROBIOLOGY/MERCURY PRESS; 21 (t, bl, br) The Good Project; 22 (bg, cr, bl) Mother Shipton's Cave; 23 Courtesy of Mary Nash Ward; 24 Sijori Images / Barcroft India; 25 (t) PETER PARKS/AFP/Getty Images, (b) PAUL KOUDOUNARIS / CATERS NEWS; 26 (tl, tr) Photo: Leah Yeung/Declan Jones. All pics. © TwinStrangers.com, (b) Photo: David Atkinson/Declan Jones. All pics. © TwinStrangers.com; 27 True Wetsuits; 28–29 More about Thomas Thwaites's project can be found in his book *GoatMan: How I Took a Holiday from Being Human*; Photographs by Tim Bowditch; 32 (t, b) MARK RALSTON/AFP/Getty Images; 32–33 Lintao Zhang/Getty Images; 34 (t) STR/AFP/Getty Images, (b) Ai xi - ImagineChina; 35 (t, b) REUTERS/Thomas Peter; 36 © Fan Jun/Xinhua Press/Corbis; 37 Müller-Stauffenberg/ullstein bild via Getty Images; 38 REUTERS/Akhtar Soomro; 39 (t) MyLoupe/Universal Images Group via Getty Images, (b) Dimas Ardian/Getty Images; 40 (cr) © milosk50 - Shutterstock.com; 40–41 © Alexey Stiop - Shutterstock.com; 42 (t) REUTERS/Jeff Topping, (b) Buddhika Weerasinghe/Getty Images; 43 (tl) Bernie Pettersen / SWNS.com, (tr) Sam Autie / SWNS.com; 44 (tc) JNS/Gamma-Rapho via Getty Images, (tr) Hk Rajashekar/The India Today Group/Getty Images; 45 (t) MARTIN BERNETTI/AFP/Getty Images, (b) ChinaFotoPress/ChinaFotoPress via Getty Images; 46 (t) Marka/UIG via Getty Images, (bl) GIUSEPPE CACACE/AFP/Getty Images; 47 ChinaFotoPress/ChinaFotoPress via Getty Images; 48 CATERS NEWS; 49 Studio City, Macau; 50–51 Photographer John Gollings; 52 View Pictures/UIG via Getty Images; 53 Pablo Blazquez Dominguez/Getty Images; 54 ASSOCIATED PRESS; 55 (t) Renaud Philippe/ CATERS NEWS, (b) ChinaFotoPress/ChinaFotoPress via Getty Images; 56 ASSOCIATED PRESS; 57 ChinaFotoPress/ChinaFotoPress via Getty Images; 58–59 JTB Photo/UIG via Getty Images; 60–61 www.aliencatmatilda.com; 62 SUSAN SCOTT / STROOP / CATERS NEWS; 63 (t) Courtesy of Angela Johnson, (b) TANJA MERENSKY-HARTINGER / CATERS NEWS; 64 (sp) Underwood Archives/Getty Images; 65 (t) Peter Stackpole/The LIFE Images Collection/Getty Images, (b) Michael Rougier/The LIFE Picture Collection/Getty Images; 66 CATERS NEWS; 67 (tr) Jeff Cremer / @JCremerPhoto, (br) © Newsteam / SWNS Group; 68 (t) Daryl Marshke/Michigan Photography, (b) DAVID GRUBER/National Geographic Creative; 69 CATERS NEWS; 70 Eye of Science / Science Source; 71 (t) The Asahi Shimbun via Getty Images, (b) © Piotr Naskrecki/Minden Pictures; 72 Photo by Noel Conrad; 73 (t) DENNIS BEEK/AFP/Getty Images, (bl) Andrew Evans / Nat Geo Stock / Barcroft Media / Getty Images, (bc) REUTERS/Marinos Meletiou, (br) R.M.Buquoi Photographics; 74 © EuroPics[CEN]; 75 (t) Ronny Adolof Buol/Pacific Press/LightRocket via Getty Images, (b) © Ross Parry / SWNS Group; 76 ChinaFotoPress/ChinaFotoPress via Getty Images; 77 ChinaFotoPress/ChinaFotoPress via Getty Images; 78 (bl) www.aliencatmatilda.com; 79 (t, b) Courtesy of Hotel Epinard Nasu; 80 (t) Dan Kitwood/Getty Images, (cr) JUSTIN TALLIS/AFP/Getty Images; 81 PAULA MASTERSON / CATERS NEWS; 82 (tl) CATERS NEWS; 83 (sp) © Ami Vitale / Alamy Stock Photo; 85 (tl) Courtesy of Martin Le-May, (br) JOANA TRINDADE/MERCURY PRESS; 86 (t) Rick Kern / Contributor, (bl) Exclusivepix Media; 87 (r) Exclusivepix Media; 88–89 © Mercy Ships Josh Callow; 90 ImagineChina; 91 © EuroPics[CEN]; 92 Cody Pickens; 94 (t) ASSOCIATED PRESS, (b) Sanjay Pandey; 95 (t) SANJAY PANDEY / CATERS NEWS, (b) Photograph by Barcroft India; 96 Courtesy of Jamie Hilton; 97 Courtesy of Science for the Masses; 98 REUTERS/Milena Georgeault; 99 © EuroPics[CEN]; 100 (t) © Mercy Ships Josh Callow, (b) ASSOCIATED PRESS; 101 (tl, tr, cr) © Mercy Ships Katie Keegan, (cl) © Mercy Ships Justine Forrest; 102 David Cheskin / PA Archive/Press Association Images; 103 (t) © EuroPics[CEN], (b) Clem Murray/Philadelphia Inquirer/TNS via Getty Images; 104 JUAN CEVALLOS/AFP/Getty Images; 105 (t) JUAN CEVALLOS/AFP/Getty Images, (b) ASSOCIATED PRESS; 106 (t) D.E MEDIA / CATERS NEWS, (b) Jacob Puritz; 107 © EuroPics[CEN]; 108 (t) CATERS NEWS, (b) ASSOCIATED PRESS; 109 ImagineChina; 110 Ajay Verma / Barcroft India via Getty Images; 111 (t) NCJ Media Ltd, (b) © Nopparat Kingkaew; 112–113 David Hedges SWNS.com; 114–115 Summers Farm; 116 (t) ANA, (b) Crummy Gummy; 117 (t) TOSHIFUMI KITAMURA/AFP/Getty Images, (cr, br) David Eger/Rex Features, (bl) Education Images/UIG via Getty Images; 118 Summers Farm; 119 (t) Courtesy of Blake and Jessica Carranza; 120 Photos credit: Gail Heidel; 121 (t) Courtesy of Uig Hotel; 123 (tr, b) Kennedy Lee Lewis; 124 (t) Courtesy of Theo Fennell Ltd., (b) ChinaFotoPress/ChinaFotoPress via Getty Images; 125 Photo courtesy Antonio Santana, https://www.facebook.com/NYCISEE; 126 (sp, br) Courtesy of the New York Historical Society; 127 (tr) United States Library of Congress, (tc) Courtesy of the New York Historical Society, (c) Courtesy of the University of Buffalo Library, (b) United States Library of Congress; 128 (t) Keystone-France/Gamma-Keystone via Getty Images, (b) United States Library of Congress; 129 (t) United States Library of Congress, (c, b) Courtesy of the New York Historical Society; 130–131 Eric Millikin; 132 (t) ASSOCIATED PRESS, (b) Laurentiu Garofeanu / Barcroft USA; 133 Quang Le; 134 (t) CATERS NEWS, (b) ASSOCIATED PRESS; 135 Thomas Voor't Hekke, Front404; 136 Picture by: David Parry / PA Wire/Press Association Images; 137 (t) Trevor Williams/WireImage, (b) TORU YAMANAKA/AFP/Getty Images; 138–139 Photos courtesy Dominic Wilcox, Stained Glass Sleeper Car of the Future/Photographer Sylvain Deleu; 140 (t) Photo: XDubai; 140–141 © Shutterstock/Ashraf Jandali; 141 (t, br) Photo: XDubai; 142 (t) EPA/HARISH TYAG, (b) ATTA KENARE/AFP/Getty Images; 143 TOSHIFUMI KITAMURA/AFP/Getty Images; 144 ASSOCIATED PRESS; 145 Photo: Bas de Meijer; 146 (t) CATERS NEWS, (b) ImagineChina; 147 QUADROFOIL/CATERS NEWS; 148 PHOTOGRAPH BY Ruaridh Connellan / Barcroft Cars UK Office/Getty Images; 149 Louisville Mega Cavern; 150 (t) SHROPSHIRE STAR/CATERS NEWS, (b) Photo by The Asahi Shimbun via Getty Images; 151 Quirky China News/Rex Shutterstock; 152 (t) Photos courtesy Dominic Wilcox, Stained Glass Sleeper Car of the Future/Photographer Sylvain Deleu, (b) MIKE JONES/CATERS NEWS; 153 JOE BROYLES/CATERS NEWS; 154–155 Photo by ChinaFotoPress/ChinaFotoPress via Getty Images; 156 Photos courtesy Sol Cinema, www.thesolcinema.org; 157 (t) BART VAN OVERBEEKE/CATERS NEWS, (b) CATERS NEWS; 158 Photo courtesy of Butch Anthony; 160–161 M-1 Global; 162–163 PHOTOGRAPH BY Alexandre Socci / Barcroft Media; 164 (t) ImagineChina; 165 Andy Cross/The Denver Post via Getty Images; 166–167 Photo by Matthias Hangst/Getty Images; 167 (t) Photo by Clive Rose/Getty Images, (b) Photo by Matthias Hangst/Getty Images; 168 Photo by ChinaFotoPress/ChinaFotoPress via Getty Images; 169 TACTICAL TRAINING SERVICES, LLC; 170 (t) Photo: Garth Milan, (b) Mohammad Izani Ramli; 170–171 Photo: Deven Stephens/DC Shoes; 172–173 MIKE MCKENZIE / CATERS NEWS; 174 CATERS NEWS; 175 ALEX BUISSE/MERCURY PRESS/CATERS NEWS; 178 (t) ALEX SUKHAREV/CATERS NEWS, (b) PHOTOGRAPH BY Rustram Saadvakass / Barcroft USA; 179 IAN MACLEAN/CATERS NEWS; 180 (t) The Asahi Shimbun via Getty Images, (b) ARCADIA / CATERS NEWS; 181 M-1 Global; 182 Photo by ChinaFotoPress/ChinaFotoPress via Getty Images; 183 Photo by ChinaFotoPress/ChinaFotoPress via Getty Images; 184–185 Courtesy of Elizabeth S. Harding; 186–187 PIC BY ROBERT GODWIN / CATERS NEWS; 188–189 HAZMAT Surfing by Michael Dyrland I DYRLANDproductions.com; 192 Chris Lee via Getty Images; 193 Liu Jiaoqing/ChinaFotoPress via Getty Images; 194 Jim Dyson/Getty Images; 195 (t) STR/AFP/Getty Images, (b) ChinaFotoPress/ChinaFotoPress via Getty Images; 196–197 Photos by Adele Schaefer; 198 Photography Erik Kwakkel; 199 (t) ImagineChina, (b) HEMEDIA/SWNS.com; 200–201 HAZMAT Surfing by Michael Dyrland I DYRLANDproductions.com; 202 SSPL/Getty Images; 203 (tl, tr) SSPL/Getty Images; 204 Oklahoma City Public Schools; 205 Courtesy of Stan Skopek; 206 Genesee Brewing Company; 208–209 Tisha Saravitaya "Tisha Cherry"; 210 (t) BRADLEY AMBROSE / CATERS NEWS, (b) ImagineChina; 211 Annabel de Vetten, Conjurer's Kitchen; 212 (tl) In the Light Urns, (tr) Craig Warga/NY Daily News Archive via Getty Images, (b) Barnes, Catmur & Friends; 213 Louisa Paintin; 215 (t) Tisha Saravitaya "Tisha Cherry"; 217 Tolga Akmen/Anadolu Agency/Getty Images; 218 (t) ChinaFotoPress/ChinaFotoPress via Getty Images, (b) ChinaFotoPress/ChinaFotoPress via Getty Images; 219 Marc Vasconcellos, The Enterprise; 220 YOSHIKAZU TSUNO/AFP/Getty Images; 221 (t) ChinaFotoPress/ChinaFotoPress via Getty Images, (b) ChinaFotoPress/ChinaFotoPress via Getty Images; 222 ImagineChina; 223 (t) REUTERS/Stefano Rellandini, (b) ChinaFotoPress/ChinaFotoPress via Getty Images; 224 Lexi Santos (www.seoulsearching.net); 225 (tr) Jason Mecier/Rex Features, (b) Henry Aldridge and Son; 226 (tl) Translation provided by JR Language Translation Services, Inc., (c) Public Domain {{PD-US}}; 227 (t) Kevin Schafer/Getty Images, (b) ChinaFotoPress/ChinaFotoPress via Getty Images; 228–229 Courtesy of Hospital de Bonecas; 230 Alek Kurniawan; 231 Robertus Pudyanto/Getty Images; 232 (bg, b) Sabrina Sieck, (tr, cr) Courtesy of Cassadaga Spiritualist Camp; 233 (tl) United States Library of Congress, (cl, c) Sabrina Sieck, (cr) Universal History Archive/UIG via Getty Images, (b) Ann Ronan Pictures/Print Collector/Getty Images; 234 (bg, tr) David McNew/Getty Images; 235 Courtesy of Hospital de Bonecas; 236 (t) ChinaFotoPress/ChinaFotoPress via Getty Images, (b) ImagineChina; 237 Photos by Estar Hyo Gyung Choi; 238 Andrew Burton/Getty Images; 239 DeAgostini/Getty Images; 240 CATERS NEWS; 241 (t) Ed Wray/Getty Images, (b) Richard Lyons, courtesy South Australian Museum; 244 © EuroPics[CEN]; 245 (t) The Asahi Shimbun via Getty Images; Master Graphics Ripley's Research: © Shutterstock/Iakov Filimonov; Features graphic: http://subtlepatterns.com/?s=symphony, made by Irfan iLias

Key: t = top, b = bottom, c = center, l = left, r = right, sp = single page, bg = background

All other photos are from Ripley Entertainment Inc. Every attempt has been made to acknowledge correctly and contact copyright holders and we apologize in advance for any unintentional errors or omissions, which will be corrected in future editions.

Connect with Ripley's Online or in Person

31 ZANY LOCATIONS

There are 31 incredible Ripley's Believe It or Not! Odditoriums all around the world, where you can experience our strange and spectacular collection and unlock even more weird!

Amsterdam THE NETHERLANDS
Atlantic City NEW JERSEY
Baltimore MARYLAND
Blackpool ENGLAND
Branson MISSOURI
Cavendish P.E.I., CANADA
Copenhagen DENMARK
Gatlinburg TENNESSEE
Genting Highlands MALAYSIA
Grand Prairie TEXAS
Guadalajara MEXICO
Hollywood CALIFORNIA
Jeju Island KOREA
Key West FLORIDA
London ENGLAND
Mexico City MEXICO
Myrtle Beach SOUTH CAROLINA
New York City NEW YORK
Newport OREGON
Niagara Falls ONTARIO, CANADA
Ocean City MARYLAND
Orlando FLORIDA
Panama City Beach FLORIDA
Pattaya THAILAND
San Antonio TEXAS
San Francisco CALIFORNIA
St. Augustine FLORIDA
Surfers Paradise AUSTRALIA
Veracruz MEXICO
Williamsburg VIRGINIA
Wisconsin Dells WISCONSIN

Stop by our website daily for new stories, photos, contests, and more!

www.ripleys.com

Don't forget to connect with us on social media for a daily dose of the weird and the wonderful.

/RipleysBelieveItOrNot
@Ripleys
youtube.com/Ripleys
@RipleysOdditorium

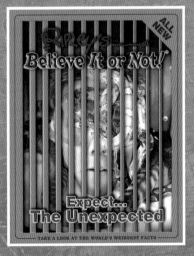

FUN FACTS & SILLY STORIES

Filled with wacky stories and colorful images of crazy animals, incredible talents, amazing people, and goofy events, readers will have a hard time putting these books down!

ODD
AROUND THE WORLD

Featuring brand new Believe It or Not! stories, puzzles, and games, Ripley's fans are guaranteed to giggle and gasp their way through *Fun Facts & Silly Stories ODD Around the World!*

TWISTS

Ripley's award-winning TWISTS books combine fascinating facts and unbelievable stories to make learning fun!

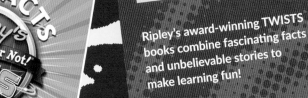